Lost Nowhere

Phoebe Garnsworthy

DEDICATION

This book is for the ones who feel like they don't belong
in this world . . .
and it's for those who have endless questions about life,
the universe, and why we are here.
I have created a safe haven that you can escape to
for awhile . . .

Come, we have been waiting for you.

CONTENTS

ACKNOWLEDGMENTS

This book would not have been possible without the ongoing love and support from my family and friends. With special mention to – John, Jacqueline, Claire, Perdita, Tobias, Ruby, Madeleine, Emerald, Leo, Woody, Katie, Courtney and Yasmin. And to the stars shining brightly in the sky looking down on me, thank you to Jack, Isobel and Alice.

You are forever in my heart.

CHAPTER ONE

THE OUROBOROS

Lily was probably more scared than anything. Moving to a new house, going to a new school and having to meet new people. Change, she hated change. *Why does anything have to change?* she thought.

"This will be your room," Father said, as he pointed to the aged wooden door on the right.

Lily looked down to the floor to avoid her father's gaze. She distracted her mind by thinking about how little her feet looked against his. She used an imaginary ruler to measure the distance between the two, and then calculated the exact ratio by which her feet were smaller, predicting the rate they would need to grow in order to catch up to his size.

"Lily . . ." Father interrupted her counting as he placed his hand on her shoulder lovingly, straightening up the collar of her sky-blue dress.

"I don't want to live here," she sulked, pushing his hand off and continuing to stare at her favorite white sandals, now admiring the contrast of dark wooden floor beneath her feet.

"Lily, we've been through this." He lifted his hands up with open palms as though surrendering, lost, with no idea on how to handle her anymore. "The doctors advised . . ."

"The doctors don't know anything," she snapped back, stomping her foot. "All they do is feed me pills and monitor how they affect me. That's not helping!" She turned and walked away as though talking to herself, fiddling with the lace trimming of her dress. "They aren't learning about me, about my thoughts and about my dreams . . ." Her mind wandered before she finished her sentence and she stood in the hallway, staring at the natural imperfections of the stained-timber wall.

Father didn't move. He stood at the door, wanting to open it, wanting to show her how proud he was to buy the new house and give her a brand new start. She turned back around slowly, realizing he wasn't following her, and she took long drawn out steps back to the bedroom door.

"Why is everyone scared of what I see?" she asked and sighed, standing directly below his gaze. "Why don't you listen? Why don't you learn to love me just the same?"

She shrugged her shoulders and looked back down, pressing the fabric of her skirt tightly between her fingers.

"I do love you, Lily," Father said as he cradled her chin in his warm cushioning hands.

She nuzzled with sadness, with a hint of acceptance, and then pushed his hands away. *You're not listening to me!* she screamed inside her mind. She could feel the heat within her body boiling with fury, her thoughts overflowing with madness, ready to explode. She wanted so badly to be heard. But there were no words left to say. There were too many questions unanswered, and she was exhausted at having the same argument over and over again. She had grown to believe that no one would ever understand her, not her father, not the doctors, not anyone.

"Didn't you like the garden outside?" Father pointed to the trees through the window behind them, as he tried to change the subject. Her mind flashed back in a photographic memory to the butterfly with pointy yellow wings and an orange zig-zag trim. It had landed on her arm and tickled her skin with its delicate toes. The gentle creature had fluttered its wings so peacefully, it had mesmerized Lily into a trance-like state. It had reminded her of her mother, and she felt as though she had been talking to her, while it softly kissed her skin to say hello.

"I chose this place because of it," Father said as he sensed her desire to come around. "And the teacher we met at your new school today, didn't you like her? She seemed so lovely, no?"

"I didn't think that she liked me very much," Lily replied stubbornly, staring back at her father with confidence in her assumption.

Lily felt no connection with the school—not the teachers, nor the students. She knew it was going to be just like the last one where she had felt rejected and alone. Even the teachers would be fed up with her before she'd begun.

"She did, darling. It's just that some people show their love in other ways."

Lily listened to her father's words resonate deeply. She noticed the way his mouth articulated slowly, and the pressure of his breath pushed out toward her, creating each individual sound as its own vibration of mismatching syllables. Father could tell she wasn't really listening, but he continued just the same. "Your life will go on just as normal here. The only difference is that they will be giving you some more one-on-one time, to help you concentrate."

Lily felt suffocated at the notion of someone watching over her, and she wondered why she needed to be forced to concentrate on subjects that were of no interest. It wasn't that she couldn't focus on the assignment. It was just that she preferred to think about other things, like how many stars there are in the sky, and how far away the closest universe really is. Her fellow peers used to laugh when the teacher would point out that her mouth was open, deep in thought. She squirmed in remembrance.

"And here you will make new friends," Father continued, massaging the back of Lily's neck lovingly.

"But, Papa, I don't even have *old* friends." She lifted her foot and stomped it lightly on the ground, repeating it over and over again in an awkward stampede.

"It's all a part of growing up, Lily," he said as he silenced her foot from moving, crouching down and holding it securely to the floor. "Sometimes we have to do things we don't want to do."

He squeezed her ankle lightly and half smiled, signaling that he too didn't want to do many things. But the idea of doing something against her own desires seemed to upset Lily more than she anticipated, and her thoughts began to pile back up, and this time they had a voice.

"But why?" she screamed back at him. "I don't want to grow up then! If growing up means living in a world that has been created for me, what's the point? Why can't I make it the way I want to?" She shook her head quickly. "But no, everyone thinks I'm crazy."

She kicked her leg out, releasing his grip, and looking away.

"I don't think you're crazy." Father winked as he stood back up and took her hands in response. "You just need to find what it is that makes you happy. Maybe here you will meet some like-minded friends? Someone who you can share your ideas with?"

He raised his eyebrows as though his idea was innovative. Lily pouted her bottom lip and pulled her hands away from her fathers'.

"I doubt it," she said, and pressed on the lace of her skirt once more. "I had no friends at my old school and I was used to it. I liked it in fact. Now everyone is going to stare at how weird I am, and I will have to relive this feeling of being so alone."

Her eyes drifted away from him as she remembered vividly the lack of interactions at her old school. Everyday she would sit in the far corner of the play yard, along the fence where the trees lined up. If her peers felt like it, they knew they could find her there. And that's where they would torment her, teasing her for talking to the trees, and the animals; the bountiful gifts from nature that were her only friends.

"Oh, don't sulk like that Lily, you look like your mother." Father sighed as he looked to the ceiling, and for a split moment, Lily felt like she could read his mind. He was asking her mother if he was making the right decision.

"Papa, am I a lot like mama?" Lily asked, leaning her back

against the wall.

"An uncanny resemblance my darling," he said and smiled with no teeth, but with love in his eyes, as he straightened one of her untamed curls between his fingers.

"Papa why is it that I feel so alone?" Her voice quivered as she asked, and she turned away from him, pressing her forehead against the wall. "Sometimes my dreams are far more exciting than real life," she confessed, feeling her eyes begin to itch. "And mama, well, she is always there. I don't want her to leave me. The drugs are making her disappear . . ." Her voice softened as she spoke truthfully, as a teardrop landed on the floor. She rubbed it into the wood with her foot, imprinting the ground with her sorrow. She stopped herself from crying any further, unaware that the release would have probably been a good thing for her. But she had spent too many nights crying over a thought that exuded the same pain as though it were physical, and she didn't want to keep hurting herself any longer.

"Mama will always be with you darling, you just can't always see her," Father soothed as he stroked her hand inside of his, turning her around to face him. He paused, selecting his next words carefully. "You're going to love this new house, Lily. There is so much to explore, and the neighborhood is full of teenagers your age. This is going to be a good change, I promise." He spoke with enthusiasm and wiped the sweat from the corner of his forehead. But instead of thinking it was the heat that made him sweat, Lily read it as pity seeping from the pores of his skin. She wanted terribly not to be a burden on him, but she couldn't stop the thoughts hammering away in her mind.

"And what will happen tomorrow?" she asked, feeling her vision get blurry.

She pulled on the soft part of her earlobe in an attempt to stop the tears from surfacing. But it was too late, the familiar emotion overwhelmed her thoughts, and she made no attempt to hide the tears. Slowly they burned along her cheek, falling down her face in one long, drawn-out breath, as though each freckle of skin melted with the reminder of just how far away she felt from acceptance.

"Don't worry about tomorrow, let's just focus on today," he

said calmly, wiping the tears from her face with his tough-skinned thumbs. They scratched the edges of her chin, his rough hands, tarnished with embedded grooves, a sign of having worked hard every single day of his life.

"But tell me," she argued again. "Is a doctor going to come into our home? And stare at me? And monitor what I do?" She tapped her ear lightly, drowning the space in between her ear and her hand. And she slapped it repetitively, creating a soft quivering noise that purred in her head.

"Lily, you know this is the new program we are trying. Don't you want to get better?" He took hold of her hand to stop it from moving, and pressed on her knuckles individually, his way of distracting her need for wanting to stir.

"Please try and give it a chance? Lily, will you? Please? For me?"

Lily felt her stomach turn with a nauseous feeling that made it difficult for her to breathe. Her heart started to beat faster and she felt dizzy—it was another panic attack coming on. She fluttered her eyelids quickly, while her breath hissed between her teeth and she felt her whole body shake with the rejection of a choice having been made for her.

"Papa, it's not right, it's not right," she repeated, hurriedly, feeling herself fixate on the words uncontrollably. "It's not right, Papa."

She pulled her hands from his grasp and tapped her fingertips repeatedly over her ears and along her neck while she looked away, knowing what was happening. She knew all too well her behavior didn't help her situation. The doctors had convinced her father that moving her was the right thing for him to do, but she couldn't help the need to scream and release all the built up anger inside. The idea of being watched like an animal under the nurses' care while they tried to diagnose her, or misdiagnose, as she believed, was too much to bear.

Father could sense the displacement in his daughter, and he held her in a tight embrace, inhaling deep breaths and encouraging her to do the same. She surrendered and listened with him as her body calmed itself as requested.

"Everything will be okay," he said, releasing his grip and staring intently at his daughter. His green eyes mirrored the same reflective features of her own, dark diamonds and drawn out ovals.

The familiarity soothed her immediately, but his words of comfort were not enough. She needed to believe it. And from her own eyes she dove; through his pupil and right into his soul. Searching for the answers. She flew so far down that she almost got lost, as though she were swimming back inside of her own mind. And she floated there for awhile, safely in the dark. She loved him so much but had no idea how to show him. They were too similar, the pair of them, broken and alone, wanting love but not sure how to give it. She held his hands to reassure him, but in truth the reassurance was to herself. For when she looked back to his eyes his exterior had faded and she had easily forgotten whose heart she felt beating. She took a deep breath and composed herself, shaking the darkness from her mind as she decided to believe. She smiled with understanding, and nodded at their agreement. Then, she twisted the metal handle and opened up her new bedroom door.

The warmth from the outside sun greeted Lily first as they entered the room. It radiated through a giant window in the far corner adjacent to where they were standing, and it lit up the entire space, every corner, every crease. Right up high into the ceilings the light shone fiercely like a gallivant display of affection. The ceiling was painted a perfect stark white, contrasting beautifully to the violet shades of walls all around. *It feels very much like my room,* Lily thought, but was too stubborn to say anything to her father, the idea of change still worrying her.

Directly ahead, a large queen-size bed was already made up, complete with thick white fluffy pillows and a soft cream bedspread. The pillows were angled to face out the window, so that Lily could daydream amongst the stars, as her father knew that she loved to do.

Such a big old house, Lily thought as she stared up at the huge ceiling. There was so much space. So much air and so much nothingness.

She felt tiny. Insignificant. But definitely not alone. *The walls had seen a lot,* she thought. "This house is a hundred years old," Father had informed her. It definitely had some stories to tell.

"Papa, where did all this furniture come from?" she asked, jumping up on the squeaky bed.

"It's ours if we want it darling. You see the family who lived here before us don't need it. Should we keep it? It's antique and suits the house, don't you think?" Father said as he touched the end of the framed brass bed.

It had three marble bulbs that decorated the base, and they twisted around when touched. Lily loved the idea of the furniture staying, and her mind immediately began to wander. She thought about who the person was that made the bed and how long it took them. When they made it, did they think about what would happen to it long after they had died? Did they know that a girl just like Lily would be lying on it? Thinking about them. The bed creaked lightly as though it were hearing her thoughts. She giggled to herself.

"Yes I think the furniture likes being here," Lily said as she leapt to the window, pulling lightly on the curtains that were stained with age. But they wouldn't move, there was something caught between the hooks and the rod. Although the curtains were old, Lily didn't want to rip them, and so she gracefully climbed up onto the side of the window to investigate further. Reaching high onto her tippy toes she tried to unhook the top corner of the curtain closest to the window.

"Papa, I can see a piece of jewelry up here!" she shrieked excitedly as she pulled an object from the curtain and floated back down to meet her father.

Using her skirt, she removed the dust on the charm, and held it up to him as they both examined her discovery. It was a serpent that formed a perfect circle, no bigger than the center of her hand. Covered in yellow gold it was embellished with dark indigo lines that etched deeply to form the scales in its skin. The serpent's wide mouth wrapped around the base of its tail, and it was eating itself, strangely, yet pleasurably. The eyes had fine white crystal stones inside of them, and they stared outwards. The edges of the serpent weren't perfectly kept, and Lily liked that. It added character she believed. She saw great beauty in the uniqueness of imperfections. Most of the time the pretty things she had collected were in fact broken objects that she showered with love, giving warmth to those who only ever felt the cold. She loved to seek beauty inside of everything that was within her reach.

"Papa, do you know what it is? No beginning and no end," Lily asked as she ran her finger inside the circle of the serpent. "There's a word for that, isn't there?"

"You're thinking of infinity. It has no beginning and no end. Yes, you are right, it does represent infinity," Father replied as Lily continued to stare at the object carefully. *To eat one's own tail. What a strange thing to do,* she thought.

"Papa I want to wear it on my necklace, do you think it will fit?"

Lily pulled the chain below her chin as she examined it carefully, seeing if the colors of gold complimented each other.

"We can certainly try darling. I think your mother would like that too," he nodded, helping to attach it to her necklace.

She fastened the jewelry back around her neck and walked over to the mirrored wardrobe sitting against the wall. The charm clicked oddly against the gold when she moved, but she wore it proudly anyway. The chain once belonged to her mother and she gave it to Lily just before she died. Lily had never taken it off, and even though she didn't know her mother, she felt closer to her just from wearing it. And now a pendant hung low across her chest, beautifully decorating her décolleté like a true adult. Lily admired herself in the reflective glass, and felt different somehow. The serpent sat flat on her chest, and Lily felt an unusual attachment to it already.

The coolness of the crystals in the eyes protruded prominently against her skin. It created an electrical current that zipped into her heart, creating a vibrational frequency that resonated loudly inside her. She placed her hand over the charm and felt the energy amplify; it calmed her and yet at the same time propelled an adrenalin rush throughout her body. She shivered. It reminded her of the ocean. How the quick cool breeze travels from the horizon and runs across the waves to touch her. She liked to think that the wind was roaming from different lands, coming to her to caress her skin and comb through the finite pieces of her curly brown hair. It made her feel awake and alive. And she smiled with wide-open eyes, turning back to her father, who was standing with his hands in his navy short pockets, eagerly awaiting her approval.

"Come on Papa, show me what else you got," she said while holding her hand out to her father, eager to explore the rest of the house.

They turned to the right and walked through the long hallway, talking about filling the empty spaces with memories gone by. Lily's favorite painting was of her mother when she was younger, sitting in the garden. She loved the way her face looked so peaceful while she stared into the distance, her body surrounded by colorful flowers. Lily chose the perfect place to hang it, so she could walk past it every day and say I love you. Her father agreed.

The living area was next—velvet lounges and a floor covered with an antique black and cream carpet, it had an intricate design that looked almost like a maze. Lily followed the lines on the ground as they weaved in and out of the labyrinth pattern. The colors of black and cream chased each other with madness. Lily hoped to find an exit but the journey brought her back to where she started from, a continuous cycle that seemed to remind her of the serpent charm she now wore around her neck.

Next, she ran her hand over the edge of the wooden frame that supported the velvet maroon lounge, and tapped alternatively between the wood and the fabric, feeling the distinction of soft and hard surfaces, left to right and right to left. The lounge was more of a seat to perch daintily on, rather than a comfy sofa to relax in. It faced two other chairs and they surrounded a low marble table. Lily could see an image of three women sitting around having tea, while a delicious cake stand sat proudly in the middle. The ladies all looked to one another as they sipped on their delicate teacups painted with floral prints and gold trimmings, and Lily could hear the sounds of classical piano music playing faintly in the distance. She blinked and they disappeared, leading her to wonder how it was that the ancient mansion was playing with her imagination, showing her past times from before she was alive.

"Papa, tell me more about this house," Lily asked inquisitively, secretly searching for answers as to whether her visions were real, as she bounced on the chairs one by one.

"Only one family ever lived here, and it was passed on generation to generation. The last lady who lived here is still alive at eighty-six years old and lives in a home not far from here. She wants to come tomorrow and see the house one last time. Would you like to meet her?"

Lily looked away, ignoring her father, which was her usual mannerism when the subject matter changed to something she wasn't interested in.

"Lily, I'm talking to you," he asked again, lifting her chin up so their eyes were synchronized. "Would you like to meet the lady who used to live here?"

Lily wriggled again uncomfortably.

"Papa, I won't know how to talk to her though. She's so old."

Lily could feel the nerves caged beneath her chest tapping on the inside of her skin. They were making noise inside her stomach, jumping up and down on her heart like a trampoline, and pulling on her intestines like a tug of war. They had the ability to take over her mind sometimes. Knowing that they were waiting for a moment to show their faces had the ability to scare Lily more than the news itself.

"Lily there is something to be learned from everyone," he tried to rationalize. "Perhaps you could ask her what her life was like when she was your age?"

"I guess." She shrugged her shoulders lightly. "I'm just not sure how knowing that would benefit me." She wiped her sweaty palms onto the base of her skirt, not caring if it got dirty.

"Just because you don't understand how something affects you, doesn't mean that it won't."

Lily rolled her eyes at her father and took a long drawn-out sigh.

Talking about it didn't help the situation. *Why do I have to do things I don't want to do?* she thought. It was going to be the same argument again, and so she prompted her father to continue exploring the house.

"What's through those doors?" Lily asked as she pointed to two colorful stained glass doors behind them. A bright light shone through the floral artwork on the doors powerfully, reminding Lily of a kaleidoscope she once had. Father shook his head as though giving in, and he unlocked the doors to the outside veranda. Leaning against a brick platform in the far edge, he invited Lily to join him.

Lily swiftly followed, but as she entered through the kaleidoscope doors, the sunlight didn't stop twirling, and it continued to flicker quickly on everything in sight. It moved so vigorously that it was distracting. She stood still trying to adjust her eyes, but all she could see was tiny particles of light floating through the air. The speckles of light seemed to dance playfully, and although she was standing perfectly still, she felt herself move too. She moved so quickly in a vibrating force of back and forth, side to side, that it made her question whether the rainbow colors of flickering light were in fact from the outside sun itself or whether she was looking at a reflection of what she was experiencing inside of her.

"You look deep in thought Lily, what is it?"

The familiar voice brought her back into the moment. It was her father.

"Papa, I saw something strange," Lily replied shyly, stopping in her footsteps, hesitant to walk out to the veranda.

"What did you see, Lily?" he asked, coming back toward her, holding his hand out to encourage her to keep moving forward.

"Sparkles of light in the air," she whispered, not wanting them to disappear, although slightly disturbed by the supernatural sensation. "I see them floating around me, just for a split second, and then my eyes calm down and when I look at the sky they are gone." She found her voice, remembering how real they had felt to look at, reliving the same vibration as though she were still experiencing that exact moment of reality. "But I still remember them, I remember seeing something amongst nothing. It's weird, isn't it?" she asked nervously, taking her father's hand and walking toward the veranda edge.

"Perhaps it's just your eyes adjusting to the light? I don't think it is anything to be concerned about darling. It is a gift to see things that no one else can."

He reassured her that her thoughts were not queer, and guided her to the brick platform that marked the end of the veranda. She gasped at the beautiful sight. For there in front of her stood an enormous backyard, full of luscious green trees, tall grass, an abundance of flowers and a beautiful three-tier fountain. And in the very far distance she could see a blue creek with a peaceful flowing stream.

"Papa, is this really all ours?" Lily asked as she looked over the land, wanting to dive off the veranda and fly through the garden.

"Yes darling, do you like it?"

Lily nodded in approval, still too proud to accept that maybe this house could be better than the last one, and that maybe her father was right.

She looked down below, staring at the different heights of the trees. A faint pebbled pathway weaved between the flowerbeds, as it made its way down the slightly slanted hill. It led to an open field of grass, where a gardener was chopping the hedges.

"Lily, the gardener is waving to you, wave at him!" Father instructed as he flapped his arms in giant swinging motions.

"No way!" Lily rebutted rudely, looking in the opposite direction. "I don't want to associate with the help."

She snubbed her nose and stared at the fountain, admiring the water pouring lavishly in excess.

"I do not believe my own child just uttered those words," her father replied with disbelief, and turned to his daughter, lifting her chin up to face his eyes. "Never discriminate that which you do not understand. You are no better than him do you hear me?"

Lily shook her head quickly in an attempt to dismiss the play of events. She felt guilty immediately and could hear voices repeating her father's words, telling her how bad she was for thinking that way. Although she knew the gardener didn't hear her she could sense that perhaps he could feel her disapproval. *No, but that's crazy, he can't telepathically hear me, can he?* she thought quietly to herself.

"Yes father. But, does he not work for us?" she said in an attempt to justify her actions.

"That is the exact reason why you should be grateful to him. He is sharing his time for your benefit, Lily. I can't believe I have raised such a spoiled girl, why is it that you even think this way?" He spoke sternly, demanding an explanation. Lily didn't even know where the words had come from, or whether she even believed them.

"Well, the girls at school. . ."

"I am so happy that you are never going to that school again if this is how the girls at your old school behaved," he interrupted her. "How could you be such a fool? You need more positive influences in your life."

Lily had never seen her father angry like that before. She realized perhaps she was being too harsh on him, and on the new house. His eyes were glaring at her, barely blinking, and she could feel the affliction her words had created.

"I think you should go to your room, Lily," he ordered, smiling greatly at the gardener as though to make up for Lily's outburst.

"No Papa, I am sorry, please forgive me. I'm so grateful for this new house, I would love to see more of it," she pleaded, running after her father who was walking back inside.

"You are acting like such a spoiled girl and I can only blame myself," he said disheartened, stopping in his steps from Lily having blocked his entrance.

"Papa it's not your fault at all. You are right; I am too impressionable from these other kids. I promise I will use my own judgment in future. Please forgive me," she begged again, realizing that perhaps she had gone too far this time. "I'm so grateful for this house, please tell me more about it."

Father nodded gravely, acknowledging her words yet reserving himself from showing too much kindness. They walked through the rest of the house—a large kitchen, laundry, three bedrooms, two living areas, another side veranda, and three bathrooms. The house was very spacious and carefully decorated with antique furniture leftover from the previous tenants. Lily felt like she had just walked in on someone else's life yet was welcomed to make it her own.

The last room they walked into was Father's bedroom. It was a welcoming room of warm golden light that dribbled through the windows upon Lily's entrance. A large king bed was positioned proudly in the middle, and in the corner sat a beautiful antique mirrored dressing table, made from dark timber with long thin draws underneath.

"Papa, I think this would look better in my room," she said as she pointed to the dressing table.

"Yes Lily, you can have it," he mechanically replied, running his finger over a small hole in the wall.

"So, if we own everything, does this mean that anything I find is now mine?" she asked with gleaming eyes, thinking about what ancient treasures she could find in unusual places.

"That's right." Father smiled as he nodded and left the room, letting Lily entertain her imagination on her own.

She started by searching through the dressing room draws. There was nothing, only the smell of dusty dry wood, which reminded her of the cut down sandalwood trees at her grandparents' farm. Disappointed, she walked along the edge of the room near the windowsill, staring at the sunlight and predicting the process of how the light is distorted when filtering through the glass.

She envisioned the distance upon which the burning star blazed and imagined the time it took to reach her, as well as how much heat would have been lost on the journey. She followed the light to the tips of the frame, along the edge of where the glass met the floor; and that's where she saw them. The crystals. They proudly shone along the window in between the wooden crevice, lined up perfectly in a row, as if they were bathing in the heat from the sun. She liked the look of them, so she picked them up.

I can feel their heartbeat, she thought, as she closed her eyes and held the crystals tightly.

And like magic, she was calm. She forgot how her crystals could talk to her soul. They had the ability to provide her with strength when she thought she had none. Lily had found crystals in her old house too; she felt as though they had somehow followed her. She would always feel magnetic energy vibrate when she was near them, but if she spent too much time thinking about it, it was too difficult for her to comprehend. So she taught herself to just accept it and continue with her day. She placed the crystals in her pocket securely. *They clink together joyfully,* she thought, *like they have been reunited again. I wonder how long they had been apart? Did they know they were lying right next to each other?*

She continued to have a conversation with herself in her head as she explored the rest of her new home. She could time herself to run from one end of the house to the other in just under fifteen seconds. Her skirt swam with the draft and streamed behind her as she ran back and forth above the creaky floorboards. Her crystals jingled loudly in her pocket and she gleamed with excitement of how much exploring she had yet to do. She knew all too well that both the attic and under the house were the best two places to search and she imagined the next discoveries to add to her collection: a random key, a small piece of painted pottery, perhaps a few words on paper. Anything that suggested another realm of what was or what could be.

She ran down the stairs to the bottom veranda, which stretched out to meet the garden. But something stopped her from touching the meadow, and she was drawn to the back corner of the wall. A fine square outline lay subtly amongst the wooden floor. The size of it was just big enough to fit a person through. She knew immediately it was meant for her. But, the empty space carved around the corners of the door was tiny, and she failed to squeeze her little fingers through. She would need something strong and thin to slide down and leverage it up. She gazed around the room accordingly, looking for an improvisation.

An antique piano stood underneath the stairs, and a hard piece of metal about the size of her hand poked out abruptly from underneath. She crawled to pick out the wire and examined it carefully, predicting the probability of it working. The piece of metal teethed perfectly between the wooden plank, and she jolted one end up high like a sea-saw. Careful not to wedge her fingers between the gap, she lifted the edge of the door up and removed it completely, revealing an open square of black nothingness below. She gasped with awe as she hovered above the space inside, allowing it to breathe deeply for the first time in however many years.

The afternoon sun pierced through the square faintly. It was enough light for Lily to predict the height between the ground and where it was that she was standing. She knew she could jump down without hurting herself, but without a ladder to get back out she would be stuck. She hovered over the hole to get a closer look. A muddy patch of dirt lay directly below her, with a slimy green layer of moss. It looked home to a growing patch of flowers, although it was difficult to say if they were indeed flowers. *What strange plants are able to grow with such little sunlight to feed them?* she thought. But when she reexamined, she saw it was not actually a flower but tiny crystals in symmetric circles pushing out through the floor, which had created a pattern similar to a flower!

Her body twitched with delight and an anticipation of needing to investigate further overwhelmed her senses. Holding her weight in her arms, Lily poked her head through the hole, and then slowly, she moved her neck around. Pitch-black darkness surrounded her completely. There was nothing in front, nothing behind nor to the left or to the right. But as she rolled her neck to come back upwards she saw a bright light flash twice in the distance quickly. One, two. *What was that?*

Eager to jump down but scared of doing so without a ladder or torch, she walked back upstairs, commencing a search for the missing pieces to complete her mission.

"Papa! Papa!" she shrieked, looking for her father to help.

But she didn't need him after all, for there in front of her lay a perfectly stable not-too- big, not-too-small, silver ladder. *Perfect!* she thought, quite pleased with her luck, and she picked it up. It was very heavy, and almost set her off-balance, but she had a goal in mind and it didn't stray her from her path. She would carry that ladder somehow. *Now for a torch,* she thought, as she ran back upstairs. She found a candle and light in her father's tool box in the shed, and hurried back to the floor opening, hearing the clunky clank of the crystals kiss once again in her pocket. They vibrated loudly together like a drumming heartbeat, and for a moment Lily thought perhaps they were singing in tune together in a chant-like rhythm, encouraging her to move forth. Okay, she was ready.

"Li-ly . . . Li-ly . . ." Father interrupted her.

She could hear his footsteps up above on the veranda.

"What is it Papa? I'm about to jump down a manhole in the floor! Is it urgent?"

"Yes darling, it is, I'm afraid there will be no exploring tonight, we have dinner plans with your grandparents."

Lily stared at the hole, and then to the ceiling to where she could hear her father standing above her on the veranda. "But Papa . . ." she whined, staring back at the hole.

"I'm sorry, darling. We have to."

Lily dragged her feet as she walked up the stairs, leaving the door to the underground wide open for her to explore tomorrow.

But that night when Lily tried to go to sleep, she had a burning desire to go and visit under the house. A little voice kept talking to her, saying, *I wonder what's downstairs, I wonder how to get inside.* She knew she had to wait until morning, but silencing the mind was such a difficult task at times, especially when she felt as though the voice was coming from her heart. *Am I really meant to hide such overwhelming desires?* she thought. *Surely, if this voice was this strong, there must be truth to it?* She tossed again, smacking the pillow to the mattress. *The jump down wasn't really that big was it?* she thought as she calculated her next moves. *If I don't go down now, I won't be able to see it until after school tomorrow, that's another day . . . I can't wait that long!* She jumped out of her bed and lit a candle in her hand. She packed a little gold jar to hold an extra candle and a match, and put it inside her cream crochet bag that carried all her favorite things, she swung it over her shoulders and tip-toed downstairs to the opening of the floor.

The jump down looked nowhere near as big as she remembered it and she threw the ladder in, measuring the distance of the fall from the time it took to land. It was only now that she realized she was barefoot, still in her long white lace nightgown she liked to wear on a hot summers night. Barefoot under the house was not a good idea—there could be broken glass, all sorts of wildlife that she could step on—but the idea of going all the way back upstairs and changing right now was not an option. *I'd like to take the risk please*, she thought. What's the worst that could happen? She pierces some skin? Tears her dress? All in the game of doing something that she loved. It would be worth it a hundred times over. There was no better moment than right now to leap into the unknown and see what she could find!

Her eyes twinkled with anticipation. She was wide awake, probably over-tired for being up at such a late hour for a young girl like her. She could hear the great grandfather clock chime up above. She counted. Twelve. *Okay, I'll be back before 5am, when Papa gets up. That gives me five hours.*

One . . . two . . . three . . . wooooooshhhhhh! Her lace dress ballooned out as she jumped down, and she floated gracefully, swaying gently from side to side. When she landed, the candle dropped to the floor, extinguishing upon doing so and leaving her in complete darkness. The space was so black, she could not even see her hand in front of her face. Only a faded charcoal light was visible through the square door high above and it streamed down as though it were a gift from the stars and the moon. But it was not enough light to see straight ahead. *Oh perhaps this was not a good idea after all.* She scared herself with the unknown and blinked her eyes quickly as the fear set in. But as she blinked, a strange light became visible in the distance. She blinked again and the light flashed once more. She closed her eyes tightly. Flash! A single white light danced in front of her eyes. It hovered toward her, gaining strength and building momentum. She opened her eyes wide. Nothing. Not a thing! She closed them again and watched as the white light reappeared, this time moving vibrantly toward her. The light began to dance, as though it now had an audience to play out in front of. And it opened up like a flower, prancing elaborately in a continuous fractal pattern, constantly evolving, constantly moving. The longer she stared, the greater the evolution, and the strength in the detail magnified, the edges now sharpened with definition. Overwhelmed with such a tantalizing display of animation, Lily held her eyes closed tightly, allowing the colored lights to dance candidly around her. They encased her entire body and created a glowing sphere that illuminated the edges of her skin as though holding her in a protective embrace. The outline of the sphere then duplicated, and moved along the circumference of the original circle, leaving a shadowed trail behind as it did so. The two spheres did not split and instead multiplied; now opening up like a flower, as though Lily was the pollen heart center, she was framed with petals all around.

She felt herself drawn toward one direction, and she followed the pull. With each footstep she marked a new circle, and the petals spun turbulently around the circumference once more. It was only now that she realized that each step she took, the circle followed her, and the petals around her continued. So each moment was completely new, completely different than the last.

Confused, she spun around again, and watched as the lights twirled around with her movements as expected. She felt a strange tingling sensation from the ground beneath as her body began to feel weightless, like she was floating in water. The light supported her body and she felt herself being pushed and pulled in all directions, into an infinite measurement of length and widths. She felt herself stretch out far and wide, completely outside of her own body. She travelled high above into a place filled with endless bright lights. It was there that she was squashed into a tiny little ball. So small and minute, she rolled around, switching between different extremes of sizes, of big to small and small to big. Squashing everything and yet nothing, rolling around and around, up and down, side to side, without actually moving her arms or legs. She couldn't feel her body anymore, she was traveling elsewhere, it was somewhere outside of herself.

A bright light ahead travelled directly toward Lily. Or was she moving toward it? She couldn't be sure, but she did know that both she and the light together were magnetically connected. And as it came closer, it grew bigger, and bigger. It grew so big that soon it completely covered any darkness around her, and she collided straight into it. And when she arrived, her body arrived too, and her dress, and her pouch. And the darkness had gone, and all that remained was the light shining brightly inside of herself.

CHAPTER TWO

JACQUES & THE LAND OF OTOR

A thick layer of black smoke blanketed the sky, while slithers of ruby red clouds clawed their way through. The gothic backdrop created a heavy impact on Lily, as she lay on the ground staring above. She could feel the smoke-like clouds run over her skin. They crushed her lungs and forced her breathing to slow down severely. Her eyes rolled back and forth gradually, as she absorbed her new surroundings, and slowly, very slowly, she moved to her side in preparation to stand. An exploding burst of thunder engulfed her ears, yet she could not see the lightning anywhere in the dark haze. Only a red dirt path with speckles of ruby sparkles lay before her feet. And the glittering path moved in waves, lighting up directly to where Lily's eyes wandered. She walked calmly with bare feet, feeling the sparkling dirt touch her skin, squeezing up between her toes and massaging what little space there was left between the weight of her body and the ground. There, the red dirt rested in the empty space, satisfied in giving support to Lily as she embarked on her journey.

Lily could see a fiery sun peeking its head in the horizon. It was patiently waiting its turn to rise up and demand the sky. And despite the comfort of seeing the normality of the sun warm up the ruby sky, it was in the splinters of light that shone through the clouds that she felt someone watching down on her, looking after her. In the darkness of black smog she felt the hope to carry forward, all through something that perhaps was just her imagination, perhaps was just all in her head. But that ray of light that she could see so far away, that could not be touched, it had somehow touched through to her heart, making her feel a glimmer of hope ever so deeply, so deeply that she had no other choice but to believe that it was real.

The thunder grew louder with each step, and as the last of the smog finally cleared, Lily could see that the noise wasn't electricity flowing down from the sky, but instead the opposite: smoke and lighting erupted like a volcano from the ground. The sparkly dots flew in a vortex, full of brightly mixed colors, each separated in their spin, almost plaited together and then unmixed and mixed again. It was as if they couldn't make up their mind if they wanted to be one or separate. Or perhaps they liked to play with one another, seeing what color they mixed best with together. Lily walked toward the tornado of smoke as the path in front rose to greet her. As she proceeded along the path it slowly turned into a long, drawn-out hill, and before she knew it, she was standing directly at the base of a giant red pyramid.

A glittery dust overlay the pyramid's surface. It sparkled with quick flickering lights like a fireworks display. The smoke that rose to the sky was coming from the tip of the pyramid, and it streamed out into a long thin line of rainbow colors shooting upwards. It was a magnificent sight to witness. As Lily stared at the smoke the dots began to transform into miniature shapes; first squares then circles, triangles, and pentagons, twirling around and moving from side to side. She walked closer to the pyramid, and could see an opening, no door, just a large circular opening in the middle of the red shimmering pyramid. The same colorful smoke that was pushing out from the tip of the pyramid swirled around the circle door in a vortex. And at the bottom of her feet in giant letters were the words 'Jacques the Healer' stamped deeply into the ground, spelled out with thick red crystals, cemented in like a welcome mat.

"Hello," Lily whispered faintly through the door.

A small hole pierced into the smoke from the power of her breath, allowing an opening to see inside. In the center of the room sat a tall skinny man. His skin was a dark caramel brown, and he was dressed in maroon loose-fitting pants with a matching short-sleeve top. He did not move, and faced the opposite wall, adjacent to where Lily was standing, which had an identical opening with a large cut-out circle.

"Hhhheeeeeellllloooooo . . ." she sang through the confined space once more, this time a bit louder, and she watched as the hole widened from the force of her breath.

She picked up a stick from the ground and used it carefully to mimic the circular motion of the hole, extending the smoke outwards, slowly around and around. Once the hole was big enough for Lily to step through, she yelled out to the man once more.

"Hello! May I come in?" Lily asked politely in a child-like sweet singing style; a voice she had learned to be most persuasive with her father.

The man turned his head without moving his body, not so much abnormally, but with a strict angle of flexibility. His eyes were wide open, almost scarily happy, alive, and bursting with energy. The white area around his pupil expanded heavily and he grinned with perfectly aligned teeth beaming harmoniously with his excited eyes, contrasting beautifully against the dark skin. He opened his mouth as if about to say something, but instead, used his hand to direct her forward. He pointed his finger, and pursed his lips together to shush Lily once she was inside. When Lily walked closer to the healer, he spoke in a soothing voice.

"Welcome to my home, please make yourself comfortable. I will be present shortly."

His voice didn't match the look of his face, nor the excitement in his smile. It sounded far too calm to coincide with the emotion that he was relaying through his facial expression alone. Lily took this opportunity to explore the rest of the house. There was no bed, no kitchen, nor any lounge area as such. *What an odd house*, she thought.

In the center of the square-shaped room lay a square table of marble, which was the perfect height to stand at without the need for chairs, and just as well because there were none to be seen at all. In one corner stood giant shelves, full of thick, heavy books, small drawn paintings, odd-shaped bottles, crystals, and metal ornaments. A large cauldron sat over an open fire on the left and a giant map-like painting hung on the far right. The fireplace had a mimic of the same pyramid structure over it, directing the smoke to follow through a pipeline. But the smoke from the fire did not exit out the center of the topmost point of the pyramid; instead it traveled through several glass tubes that were directed into separated small holes along the wall. This reminded Lily of a piece of artwork as opposed to a chimney. After observing her surroundings, she looked back to the healer to try and figure out exactly what it was that he was doing. Jacques stood in a hunched over position with hands on both knees as he stared at his navel, breathing deeply and quickly. He was moving his stomach in waving ripples as he inhaled and exhaled noisily. Lily looked away uncomfortably. But as she looked to the right, he appeared again, in the same manner, waving ripples through his stomach. She looked to the left, he reappeared, but this time he stopped and smiled.

"Follow my actions; it will breathe life into your lungs." He wavered his hand, encouraging Lily to oblige, but she looked down to the floor awkwardly, straining to understand his sharp English accent.

The man did not seem to be offended and he continued to talk. "I like to do this every morning when I wake up. It moves my breath around my body, giving me energy and keeping my mind active." His voice hushed. She peeked up to look at him. He continued to breathe deeply while he rotated his stomach from top to bottom in a fluid motion, repeatedly, making a loud sound from his nose and his mouth.

She shook her head quickly and avoided his eyes, looking around the room once more, wondering whether she should leave. But something was keeping her there and she peeked back to spy on the man in his natural habitat.

Jacques pretended to ignore her response, knowing she was watching. He held up his hand with a thin, crooked finger pointing above as if to attract her attention. He then dove his finger up and over to point at his stomach, and he lifted his cotton cloth shirt up to reveal his boney frame. He hunched over again aggressively, twisting his head toward his belly as far as it would go, breathing all the air out and then moving the skin over his stomach in and out quickly.

Lily had never seen anything like it before and continued to stare in an awkward silence. She wanted to look away, but knew that the strange man could feel her eyes upon him, and she was nervous he would have ordered her to look back. He continued to breathe in deeply, once again, *Wooooooooosh* came a loud noise from his mouth as he pushed all of the air from out of his stomach.

After several breaths he stood upright and walked toward Lily. He looked different than before, as though something had overtaken his body. His eyes became both whiter and brighter, and he smiled calmly with his perfectly straight white teeth.

"This breathing technique I was willing to share with you. Why did you say no? You have never tried it before have you?"

Lily shrugged her shoulders and looked away, doubtful on how to reply. She pointed her toe into the dusty floor, circling it around to distract her mind.

"So, how would you know what kind of affect it would have unless you tried? You should try different things," he poked at her again. "Nothing will change if you don't change."

"But I don't want anything to change," Lily replied with a small outburst as she thought about her whole life consisting of one big change after the other, all happening without her control.

She had felt it impossible to welcome such notions when they always seemed to follow with such heartache.

"That's a very sad outlook on life little girl."

Lily looked away again shyly, feeling tears well in her eyes from having been confronted with honesty by a complete stranger. And the idea of being alone in another world where she felt like she didn't belong leaked into her thoughts. But Jacques wasn't letting her sulk, and he leapt into the air, twirling around as he continued to preach his advice at the lost young girl.

"Those who welcome change are the happiest! Those who relish in the glory of the constantly evolving life lessons are the wisest and live the longest! Those who . . ."

Lily shook her head and walked away, back toward the door. She wasn't sure how to handle the situation anymore and had concluded it was best if she just escaped.

"Not listening to me is the highest form of disrespect young girl," Jacques called out after her, the words hovering in the air like a speech bubble, blocking her exit.

She turned back to face Jacques as though a teacher at school were scolding her and nodded hurriedly. Then she walked back toward the door, holding the tears inside with strength.

"Where are you going?" Jacques questioned, stomping after the girl.

"I think I want to go home," she replied timidly, stopping in her footsteps, and turning back around, clearly unsure of her decision.

"You think?" Jacques smirked as he questioned, tipping his face down but his eyebrows up. "You don't know?"

"I don't know," Lily agreed.

"If you are unsure of the decision then it is not the right time to make it," Jacques stated proudly as he clicked his fingers with emphasis. "Why force yourself to choose? Learn to be patient and allow the moment to present itself to you." He placed his hands on his hips, and wiggled from side to side.

"I feel like I just insulted you," Lily replied nervously, "Wouldn't you prefer it if I left?" she asked as she looked down to her crochet bag, fiddling with the straps over her arm.

"You didn't insult me at all. You actually only hurt yourself," Jacques replied soothingly as he tiptoed closer to Lily. "And I will love you anyway. For I know you didn't know any better at the time."

Lily looked to Jacques, puzzled, as she wiped small droplets of sweat off her brow and she pushed her curls back behind her ear. The sun was now burning brightly through the circled doorways, and attached to the light was a calming warm breeze. It had made the space inside of the pyramid intensely humid. "You love me?" she rebutted, confused, lifting her shoulders up slightly. "You don't even know me."

She raised her eyebrows in disbelief of Jacques' words, remembering back to her days at the schoolyard where no one would even be spending this much time talking to her.

"Do I need to know you to love you?" he asked, his teeth still shining from the beaming smile painted across his face.

Lily looked more confused than she was when she had seen him breathing hunched over like a madman. A part of her wanted to stay and find out more, as she was oddly attracted to the demeanor of the old man. He was rightfully kind, orderly, and vastly strange. She didn't want to leave him.

"What's your name?" he asked.

"Lily," she replied shyly, looking down to the ground once more.

"Oh Lily, wow. That is such a beautiful name!" Jacques replied with lively enthusiasm, as though he had never heard it before.

"Really? I think it's kind of boring," she shrugged her shoulders, "like me I guess."

"Lily, why put yourself down like that? You know that's not true at all. Your name is so elegant and smooth-sounding. It's perfectly even, four letters. Lil-leee, Lil-leee. Two, two, the same!" Jacques said as he picked up a long, wooden stick from the floor and drew her name in pink letters in the air. He underlined the two syllables of her name, spelling it out again and again. His repetitive behavior reminded her of herself, and she smiled with gratitude, utterly appreciative to have met such a creature.

"I have never thought about my name like that before," she admitted, wondering how she could have overlooked something as obvious of her own self when she loved to find similarities in everything around her.

"Well you should! There is a great deal to learn about a name." Jacques nodded in approval, writing his own name in red letters just below Lily's.

"And so are you Jacques the healer, as it says out front?"

He smiled with a cheesy grin, his thick lips pushed up to cushion his cheeks and he squinted his eyes, wriggling his body in a dance again. "Yes, yes that's right! My name is Jacques. I live here in Otor, and I am the greatest healer in all of the land."

He twirled again, levitating high into the air and gliding back down to the ground in slow motion. Lily smiled with anticipation, waiting for him to lead the conversation, but he didn't and they just stared at each other in silence. Lily looked away nervously.

"Are you quite shy?" Jacques asked intrigued, taking one step closer. "Are you a bit of an introvert?"

"What's an introvert?" Lily replied, as she moved one step back, slightly guarded.

"It's someone who keeps more to themselves as opposed to interacting with their outside world. It's okay, you don't need to pretend with me. I like introverts. Some people never shut up. Talk, talk, talk, all the time. Thinking that their voices show their intelligence, but it just shows their stupidity!"

Lily giggled as she thought of her grade ten teacher who talked so much that Lily often dozed off, thinking she was the dullest person she had ever met. Finally, she met someone who was agreeing with her thoughts!

"I . . . I guess I don't really know how to talk to grown-ups," Lily replied as she diverted her eyes to the side. "Or anyone really," she mumbled underneath her breath.

Lily looked back down to the ground, wishing that Jacques wouldn't focus his attention on her anymore. But still, a small part of her was interested in hearing what he had to say. There was something special about Jacques and she felt safe with him.

"I don't believe that for a moment," Jacques intervened as he crouched down to the ground, attempting to make eye contact with the timid girl. "Perhaps you need to believe in yourself more."

"But you're so much older than me? As if I am going to say anything that could be of interest to you?"

"Why present yourself in that way to me Lily? You have just as much right to voice your thoughts as I do," he corrected her. "We are always learning, both you and me. No matter what age."

Lily listened carefully to Jacques explain. It was as though she was being told a secret that only adults knew, and she smiled at being allowed such a privilege.

"I would like to voice my opinions more, really I do. I just . . . I don't know why I think I can't."

Jacques waved his hand encouraging Lily to move closer.

"Do you know what the secret is?" he whispered. "Knowing how incredibly wonderful it is to be unique! It makes you irreplaceable, didn't you know?" Jacques winked with one eyebrow raised as he continued louder. "Sometimes it's better to be an introvert anyway. Silence lets you observe not only your surroundings, but yourself too. Oh if only all of Sa Neo would be silent, perhaps we would live like the most powerful empress, Violetta in the land Neveah where all is telepathic and no words are uttered!"

"Sa Neo? Violetta? Neveah? I would love to go to such a place," Lily replied with excitement as she thought about all the marvelous places she had yet to discover.

"And so it shall be!" Jacques smirked as he lifted some of the sparkly red dirt from the ground and cast it up above their heads. It flew directly up to the center point of the pyramid and drifted down slowly like a glittery rainfall.

"How so?" she asked.

He held his hand out and Lily watched as the sparkly dust fell perfectly into his palm, as though it were being magnetically pulled.

"Whatever you think, you shall receive," Jacques said as he blew slowly on the glittery sandcastle piled in his hand. The dust swooshed upwards in a giant wave, forming a fiery red dragon. Each point on the dragon's back held a large ruby crystal, and it took a deep breath, blowing thin sparkles of dust from its mouth. The dust then swirled around its body until it completely disappeared.

"So, I can think of anything at all and it will happen?" Lily's eyes opened wider than they ever had before. She almost felt like they were popping out of her head, they had dramatized so much. But when she caught a glimpse of herself in the reflection of Jacques' eyes, he didn't seem to be fazed at all.

"To an extent," he replied.

"And what extent is that?"

"To the extent of that which you believe . . . but if you are here you already must be believing somehow, or how would you manifest for such a place to exist?"

Lily combed her fingers through her hair as she stood confused and she dismissed his comment swiftly.

"But I didn't Jacques. I followed the light and here I am."

"Hmm . . . I see. So, you don't understand inside or outside of yourself yet do you? Is that why you have come to me?" Jacques asked rhetorically, as he tapped on his cheek, pondering how to educate the child on such matters.

"But I didn't come to you, I just walked up the path and here you were." Lily pointed to the circle door that she had first walked through in an attempt to show Jacques the road that she had followed. But the smoke-filled dust that whirled around the sphere clouded her vision and the path was nowhere to be seen.

"My dear, there are never any accidents; you had planned to come here all along!"

"Planned to come here all along?" Lily repeated with a puzzled pout, remembering that she had only by chance decided to explore under the house that afternoon. How was it possible that she had thought of exploring the house when she didn't even know that they were moving up until a few months ago.

"Yes, you decided this before you were born," Jacques replied with a matter-of-fact attitude. "You have come to me for a reason, there is something that I am meant to be giving you," he said as he crossed over to the wall where the shelves were filled with metal ornaments and crystal bottles. "Hmm . . . What is it though?" he muttered to himself as he picked each one up individually and weighed them carefully with closed eyes. "For only you can heal yourself, I can merely guide you on your way."

"But how could I have always known I was coming here when we only just moved into the new house?" Lily asked as she followed the tall lanky man to the corner of the pyramid. He ignored her question and proceeded to pick up random objects, holding them for several seconds before dismissing them.

"A copper horse? No. A silver spoon? No. A golden bridge? No." He muttered to himself as he continued, oblivious to Lily's confusion.

"Ahuh!" he said, picking up two small ruby bottles and handing them to Lily.

"Smell them and tell me which one you like," he said, raising his hand to hurry her along.

"I don't really understand," she protested, although she lifted up each one to inhale the scent thoroughly as requested. She closed her eyes as she smelled the long thin neck of the first bottle. It smelled like a great barrel of spicy cinnamon, and with her eyes closed she could feel herself transported to a marketplace. Many tradesmen were yelling at her to buy the spices, and she looked down, feeling the powdery substance between her fingers.

She shook her head quickly and opened her eyes to see lanky Jacques standing with an open mouth, eagerly awaiting her response. But before she could talk, he replaced the cinnamon smell with a short fat bottle, and pushed it up under her nose. Again she closed her eyes as she inhaled, this time a warming sensation overtook her body, and it reminded her of eucalyptus leaves and frangipani flowers. When she closed her eyes she was running through an open field of tall grass, the warm sunshine on her hair. She didn't want to leave, but Jacques tapped her on the shoulder to come back. She sighed with a pleasing moan as the fragrance delighted her senses.

"Oh, of course you picked rosemary. You had dreamt about it before. Silly me." He took back the long thin-necked bottle and placed it on the shelf, and he pointed to her bag, encouraging her to put the fat bottle with rosemary oil inside. "You need help with your memory right?"

Lily looked to Jacques uneasily. "How do you know I've dreamt about rosemary before?" Lily asked worryingly, remembering the dream she had not too long ago where she laid in a field of rosemary, smelling the scents of pine and lemon. "I think I want to go back to where I came from," she concluded, accepting the gift of bottled essence and placing it in her bag.

"You think you want to?" Jacques stopped his calculations and pointed to his head. "You thought? Or you think?" He pointed with his other hand and rewound an imaginary wheel, as though he had moved back their time to when Lily had first wanted to leave. She was now standing back at the door, having just insulted the fellow. Well she thought she had insulted him. Lily stood alarmed that she had just teleported to another location within the pyramid and she closed her eyes, trying to make sense of the situation.

"Oh, well now you really have no idea what you're doing, do you?" Jacques smirked as he yelled from across the room. "You cannot go back just now anyway. You are a gift to this world. You are meant to be here. Welcome to Sa Neo!" Jacques exclaimed as he pointed to the map on the wall and opened his arms wide as if representing the land. His eyes squinted to a half moon while he grinned, lifting his thick pink lips to push up and touch his nose. Lily felt the kindness in his heart shine straight through his eyes and magnetically connecting to hers, she was unable to look away. He hopped on both feet jumping back and forth in excitement while dancing with both hands.

Lily walked over to the giant map on the wall. The seas were painted on a wax-like paper, and above it, hovered the seven lands in mid-air. She stared at the outlines carefully, there were faint little paths carved into the mountains, and various houses with names and signs etched in between the trees.

"Can I draw a copy of it?" she asked politely, "to help me find my way around here?"

"But that's my map! That's my way around here," he replied as he wiped the pathways clean on the lands like a duster on a blackboard. "Go and make your own mark."

Jacques wasn't being mean, but Lily felt a bit insecure.

"What's wrong?" he asked, reading Lily's withdrawal.

"You could have said it nicer to me," she replied quietly, more so as a reaction of being embarrassed.

"Not really. It's just the way you interpreted it Lily. If anything, I am h-e-l-p-ing you." Jacques sounded the word out slowly, wanting it to sink into her mind deeply.

"Helping me? Helping me how?" she questioned, wanting to believe Jacques, but she still felt quite conflicted as her mind was telling her otherwise.

"I am helping you by encouraging you to follow your own path and not mine. As well as giving you a little lesson on interpreting words." He chuckled to himself and circled his finger as he tapped Lily playfully on the nose. His likable behavior made it impossible to be angry with him, and she smiled reassuringly.

"Okay, shall we look at the planetary alignments from when you arrived?" Jacques asked as he sharpened the burnt amber stick and drew on the dirt floor of his home. He started to draw triangles, hexagons, and squares. It evolved more and more and more. He drew a long timeline map from one side of the room to the other. Back and forth he went, drawing long figurines that connected in one long line.

"This is all fascinating Jacques, but what does it mean?" Lily asked, having waited quite awhile and excited for some answers.

"Nothing, I just felt like drawing." Jacques opened his mouth to let out a loud roar of laughter, and he bent the stick over his knee, breaking it in two pieces in one quick motion.

"So, what I am to do here? I do not know my purpose?"

"Your purpose is to be exactly who you are. Why must you define it anymore than that? Why can't you just beeee?"

Lily stared at Jacques, allowing the weight of his words to crush down on her fears. She never thought about the idea of 'just being' before. She always thought she needed to do something or go somewhere. He was right, why did she have to have a purpose, why couldn't she just enjoy the journey?

"Okay. So . . . what now?"

"Perhaps show me your hands? I will let them tell me."

Jacques opened Lily's palms and stared carefully. He held his finger up and signaled for her to wait as he went and got a microscope that was resting on the shelf in the far right of the pyramid.

"Ahuh . . . ahuh . . . hmm . . . interesting . . . Yes . . . okay . . . sure . . . alright . . . Good . . . very good!" Jacques muttered to himself as he held a piece of crystal over Lily's hand and stared diligently.

"So what did you see?" she asked impatiently, looking to her own hands carefully as well.

"Right now, your head line overtakes your heart. It's not good."

Jacques drew a red line over Lily's hand to outline what he could see. The ripples of the line bled outwards, growing in thickness and in size.

"But you said very good?" She looked up puzzled, although when she looked back to her hand, the painted line had disappeared.

"I meant very good to myself, giving myself a compliment for reading, you know."

Lily shook her head and pulled on the lace edge of her dress, a defense mechanism she seemed to resort to often when she didn't know how to handle the conversation. But instead of Jacques talking, he was quiet, and the stillness between the two became increasingly loud. She was forced to talk.

"I don't understand why you would compliment yourself?" she asked nervously.

"You never give yourself a compliment?" Jacques opened his eyes wide with disbelief. "Why?"

"Isn't giving myself a compliment vain?"

"Vain? Vain?" Jacques shook his head quickly and pointed back up above to the ceiling. "No my dear, vain is when you see beauty in only yourself and nothing else. But, if you can see beauty in yourself and realize that the outside surrounding you is a reflection of your own thoughts, then everything around you will always be beautiful. Then you can compliment yourself for seeing the greater good in everything around you." He nodded to himself, pleased with his response and shook his head as he muttered the words vain again. "Goodness, no wonder your head controls your heart."

My head controls my heart? Lily repeated as she thought about herself separately inside of her body. "Isn't my heart just a function to keep the blood moving, and my head, isn't that where my brain thinks? If my brain isn't thinking, then who is telling me what to do?"

"Sweet Lily, oh you darling Lily. You are not your thoughts." Jacques pointed to Lily as an additional version of herself extracted as a shadow and stepped forward. "Your head and your heart are two different things. Your heart will always rule, but sometimes the noise in your head can be distracting."

A glowing red love heart protruded from her shadow, and it beat vibrantly, loudly, and lovingly. The whole room filled with a warm light, and Lily felt completely immersed in warm water, as though she had dived into a salty sun-kissed rock pool. But as she closed her eyes to enjoy the untouchable feeling, an antenna-like radio reception buzzed through, it overkilled the warmth and drowned the therapeutic heartbeat.

"So how do I fix it?" she yelled as she covered her ears, trying to ignore the noise, which was saturating the peace.

The shadow disappeared and the noise immediately stopped.

"Start by listening to yourself. You should spend some time alone everyday to clear your mind and just focus on loving yourself."

Jacques edged closer as he spoke clearly, ensuring that each word he uttered was being listened to intently.

"Shouldn't I learn to love other people before I love myself? I have a hard time making friends," Lily admitted, looking down to the ground and digging another little hole into the red dirt with her bare toes. She sighed as she continued, "well, I don't have any friends, actually."

"How can you expect to make friends when you are not friends with yourself?" he objected, placing his hands together across his chest and bowing his head lightly. "If you love yourself completely first, then and only then are you are able to give love to others limitlessly. How can you feed the world when you, yourself are hungry?" he asked, keeping one hand on his chest he held the other open toward her.

"I still see loving myself as vain though, Jacques." She pleaded for understanding, taking his open palm as the two of them walked hand-in-hand around the room.

"It's arrogance of the ego that is vain, but if you loved yourself, I mean truly loved and respected yourself, nothing would ever harm you."

Lily thought about nothing ever hurting her again. She thought about the outside world and all the people in it with their judgment and the problems she faced everyday. How was it possible for all of that to just disappear? If what Jacques said was right, and if learning how to love yourself was the key to being invisible, well she ought to give it a try, she thought.

"So, how will I know if I love myself?" She stopped the two of them in their tracks, as they stood in front of the giant cauldron that overhung on the fireplace.

"Loving yourself comes hand in hand with knowing yourself," he said.

"And, how am I meant to know myself?" Lily argued, feeling the anguish of frustration creeping back through. And she pondered on the idea further. Although she spent a lot of time alone, knowing herself felt so foreign. She knew what she liked to do, and what she didn't like. But how could she know everything?

"Just trust that one day it will all make sense."

"Jacques nothing makes sense to me. I don't even know where I am!" Lily argued back exhausted, and she used the edge of her skirt to rub her eyes, realizing she had been awake for quite awhile. Her legs were sore and she wanted to sit down, but there was nowhere to sit. And the tiredness in her eyes made her feel weary. She needed some water and a soft bed to sleep on, as her body was starting to feel heavy.

"Come sit by the fireplace and I will make a special potion to re-energize you," Jacques said as he encouraged Lily closer to the fire.

"Can you read my thoughts?" Lily asked puzzled.

"No, the idea just came to me then. Did I guess right?"

"Strangely yes, I was just thinking how tired I was."

"I'm not surprised really," Jacques chuckled as he twirled his finger around in the air and sprinkled some dust in a circle. He then pointed to the ground where a large cushion appeared on the floor. Lily looked around confused. *Had it always been there?* she thought. Too tired to question, she sat down on the cushion and watched while Jacques walked to the large cauldron over the fire. It swayed from side to side and he sang to himself as he worked.

"Some prana and zirin oh chi la di da, some coco and maca and you see . . . voila!"

Jacques wobbled his head as he picked up invisible items from the air and poured them into the large cauldron. They created a loud smashing noise as though components were falling inside the pot, but there was nothing to be seen on the outside at all.

"Are my eyes playing tricks on me?" Lily asked, sitting wide awake from the aroma of Jacques' cooking. "Nothing is there, right?"

"Nothing is here?"

"Yes, nothing is there."

"Who says?"

"Me!" she squeaked, and she jumped up to have a closer look inside.

"Are you saying it doesn't exist?"

"I'm saying I can't see anything." She blinked her eyes several times in an attempt to see, although a sweet smell of cedar-wood was striking through the air. Jacques held her sight and stared directly.

"Haven't you realized yet?"

"Realized what?" she retorted as she looked around uneasily.

"You and I do not see things the same," Jacques chuckled with his rosy fat lips and he picked up a large spoon, stirring inside the pot with wide slow strokes.

Lily looked at the large cauldron and back to Jacques, wondering how they were seeing different pots when they were standing right next to each other.

"But aren't we in this world together?"

Jacques shook and nodded his head at the same time.

"This is precisely the notion you are missing that I tried to point out to you before. We interact separately but we are connected as one." Jacques pointed to the air as a line of pink marshmallow-looking clouds streamed down, splitting and reconnecting together into a knotted bow. It disappeared into nothing and yet Jacques continued to stare.

"So, why can't I see what you can see?"

"It will come, when you learn how to love yourself. Now, drink this. It will make you feel better." Jacques handed Lily a glass cup that looked completely empty. But after the last conversation, Lily was nervous to reveal that she couldn't see anything, and instead decided to pretend as well, drinking the nothingness drink, down her throat and into her tummy.

"It's delicious!" she exclaimed.

"It's my special recipe!" He winked back, nodding his head happily.

Bizarrely though, she did feel different. And within seconds a shot of energy poured through her entire body making her leap ever so slightly into the air. She now stood tall with perfect posture and a very straight back.

"What now?" she asked, her eyes opened wide, eager to go back out into the wilderness.

"I'm not sure. Perhaps show me what you brought in with you in case there is anything else I need to tell you," he said as he pointed to her crochet bag.

Lily started to take off her bag and give her only possessions to the odd man, realizing how much trust she had automatically granted him after such a short time. *Am I wrong to believe the goodness in someone so quickly?* she thought.

"You look confused?"

"I just . . . I don't know you that well, that's all," she admitted fearfully, holding her bag tightly in her hand.

"I understand completely. You're a young girl, in a new place, with new people. It can be quite scary. So just be still and ask yourself if you can trust me."

Lily didn't even need to close her eyes and take a moment. As soon as Jacques finished his sentence a huge *YES* screamed from her heart; and she handed her favorite bag over in one motion, without hesitation.

Jacques held the cream pouch up to his nose and smelled the edges from right to left. It was slightly old and tattered, and the crochet was worn down. It was hand made by her mother when she was a similar age to Lily's, and in memory of her, Lily liked to carry it always.

"This bag doesn't belong to you," Jacques said as he walked to the center table and placed the bag down, holding his right hand just above it to read the bag some more. "But it was somehow made for you, before you were born. And it likes to be with you." He continued smiling, as though he could hear the bag speaking words of happiness to him.

Lily's mouth gasped at his statement, and she promptly followed him to the center table. Anything that brought up memories of her mother always caught her attention.

"How do you know Jacques?" she asked excitedly, resting her hands on the cool marble bench.

"Because voices are telling me. I am told that with every stitch that was sewn, there was a great deal of love that went into it. With each movement of energy that was used to create such a masterpiece, all of it was transformed purely into love, just for you."

Lily looked at Jacques with admiration and happiness to have met him. And the fact that he cherished her mother's work just as much as she did made her realize that it was a quality in him that she hoped to find in other people that she would meet over the course of her life.

"That's very sweet Jacques, thank you. It was my mother's. I liked to think that she created this for me, although I never really got to ask her. She died just shortly after I was born. I never knew what it was like to have her in my life, but I talk to her often. Is that strange? To talk to someone I never knew or saw?" She looked shyly to the ground as she asked, lifting her eyes up to meet Jacques intermittently.

"No my dear, don't ever question these things. Just believe it is to be so. She is always with you. She is everywhere. In this bag, the sun, the moon, even in the flowers that grow from the ground. She is always watching you. Talk to her still, she really loves it. And she will always be listening." Jacques held Lily's hand securely between his two like a sandwich. Pushing warmth from each side, to display empathy to her loss.

"They think I'm crazy because I talk to her," she confided, looking down to the ground at to the red sparkly dirt.

"They?" Jacques asked inquisitively.

"The doctors, my father. Everyone in my world. They think I blame myself for her death."

"And do you?"

Lily had never really asked herself that question before. She had never pinpointed what it was that made her act strangely. She thought it was just her hobbies that didn't really match to those around her. She opted to spend time by herself, without that many people. She felt safe not getting close to anyone, constantly worrying that something bad would happen to them if she did.

"I don't know. Sometimes I feel guilty, but I feel like it's expected of me. And that it makes everyone happy because now they have a reason as to why I act so weird. And now they can put me aside and say this is why. Maybe I'm looking for an answer too." She answered solemnly, running her fingertips along the edge of the marble table as she spoke. "But Jacques something doesn't feel right and I want to think differently, I do. But I'm just used to thinking this way, I don't know any different."

Jacques slapped his hand on his knee fiercely. It was so loud and startling the whole pyramid shook as it echoed.

"You do know different! Well, you can learn. Have you never thought of that before?"

"Every now and again," she replied honestly. Those kinds of thoughts had presented themselves to her before, but she had learned how to dismiss them.

"Hold onto that idea," Jacques said as his hand formed a tight fist as though he was grabbing something strong. "That's the thought you should be listening to."

"But they tell me I have abnormal thoughts."

"They?" He raised his eyebrows.

"They, as in, the doctors . . . my school peers . . . my father." She had recited the proposed group of 'they' so many times before.

"Why are you listening to anyone other than yourself?" Jacques asked sternly. "You know the answers."

Lily had never heard of herself been thrown into the group of 'they.' *Why was that?* she wondered. *When did the group of 'they' become more important than I?*

"I thought I knew the answers Jacques, but when there is so much noise around you, it's hard to remember, do you know what I mean?"

"No, I think I need you to elaborate more." He stepped closer to Lily, and stared intimately into her green eyes. The backdrop of the pyramid disappeared behind him and she felt obliged to tell him the truth. The awful statement that deep down she knew was wrong to believe, yet it still very much existed inside of her.

"What about if I have thoughts about not being good enough?" Lily covered her mouth quickly, terrified that she had said too much. She had just let a complete stranger into the darkest parts of her mind. How would he take it?

"It sounds like your problem is actually a disconnect between what is here now, and what you aspire to. There is a missing link between loving yourself as you are now, and allowing your imagination to run wild." The backdrop of the pyramid came back into vision, and as Jacques said the words *run wild*, the entire room spun around behind him, as though it was chasing itself.

"Believe me, my imagination runs pretty wild," she chuckled to herself as the pyramid spinning stopped, thinking of how her current surroundings didn't really surprise her at all.

"Well of course it does. But has it run as far to the edges as it possibly can? Have you pushed the question of the stars so far that you can't push them anymore?"

Lily thought about the universe a lot. The stars and the planets fascinated her beyond comprehension. But that was just it. The idea made sense to her more than any other school subject, the thought of infinite possibilities excited her more than a conversation with her fellow peers. But this behavior was considered strange, and so she learned to keep her ideas to herself.

"No," she replied, upset with her now obvious lack of being true to herself.

"No?" he repeated abruptly.

"No! You are right. I haven't," she admitted, hitting the marble counter lightly, dissatisfied with herself.

"Then you are holding short of your dreams, no one else's. You don't need to be interested in what other people are interested in. Why can't you just be yourself?"

Lily rarely gave herself that kind of encouragement. When she was younger she didn't care what anyone thought, but as she grew into a teenager it became apparent that her thoughts did not match those of her fellow classmates. Her unique ideas drew a lot of unwanted attention. She wondered how different her life would be if they had just accepted her for who she was.

"I guess because I have been told that my thoughts are not normal," she replied, remembering the hours she had spent at the doctors throughout her childhood.

"Nonsense! You sound perfectly normal to me," he argued back loudly, kicking out whatever horrid doctor memory she was reliving in her mind. "Your gift is a positive, not a negative. Won't you just be open to thinking that you are love?"

"I am love?"

"Yes, you are love! If love is present, then nothing bad can come from these ideas."

"But I thought I am a sick girl."

"If you keep thinking that you will become one. For what other option does your body have other than to believe that it is so?"

Lily smiled at the man and looked away to the ground. And as she looked down she felt his words sink deeply into her skull, she felt the courage to look back up to his eyes, as she tried to process his message. His smiling rouge eyes were staring right back at her, waiting for a response. But she didn't say anything. And after several seconds of comfortable silence, he continued to pursue her attention.

"Shall we see what's inside this beautiful creation of your mother's?" Jacques said as he pushed his bony fingers inside the crochet satchel and pulled out the contents.

"Ahuh, ahuh," he mumbled quietly while examining each and every item with scrutiny. "This little envelope with the 'I love you' card is interesting. How sweet!" he said as he picked up a very tiny silver metal envelope and engraved card.

"My papa gave it to me not long after my mother died. He gave it with the bag, as a little symbol of him, my mother and me."

"Is this a seashell? I have heard about such a miraculous piece of nature existing, but never in my whole six hundred and eighty-eight years of life have I seen one! Oh Lily . . . you are not just a gift to this world, meeting you has been a blessing to me!"

Lily smiled from Jacques' compliment. *How kind,* she thought. And she thanked him dearly. She had never felt so happy to be somewhere with someone other than her family, and was so grateful not to have left after their first quarrel.

"Do you know where seashells come from?" he asked as he rubbed the smooth shell over his fat lips.

"They are home to the creatures at the bottom of the ocean, I believe."

He nodded in agreement, smiling with tremendous animation and continued to pick through the pouch.

"Lily, now you have a choice not to choose, but if you so shall, I will foretell you a secret."

She nodded her head in reply.

"The world of Sa Neo has seven different lands. In your pouch, you are already carrying a crystal from each land!"

Lily stared with astonishment as Jacques laid down each of the crystals out into a line to display them. But as he pulled them out of the bag, they transformed from rough edged stones to smooth, lustrous shapes. The amethyst a pointing dagger arrow, the carnelian a tear drop cluster; and the garnet stone upon the land they now stood was perfectly round, a polished sphere.

"You have red garnet, yellow carnelian, orange citrine, green malachite, blue kyanite, indigo azurite and purple amethyst." He pointed to each crystal as he pronounced their name. "Now, I would like you to choose three that you are, hmm . . . let's say, most attracted to."

Lily looked to the crystals as exactly three of them glistened extraordinarily, almost calling her name. *How odd,* she thought. She moved the following stones toward Jacques—the red garnet, blue kyanite and green malachite.

"What does it mean?"

"It means that you are going to visit these lands," Jacques replied with confidence as he lifted up the three crystals and juggled them in the air. "The garnet stone is the land of Otor which you stand upon now. This tells me that I should direct you to Karisma, the queen who rules this land."

"I'm going to meet a queen?" Lily shrieked with her eyes opened as wide as Jacques, the white around her pupil popping out with fascination.

"Perhaps my dear, if you desire it to be so. Then after Otor you may visit the land of Deia, where the crusts of the islands are decorated with sliced blue kyanite. And then my dear, the land of Tehar, where Queen Jade resides. But please be careful of the green sweet Lily. Play with it, but do not let it consume you."

Lily jumped up and down with excitement, and accidentally knocked the amethyst crystal off the table. It fell down very slowly to the ground, and the tip of the arrow pierced the dirt to a hold.

"Lily!" he shouted as he smiled with his chubby lips and white teeth.

"I'm sorry!" she cried. "It was an accident."

"No, no! There are no accidents; this is a sign! You are going to visit Neveah too! That means you will meet Violetta, the most powerful empress in all of Sa Neo." He juggled the three stones with one hand as he pointed to the purple crystal on the ground for her to bring it over.

"Me? Meet Violetta, the most powerful empress in all of Sa Neo?"

Jacques nodded in response as Lily ran to pick up the amethyst stone. But as she bent down, her serpent necklace fell out of her lace nightgown, proudly displaying itself in the center of her chest. She stood back up to face Jacques, and the sound of three juggling stones fell to the ground as Jacques froze, mesmerized by the necklace.

"Wheeeeeere did you get that necklace, Li-ly?" Jacques voice cooed in a long drawn out breath.

The feeling in the air turned incredibly sharp and silent, time moved by slowly as Jacques' persona changed from a bouncing bunny into a motionless shocked statue.

"I . . . I found it in my new house, we just moved there, Father and I," Lily replied. She was thrown off-guard by his quick change in personality, and although she replied cautiously, she knew that she had complete trust in her new friend. She held the necklace out for Jacques to get a closer look.

"I've never seen one in the flesh before," Jacques said as he stared intently at the symbol and stroked his cheek with an astonishing look of wondrous lust in his eyes.

"Do you know what it means?" she asked, looking to the serpent's eyes.

"Only from these books, these history books that were written by the people before my time. No one has lived long enough to tell the truth, so most of these stories are considered just myths."

He walked to the bookshelf in the corner of the pyramid and studied each name carefully, mumbling words and looking back over to Lily's necklace, still in disbelief. He finally found the book he had been searching for and jumped in the air excited like a child as he raced back to the center table where Lily was standing. He turned his book to the fourth page and pointed his dark bony fingers to a pencil-drawn symbol identical to that of Lily's necklace.

"The symbol is called an ouroboros."

"An ouro what?"

"Ouroboros."

"Ouro . . . oh Jacques I can't pronounce it!" squirmed Lily.

He smiled with squinted slithers of almond eyes, and showed his patience calmly.

"Whenever you have difficulty pronouncing or understanding something, just break it up. Start with the first, and don't move on to the next until you understand what it means! Ouro, means tail and boros means to eat, so . . . to eat ones tail!" Jacques used his hands frantically to emphasize the pronunciation and shuffled his feet side to side with excitement like he was performing a dance.

"Ouro . . . boros.." Lily tried again.

"Ouroboros!"

"Ouroboros!"

"Yes! Yes!" Jacques jumped up and down as his pants parachuted out from the wind between his bony thighs.

"So Jacques, why does the ouroboros eat its own tail? Why would ANYONE eat themselves?"

Lily's face shriveled up at the idea of eating her own skin and she licked her lips, clenching her teeth together tightly. Jacques smirked.

"He's not actually eating his own tail so to speak, for you see, his tail is still in existence elsewhere. It's just not where we can see it."

"So where did it go?" Lily asked confused, staring closely at the tail being gobbled by the serpent's jaw.

"Into another reality. He is recreating himself differently than expected," Jacques explained. "From all death comes life, and the serpent is renewing himself. The outside of himself is actually the inside of himself manifesting in a new form, so what you see is not what he sees, do you see?"

"No, I don't see," Lily huffed, rubbing the crystal eyes with her thumb.

Jacques lightly tickled his fingers together and pointed at the necklace, as the serpent became alive and wriggled around while it ate its own tail. Munching around and around, as though on repeat, it did not get fatter, nor did the size of the tail shorten. It just continued in one infinite circle.

"Our existence is the product of our own projections, so his tail isn't actually his tail to him. It looks like it to us but not to him, because we see a different reality to what the serpent sees. You start from the core, the root of the matter. And up you go, through heads and tails, inside and out, backwards and forwards. From dark to light and back around again."

"And what happens after that?"

"That's when the clarity begins. The rebirth of new ideas and everything will be forever different to how it was before."

He grinned, wrinkling up his great big nose, lifting his elbow up to nuzzle Lily playfully. She couldn't help but like the strange creature. He was spontaneous and unpredictable and she loved his uniqueness. Never before had she met such a character, he didn't seem to take himself too seriously either. *Maybe he was right about the greatness of being unique,* she thought.

"There's something else very special I want to tell you."

"Oh Jacques, do please tell me!" Lily replied, leaning her elbows on the table and cupping her chin adoringly at Jacques. Although sometimes his words were confusing and washed over her, she liked the sound of everything that came forth from his mouth.

"Well . . . it's a symbol of the mermaids. Because you hold the ouroboros, it shows that you are one of them. You are part of their family."

"I could be a mermaid?" Lily had never thought of herself being a part of someone else's family before. And for so long she wished that mermaids were real, that she could swim and meet them. Oh how grand that would be!

"Ah . . . well my dear, you can be anything you want to be. But no one has ever met a mermaid, that we know of . . ." Jacques nodded to himself, as though he was reiterating the information to himself disappointingly.

"How do we know they exist or that they are connected to this serpent symbol if no one has ever seen them?"

"My great grandfather wrote this book." Jacques drummed his fingers on the leather edge as he spoke with pride. "It's full of mermaid drawings, all of them wearing this special symbol. We don't know where the ideas came from, or if he ever saw them. But I believe in him. Lily, promise me one thing . . ." He lifted his finger up, showing his seriousness.

"What is it Jacques?" Lily tried hard not to giggle.

"If you meet the mermaids on your travels, which I suspect you might, you should keep this secret to yourself. Knowledge such as this may encourage jealousy amongst others and it could lead you into great danger."

"I promise."

The way he spoke reminded Lily of her father. He was soothing and sweet, yet stern and direct. She knew what he was telling her was important, and now was not the time to question what was going on. *Just play along with him, perhaps he hasn't talked to anyone in awhile and wants company. Or maybe he doesn't have any family to pass down this wisdom to,* she thought. So with her eyes wide and eager with anticipation of what he had to say, she prepared herself to listen intently.

"Lily, I think it's time for you to move on. Will you walk outside with me?" he asked, pointing to the opened circle that lay opposite to the one she had entered through. She followed willingly, although surprised, as she thought she had much more to learn from him.

As they walked through the door the sky had changed drastically. Day had definitely broken, and the deep rouge sky had now lightened up into a creamy pink. The sun was blazing high up above them, and the heat it exuded was powerfully dominating. The land that outlaid in front extended for miles, and a single path led the way between two giant hills.

Jacques pulled a long walking stick from the ground and drew into the red sparkly dirt a single dot. Then a circle around it, and then a line straight ahead, and he curved it to the left.

"Down the hill and through the forest you will reach the ocean's edge. Here you will find a small beach and to the right, some mountains. In between the mountains lies a path which leads to Karisma's house, the ruler of Otor." He drew some pointed tips to display the hills and the line upon which she was to follow. "But if you get to the beach and a sign hints for you to explore elsewhere, listen to the noise and make your necklace visible. For it will be your key into their world."

Lily nodded, knowing he was referring to the mermaids, although the idea of the unknown still frightened her. He could sense her struggle and held her hand with reassurance. "Do not let the darkness scare you, Lily; for you have infinite light brewing inside of you, just waiting to be ignited. All you have to do is listen to yourself."

"How can I thank you?" she asked politely.

"You just did." He winked as she turned to walk down the hill. "Li-ly, may I hug you goodbye?" Jacques opened his arms as she turned to face him.

She nodded in reply, as he threw the stick away, and lifted his left hand just slightly higher than above his shoulder, and he held his right arm slightly lower, suggesting Lily do the same thing. "Here sweet Lily. Let our hearts cross over one another as we hug tightly. Feel the energy of my body pour strength into your spirit." His voice soothed as he hugged her tightly.

"We are sharing something special when we hug. We are giving each other life. We are saying to the other person. Here is my heart. Let my heart touch your heart, and let them beat together as one."

Lily did as Jacques suggested, and they held a tight embrace for several breaths. Lily closed her eyes tightly, immersing herself in the warm love she was feeling from her friend. Upon doing so, she felt a strange tingling from inside of her body and she could see bright flashing lights suddenly all around. The same dancing lights that she had seen under the house were presenting themselves to her once more, and in this moment, Jacques lit up too. They became a glowing sphere of white light together. But, when she opened her eyes, she was standing by herself, arms around her shoulders, completely alone, on top of a hill, staring out to the horizon, with no pyramid in sight.

CHAPTER THREE

CRYANTHE & THE UNDERWATER WORLD

The heat from the sun was proving to be unbearable, and the ripples of water on the beach were more than inviting. There appeared to be no one around, and the idea of going into the ocean to cool off was simmering in Lily's mind. She stood on the shore with her ankles immersed in the water as the cool ocean's breath foamed life around her stick-like legs, creating a shiny gleam on the red crystal pebbles beneath her feet. She stared at the horizon in the distance. The thin line between ocean and sky looked as though they were touching, but in reality, were far away from each other. She wondered if they knew that one another existed, and the importance they held to define that which they were not. Next to the beach where she stood, enormous mountains of red crystal rocks framed the coast in synchrony. The breeze purred softly, almost non-existent, and the sound of the ocean lapping on the pebbles chimed therapeutically into Lily's ears.

Where do I go from here? she thought, dismissing her craving to dive deep into the ocean.

She looked to the right, and watched as a group of turtles ignored her presence and played out her inner desires; they slowly entered into the gentle, cool water to escape the heat of the sun. In the corner of her eye, she felt movement from behind, and she turned her head at the exact moment a bird glided by in extreme slow motion. It flew steadily along an invisible straight line, directly toward the end of the ocean. The white feathers of its wings stretched out, marking a perfect outline of its being, and a black, beady eye stared back at Lily. She felt her heart beat faster as she connected with the creature, and she stood strong and calm as a feeling of electricity exploded loudly inside of her.

She remembered Jacques' advice and felt it was a sign. Without giving it much thought, she stripped off her nightgown, threw her bag on top of it, and leapt gracefully into the rippling waters of the sea.

The salt water immediately refreshed the teenage girl and she gleefully splashed while she pondered how splendid being a mermaid would be, living amongst the ocean forever. *Mermaids*, she thought. *Mermaids, are you real?* And the idea of meeting an actual mermaid played out in her mind; alas it was only a thought, and she told herself she was being silly.

Lily stared at the necklace again and unclipped the back of it mechanically to examine it further. She hovered the piece of jewelry over the water, staring at the eyes of the serpent, mesmerized.

To eat one's own tail, she thought again, dipping the circle into the water. But as she did so, a trail of sparkling dust detached itself from the charm and swam deep into the ocean.

Revitalized from the water, Lily walked back to land. She redressed herself in her white nightgown, picked up her crochet satchel and looked to the forest to start her journey to visit Karisma. But like the bird in the sky, she felt something behind her, and she spun around quickly, looking back to the ocean.

The first thing that Lily noticed was how round and plump the mermaids' breasts were. Upon her chest hung a beautiful clear crystal and pearl necklace, which covered her skin like a protective armor, allowing her breasts to protrude so perfectly from underneath that the nipples peaked through in a plum shade of pink, perfectly erect, looking ready to burst. Her white hair floated delicately around the edge of the breasts, suckling against the skin and she rose grandly above the sea, floating like a dolphin in midair.

And on her head, she wore a crown of uneven, clear crystal quartz stones, rough and imperfect, the way that Lily liked objects of beauty to appear. Different shapes and sizes of thickness, they magnetically stuck together, thicker in the front, and thinner at the back, like the bagpipes of a large piano. A silver ouroboros hung just below the crown, on a small plaited chain and it touched her skin where her hairline caressed her face. The crown looked like it would be incredibly heavy, but the mermaid wore it with no discomfort. She truly was the most beautiful creature that Lily had ever seen.

The mermaid drifted closer to Lily and it was only then that Lily could see the true depths of her eyes, a light purple shade of violet which stared intensely at the ouroboros charm that hung around Lily's neck.

"Where did you get that?" the mermaid whispered, almost too faint for Lily to hear, and with thin fingers, she pointed to the necklace.

"I found it in my bedroom back home."

Lily looked down and covered the gold serpent with her hand as she replied with a polite yet cautious tone to the foreign creature. The waves behind the mermaid moved fiercely with her words, they rose high and crowded the sight of the beach, making it difficult for Lily to focus exactly on what was happening.

"Are you frightened of me?" The mermaid asked mischievously, half-smiling as she floated closer to Lily, allowing the waves behind her to grow in height, displaying the strength of her power.

"No . . ." Lily pretended. "Should I be?"

"I am Crysanthe, Queen of the Neosa Underworld. Come closer girl, look into my eyes, tell me, is there anything to fear?"

Crysanthe enlarged her purple eyes and her silver white eyelashes framed the almond shape spaciously. Lily returned her gaze, watching as the violet colors swirled inside her iris in a clockwise motion continuously. And while Lily stared, she felt like she was falling through the middle of the center pupil, although now the pupil was an empty hole of milky white liquid, and it swirled around quickly in the opposite direction. Lily felt like she was stuck inside a whirlpool, and it had made her feel dizzy, but she could not look away and was majestically drawn to stare deeper into the mermaid's eyes.

"Re wae nod te cen Sa Neo," Crysanthe whispered smiling in a strange satisfied kind of way.

What did that mean? Lily thought. But she didn't think for too long about it. Instead she noticed how all of her senses had pricked up at once. The sound of the water around her splashed extra loudly, and the warmth from the sun gave her a content feeling of safety. Lily tried to smile in response, but she was unable to do so. She tried to move her head. Nope, nothing. The only thing she could move were her eyes. And she stared at her surroundings, hurriedly. Straining her eyes, she looked as far left as possible, but could only see clear red water and a light pink sky. She darted her eyes over to the right, hurting the concentration in her brain as she pushed them far away, trying to see the beach, or trees, or anything other than the clear red sea, and light pink sky. For no longer was Lily standing on the edge of the beach, she was now up close to the mermaid, hovering over the water as well. She felt no weight in her body, she was levitating so gracefully over the deep hollow water staring back at the mermaid. Yet there was no fear in Lily's mind, she knew there was nothing she could do. She could not struggle in order to free herself, nor could she deny the situation for a moment. She could panic, or she could be still and breathe. And so she did, and she observed herself, floating above the impossible, staring at what could very well be a figment of Lily's imagination.

Her breasts were even plumper up close, Lily thought. The mermaid giggled, as if able to read Lily's mind and she moved her right arm out and placed the palm of her hand on Lily's forehead, closing her eyes while doing so. Lily felt as though something was being pulled from her mind, as a great deal of warmth leaked from the mermaids' hand. Crysanthe smiled. Content with her discovery, she grasped Lily's hand tightly and dove deep beneath the oceans' edge.

The mermaid's tail shook violently through the current while Lily's body shook lifelessly alongside hers. Lily realized that she was somehow breathing under water, but it wasn't unusual at all. It felt strangely normal. Her exterior was completely frozen, but she could see, hear, think and breathe. Her eyes were adjusting to the dark waters that were now thickening. And as they swam deeper, she noticed that the fish swimming around her were brightening in color, some becoming so bright, they were glowing. With silvery rays they reminded Lily of the moon, creating their own light from within in order to triumph over the darkness. A spectacular circle of yellow and green colors stained the head of a jellyfish nearby, shooting up through the center and spurting out like an umbrella.

As the jellyfish hovered above, a beautiful spinning flower with contrasting hues of blue and pink blossomed inside of the circle. The tentacles of the jellyfish were thin spaghetti-like legs of what could only be described as electrical currents of sizzling wires, moving so magnificently that Lily ached to touch such a creature. *I would stare at the sea animals all day and forever be happy,* she thought.

Next, a translucent fish swam alongside Lily's leg, so close she feared it was going to eat her! The bones in its body lit up in a rippling effect of rainbow lights, starting from the center of its heart and moving out to the fins. Its eyes were bustling balls which looked like clear bubbling glue and they stared and moved from side to side, while its mouth bobbed open and closed, oblivious to Lily and the mermaid. Deeper and deeper they glided through the ocean. Swimming over colonies of coral reef and giant seaweed trees full of brilliant colors and different shapes and sizes. The forest, so rich in texture created great depths of shadows which reminded Lily of tall buildings and cities back home. It certainly was a very dream-like state of pure bliss to be floating over such a magical presentation of nature, overgrowing wildly in its native environment. Faster and faster the mermaid swam, still holding Lily's hand ever-so-tightly, careful not to let her go.

The darkness started to become lighter. *Can I finally see in the dark?* Lily wondered. But no, the sea was turning lighter, and in the distance, Lily could see a large glowing ball of a fire-like substance that rotated in a rapid motion. Mermaids were gathered everywhere around this circle, both male and female. All with similar white silver hair, but each with varying lengths and shades of it. They all had the same ouroboros symbol attached to some part of their body, whether it was on their neck, their wrist, or above the elbow.

Crysanthe finally stopped in front of a well-built merman. He had a thin string necklace that hung loosely around his neck and a sliced clear crystal ornament that crossed directly over his heart. His silver hair sat just above his shoulders, and the ouroboros symbol was secured around his wrist with a thick silver clasp.

"Crysanthe! Have you gone completely mad?" he screamed, outraged at the beautiful mermaid. "Why have you brought down a land creature?"

Crysanthe promptly swam over to the merman, and in the process, let Lily's hand go. But Lily didn't float back up to the surface; instead, she stayed exactly where she was, absorbed within the water, becoming one inside the sea. The water continued to move around her, constantly changing yet staying the same, and slowly, very slowly, she was gravitated toward the base of the ocean floor. Here, she stood as a statue, frozen to the ground, with only her eyes moving, and the sound in her ears, as she watched and listened to the mercreatures quarrel.

"Oh my love, don't be sour with me," Crysanthe pouted, swimming up close. "I have good reasons, will you please let me explain?"

She turned slightly and looked over her shoulder with flirting eyes, smiling mischievously as she spoke. But he wasn't giving in easily and he replied with the strength of a leader.

"For thousands of years we have kept ourselves safe from the land, and now you choose to spoil our peace?"

The merman's anger scared Lily. It rumbled in her stomach with the same vibration that she felt when she heard thunder in the sky.

"Zavier, will you just let me finish?" Crysanthe bit back; but there was laughter in her eyes and she smiled as she did so, playing with his emotions.

"I don't want to hear it," he argued. "Look what you have done with your curiosity!"

Zavier pointed to the crowd who were all staring and whispering to each other while pointing to Lily's legs. There was a mixture of giggles and gasps as they all glared at such an unknown sight.

Ordinarily, for Lily to be on display like that, she would have been mortified, wanting to run and hide. But, to escape was not an option, she couldn't move. She was forced to endure it, inside her cemented statue of human legs.

"But Zavier . . ." Crysanthe begged as she spoke louder wanting to be heard.

"No, Crysanthe, no! You take her back to land right now, or I will do it myself!" Zavier commanded, as he placed his hand proudly over his chest while referring to himself.

"But she's wearing our necklace! Look . . ."

Crysanthe pulled the necklace out from Lily's dress and presented it to Zavier. He paused for a moment and looked back to Crysanthe, staring dumbfounded. Lily watched his whole persona change quickly and although Lily was unable to move, she could feel his emotion transform through his movements and his voice as he surrendered to Crysanthe.

"My love, please forgive me for doubting you." Zavier replied with a soft tone, and he shook his head in confusion, tucking his silvery hair behind his ears while looking Lily up and down. "What could this mean?"

His stance was still cautious of the incident but his words did not shy, and he acknowledged that perhaps Crysanthe was right. She melted inwards to Zavier, mirroring his vulnerability of accepting his wrong, and she wrapped her skinny arms around him in a tight embrace, kissing him repeatedly on the cheek in reward. With her crystal crown fastened tightly on her head, the ends of her hair floated upwards.

"I'm not sure my love, but I think I should find out. It must mean something right?" Her purple eyes gleamed as she spoke, full of excitement and anticipation. The crowds of merpeople gathered in a tighter circle toward Lily and chatted to each other loudly as they too deciphered the news.

"Shh my fellow merpeople," Zavier said as he removed Crysanthe's arms and faced the crowd that had now doubled in size. "We are unsure of this message. Is it a blessing or a curse? Never have we come across an outsider with this symbol. Has anyone here ever given this piece of jewelry to another?"

The crowd was a complete mix of mermaids and mermen, various ages, each with a unique pattern of beautifully colored scales below their waists. They all pointed to their ouroboros which was displayed somewhere on their bodies, either around their wrist, arm, neck, or head.

"But darling that's impossible. Without this don't we die?"

A few squeals and terrifying gasps hushed through the crowd as such words were uttered, and Zavier twisted his fin quickly as he scolded Crysanthe.

"Crysanthe, do not tell them what you fear."

"But it's the truth! Why must we hide the truth?"

The crowds of merpeople now tripled in size and continued to mutter loudly over the squabble. Their faces all held mixed reactions, some with anger, some with pity, some with fear, and some who didn't seem to understand what was going on, but were just excited from the attention it had caused.

"Crysanthe, it is not the truth it is only an idea. What has come over you? I think you should return this girl, purely for your outspokenness. You should never impose your beliefs onto another." He shook his head and rubbed his eyes as though traumatized by the mermaid's outburst. "Your questions and comments are always welcome but not at this expense," he continued, pointing to the crowd. "And right now, I can see our friends are all feeling the emotion of being scared at what it is that you call death."

Crysanthe took hold of his hands lovingly and stroked his skin with her fingers. She was the complete opposite of her partner and she calmed him with her presence.

"But there is nothing to be feared. Surely in our time, there must have been someone who decided to die?" she asked. "There are mermaids in this ocean that we have not met, aren't there? Isn't it possible that there isn't just one way of life?" Crysanthe's voice climbed to a high-sounding pitch as she asked her endless questions with worry.

"Of course my love, but if you are searching for an answer, I am trying to give you an answer. Satisfied?" He held her hands tightly, showing his respect was mirrored to her, but now she was the one upset.

"No, I would rather you just say, 'I don't know' and let us make up our own minds."

Crysanthe turned to swim away; she was annoyed at Zavier, but he intervened, grabbing her by the waist with his muscly arms.

"This is the fire I love inside of you," he smiled proudly and turned to the crowd as he continued, "my fellow mercreatures, look at my beautiful wife and the way her mind works. Do not accept something just because you are told it! Let her be an example to you all." He turned back to Crysanthe and held her hand lovingly. "What is it that you wish to achieve by bringing this girl into our world?"

Crysanthe cuddled into Zavier once more, as he had given her the freedom of speech in allowing her to prove him wrong. And Lily could feel that it was in his change of heart that he showed her how important she was to him.

"I still have questions inside of me that are not yet answered," Crysanthe said, speaking with rushed excitement and moving her hands around quickly, "I would like to know more about this girl. About her life, her way of being. Where did she come from? What is she doing in this world?"

"I will let you do as you please, but my love, be warned—I have a bad feeling about this. What if the land people were to see you?"

The crowd all hushed and whispered loudly amongst themselves as Zavier told of his premonition. Lily felt nervous too. She finally realized why Jacques had made special mention to keep the mermaids secret, for their own safety.

"They have never seen me, not in a thousand years. Why now?"

"Why not?"

"Because I have someone looking over me, you know that."

She pointed to the ball of fire near them, and as everyone turned to look, a release of flames burst through the ocean, up to the sea level as though agreeing with the mermaid.

"Crysanthe, you have everything here that you could ever want. Everything you could ask to make you happy. Why risk your life to learn about someone that is not of your own kind? What am I not giving you to make you happy?" Zavier lowered his gaze to stare at her eyes intently, eagerly awaiting Crysanthe's response.

"You give me everything I could ever ask for my love, and more. You do. But I want to learn about their music, and what it is that the land people laugh at. What simple acts bring them joy? Is it a pleasure I am unable to attain?" She pleaded, the wondrous questions flowing freely from her mind, as though she had been holding onto them for some time.

"Well, there is no more to be discussed then. You may do as you please, if this is your heart's desire. I will not stand in your way. But please, my love, please, be careful."

Zavier pulled Crysanthe closer as he kissed her sweetly. And the crowd roared with applause as their king and queen united.

"I love you Zavier, thank you," she whispered beneath the cheering.

"My love for you is unconditional Crysanthe. I will let you be free and always respect your decision. But, I do ask one favor if you please?"

"Anything my love," she replied, massaging the back of his neck with her fingers.

"Please ask her these questions tomorrow, after the dance of Neo?"

"Certainly. I will return her now and explain how she is to find me through the shells in the water. If anyone is to hear this girl's vibration through the current, please ensure I am informed and go to her first."

Crysanthe's finger twitched first. It jolted with an electrical current and wiggled again. Lily was suddenly back at the beach, standing on the garnet pebbles once more, staring out to the far horizon. Crysanthe was hovering with her waist above the water, but her face was different; this time she radiated warmness, and Lily felt like she knew her already.

"Dear sweet girl, it was rude of me to have not asked your name before. Please forgive me. I am Crysanthe."

Lily stared around quite disoriented, unsure as to what had just happened. She moved her hands to wipe her eyes and comb through her hair. But both her hair and skin were dry. She felt down to touch the lace on her white gown, and it was softer than ever. Even the dirt marks from where she had jumped through the manhole were clean. She was completely fresh and dry. Her crochet bag once again slung over her shoulder, and her necklace was perfectly secured next to her chest.

"How did you move me without my knowledge? And now I am dry?" Lily asked, pushing her curls behind her shoulders.

"When I take you into my world, I create a protective barrier around your body. I imagine it to be so, and when I place my hand over your head, the seal is formed. Do not be scared, I will never harm you. I don't know how." She giggled as she declared her weakness, while rainbow bubbles protruded from her mouth, floating up into the air.

The rainbow sheen sparkled with intensity from the blazing sun in the distance and Lily smiled sweetly, watching the bubbles drift through the sky like floating balloons.

"What is it like to be a human? To walk upon the ground? To have legs and dance?"

Lily tried not to laugh at such questions that she had never been asked of before and looked around shyly, unsure of how to respond.

"Where is it that you are walking to now?" Crysanthe continued, ignoring Lily's absence of words, eager to continue the conversation.

"I was told by Jacques, the healer who lives up on the hill over there, that I am to walk along this path and that it will lead me to Karisma, the ruler of this land. Apparently I am a gift to this world, and my purpose here is just to enjoy, experience, and learn," Lily replied, stating the facts as though reciting a lesson.

"Apparently? Do you not think that it is true?" Crysanthe asked, as her royal demeanor diminished quickly, and Lily felt as though she were staring at a fellow playmate, wearing a dress-up crown of crystals on her head.

Lily felt confidence rise in her heart, as though she was conversing with someone who was just like herself, curious and courteous.

"I don't know," Lily replied, shrugging her shoulders. "Do we ever know?"

"Maybe that is your purpose here with me as well. I am to teach you also?" Crysanthe flickered the water through her fingers and it dazzled above her, dripping down in a beautiful synchronized waterfall.

"I hope so. I would love to know more about your world. You seem so happy."

Crysanthe giggled again, the rainbow bubbles escaping from her mouth once more. "That's because we believe that the purpose of life is just to be happy."

Lily tried to think about how often it was that she purposely thought about being happy. It was difficult to recall. Between the doctor visits, and the agony from her mother's death, she didn't really have much room inside her mind to think about what it was that made her happy. And she envied the beautiful mermaid with her simplistic approach to life. *Could it really be that easy?*

"How wonderful! So, are you the queen or princess of the underwater world, and what do you call the underwater world?" Lily asked, taking a seat on the red crystal beach as though she were in school listening to her teacher.

"Yes, I am the Queen of Neosa. That is what we call our world. Neo means life, and Sa is Beautiful."

"Life is beautiful." The two chanted at the same time together, as simultaneously two dolphins jumped through the water, as though cementing their ideas. Lily smiled to herself, thinking how glorious it would be for her life to be only ever beautiful.

"How is it that you came to be Queen of Neosa?" Lily asked, picking up some crystals and playing with the textures in her hand. She enjoyed rubbing the polished gems on her skin, and she dipped them in the water, cooling them off from their time in the sun.

"To understand that, you must first understand our history. We are immortal. We choose when we are going to die. For when we die, another life is born. So, Zavier and I do not know why we are as we are; we were born and the merpeople told us that we were king and queen in our lives before, and so this time we are once again."

"So you will forever be together?" Lily asked, smiling at such a lovely thought of having a twin soul reconnect time after time.

"Yes although it doesn't necessarily mean we will be lovers. Maybe next time we will be siblings."

"Always royalty?" Lily asked as she looked to the beautiful crown that framed Crysanthe's silver hair.

The crystals appeared so heavy and chunky, with such magnificent weight. But alas, perhaps it was magic inside of them, maybe the sun that shone above filled each cube with such encompassing light it was full to the brim.

"Zavier and I do not think of ourselves as that," she replied, taking her crown off her head and spinning it around her finger like a hoola hoop around one's waist. "The merpeople desired to have a leader and so that is who we are. We create the world in which they want to live in too. It is their choice just as much as it is ours."

She placed the crown back on her head, fastening the ouroboros low in between her brows.

"You say you want to learn about the beauty behind dancing and singing and other pleasures, but do you not think that perhaps you bring joy that we do not have and do not understand also?"

"You are right Lily. See, I am already learning from you."

"And I, from you."

Crysanthe smiled warmly and the pinkness in her lips turned a deep rouge as she swam closer to where Lily was sitting.

"Will you come back and visit me?" she asked, with a glimmer of hope in her eyes.

Lily stood up proudly. "Yes, I would love to. But how will I find you again?"

Crysanthe handed Lily a small cockle seashell, no bigger than the size of her fingernail, and her face changed from a giggling smile to a grave stare.

"Our senses are more heightened than you realize," she whispered as Lily moved closer, immersing her ankles into the water. "Imagine a line of vibrating energy that runs across a cord from the tip of your head to the top of my head. Do it, close your eyes."

Lily closed her eyes as instructed. She felt no fear from the mermaid, not after their conversation. And she envisioned the line of electrical currents, extracting from her head directly toward Crysanthe.

"Whenever you want to talk to me, close your eyes, imagine our connection and envision my face. Throw this shell into the water, say my name and I will hear you." Her violet eyes shone brightly as she smiled with relief, as though she could see the cord connection that Lily was imagining. "This will be our secret Lily." She spoke again in whispers. "You must not tell anyone! It is only you who I trust. And no matter where I am, I will find you. Do you understand?"

"Yes," Lily replied, placing the seashell inside her satchel.

"If you come tonight, we are performing the dance of Neo. I would love for you to witness such an event. It would be a true honor."

"What about Zavier?"

The image of Zavier with his silver mane and beastly chest flashed into Lily's mind, and she worried for her safety, even though she was returned back to shore without any harm.

"Don't mind Zavier. He has no interest in outside life, he is perfectly content living inside. But we are half human, half sea creature; I feel connected to you. I want to know more about my other half."

Hearing Crysanthe say the two of them shared the same half, echoed deeply within Lily's soul. And although she knew they were completely different, there was an obvious underlying connection they shared; a zest for life to understand the unimaginable. And Lily sensed that by helping Crysanthe find the answers she was seeking, it would in turn satisfy her own cravings. For the questions the mermaid asked were the answers Lily knew, and the misunderstandings of life that Lily felt conflicted with, Crysanthe held the expert knowledge. Their friendship was already hinting a mutual transaction that would benefit both of them, alongside the agreement of loving each other's company in the interim.

"I promise Crysanthe. Your secret is safe with me."

Lily wanted to hug Crysanthe but she wasn't sure on how to go about it. And just like Jacques had taught her how to hug, she asked Crysanthe the same question and then embraced her. Showing her the universal love that connected two human beings together, the essence of touch. They held the embrace for several seconds, the cool feeling of Crysanthe's dewy skin, and Lily's warm touch. The two together, complete opposites yet strangely attracted to each other.

Lily waved goodbye and watched Crysanthe swim away. Her flesh touched the ocean as she dived through. Strong as an arrow she glided in the air and pierced through the water, eroding ripples behind like a rocket, the smoke trailing by afterwards, as the rising air burst hurriedly through the water.

And Lily was left once again on her own, to explore the magical world of Sa Neo.

CHAPTER FOUR

KARISMA TEACHES TO TEDIMETA

Lily turned her back to the ocean and walked into the depths of the rainforest where a path was laid out in burnt orange dirt just as Jacques had described. The sun in the distance had lowered in the sky; it was now blazing a marvelous red, feeding warmth to the planet and all living creatures inside.

She looked up to the endless row of trees that towered above. They created a large canopy, a giant umbrella of luscious green leaves with shiny detail. And the sound of trees hustling grew louder as she walked deeper into the density of the forest. It was as if the trees had their own language, and she felt like they were sharing secrets with her. If she closed her eyes she could still see them. Not as the mighty tall trees that they were, but as light beings of living energy, connecting through their roots underneath her feet, stretching down below the dirt, they interwove together harmoniously. And the singing of the leaves swishing back and forth vibrated electricity right beneath her toes, transforming the path into thick slabs of colored marble stones. Casually thrown in uneven grids, the tiled pathway danced in swirling colors.

But when Lily stopped to stare at the whirling floor beneath her feet, it was as though the marble knew it was being watched, and they played dead; freezing their life to stand still to protect themselves from danger. *But what was the danger?* Lily thought. Perhaps she was causing harm without her knowledge. Either that or maybe the tiles assumed she was not ready to accept the daily miracles present in simply ordinary things.

The sound of the birds and animals grew louder the deeper she traveled, and she began to skip. She levitated her body high while she jumped into the air, patting her feet down onto the marble steps loudly, dancing to a beating drum that only she could hear.

The pathway finally ended when she reached the largest tree of them all. The branches were an outline of black charcoal, like drawings, and on the tips of their tongues hung bright red flowers, full in bloom. Each branch of the tree crossed over in a strong geometric pattern, almost like a spider's web, yet there was no clear outline to know how the branch was to cross over to the next. They weaved in curls, spiraling upwards toward the sky, reaching far past the clouds. When the wind whispered through the trees, the petals from the flowers floated gently down in a therapeutic display of affection, as though they were softly kissing the ground below. Too eager to detach themselves from their home they wandered alone, not knowing where they would go but trusting the wind would move them to where they needed to be. They were thankful to be created and yet they sacrificed themselves in the process. And even if it was for a short moment, they lived like they have never lived before. Completely alone, floating in the air, until they peacefully molded themselves back to the ground where they originally came from.

At the base of the tree stood a large sign, 'Karisma Garnet', and a similar opening to Jacques, with a mysterious smoky doorway cut out of the trunk. Lily once again felt uneasy about crossing through the strange barrier, and she stood a good distance, trying to get someone's attention.

"Karisma . . ." Her soft voice echoed through the smoky spray, creating the same hole as before.

A large butterfly, with pointy wings splashed in orange, pink and yellow, flew through the door and up close to Lily. Mesmerized by the enchanted creature fluttering so delicately by her nose, Lily stared in awe, wondering where the creature was going to go next. In slow movements, the butterfly waved her wings peacefully, and landed ever so gently on Lily's arm, which had naturally swung open in a perfect right-angled elbow and lifted up high like a ballerina. The butterfly's black thin legs perched onto Lily's skin, tickling her lightly. As if contemplating her actions, the butterfly took a few moments to stretch her wings out, opening them up like huge peacock feathers.

Lily looked intensely to the eyes of the butterfly, holding her gaze strongly. She felt like the butterfly understood her as they shared their exchange. But just as Lily was feeling the connection to the mystical creature, it escaped, leaping quickly into the air. Fluttering its wings fiercely, it shot straight up high, twirling into a thick smoky cloud of orange, pink and yellow. The smoke swirled around Lily until her eyes were clouded and she was unable to see, almost unable to breathe. But it only lasted for a moment, and when the cloud parted, and the smoke cleared, and the emotion of confusion had stopped, everything was clear. And a radiant, red-haired lady now stood directly in front of Lily, smirking with a 'know-it-all' kind of face. She stood tall, holding a painted red linen fan with fine black edges made from a very thin silk.

"Helllloooo there, Lily." She spoke with a sweet-sounding voice that paused directly after hello and fast forwarded over her name quickly, like the sound of water washing quickly over rocks on the shore. "You may call me Karisma," she continued softly, her eyes staring deeply into Lily's, searching for information.

Karisma stepped closer to the girl, the pupils of her eyes magnified, creating a glacier overlay. Lily could see the reflection of herself in them, as though she were gazing into a mirror, but the longer she looked, the less she was able to recognize the person gazing back to her, even though it would have appeared to have been just herself.

"Lovely to meet you, Karisma," Lily replied as she bowed in response, looking down to the marbled floor that was dancing with movement beneath the queen's feet.

Karisma fluttered the fan down near her exposed belly, which was a thin milky complexion sandwiched between a cropped red shirt and a flowing red skirt. A fine gold chain looped around her neck, through her chest and down to her waist. It moved gradually with the breeze of the strumming fan.

"How did you know my name?" Lily asked, admiring the delicate features of the black silk trimming sewn into the fan.

"Voices are telling me, I can't explain it," she replied, holding the fan up high above her nose so that only her eyes were exposed. "There is something extremely powerful and special about you." Karisma stopped herself, and looked around cautiously. It was as though she was hesitant to let her know too much. "Do you know why it is that you are you are here?"

The sound of the insects and animals around them buzzed with great strength, and Lily could feel their vibration stronger than before, their liveliness, their movements, everything was dominant. She could feel the solitude of each breath.

Lily looked down shyly, not knowing what to say.

"Do you know why I am here?" Lily asked, looking around to the trees whose leaves appeared to have moved closer to the girls, as though listening in on their conversation.

Karisma fluttered the palm of her hand fiercely as she continued to fan her face, directing the wind through her fiery red hair. She moved her hand high into the direct sunlight, allowing a large ruby ring on her finger to sparkle. As the fan met the light, the intricate detail of finely sewn black silk moved underneath the heat, and it joyously swirled in motion, evolving in patterns as though loving the change of scenery.

"No one knows why they are here," she smiled, turning around to walk inside. "Come with me," she said, as she entered through the smoky door that was carved into the trunk of the gigantic tree.

A long stone archway was paved inside, stacked like bricks, it towered above. In the holes between the stones grew bright red flowers and shiny green leaves which crawled out through the empty spaces as the girls walked by, eager to see what was happening. Lily followed Karisma through the long hallway that was built like an underground city, full of secret pathways and open doors. They stopped inside a lounge room that was full of soft cushions and draped colored silks. Smaller pot plants hung from the ceilings, with an abundance of leaves falling down to the ground like a frozen waterfall, as though they were too confined inside the pot and needed to spread out, extending their leaves through the air for the whole world to witness their beauty. Karisma motioned for Lily to sit on a soft pile of pillows whose silk was painted in beautiful geometric patterns. The plentiful pillows cushioned Lily in a cloud-like formation, and she laid her head down to rest, feeling herself get quite sleepy. Her eyes began to feel heavy, and she thought, *perhaps I can just rest for a moment. . .*

"No!" Karisma said assertively. "There is far too much to do today."

Lily looked outside. The sun had been kissing the ground for some time now, and it was close to disappearing.

"But, I haven't slept in so long! I am tired," Lily replied wearily, remembering how long it had been since she had played in her dreams.

"You can sleep after. Let's eat some stew and then we will begin the lessons," Karisma said, collecting two bowls that were sitting on a shelf carved into the wood, as though they had been waiting for Lily's arrival.

"The lessons?" Lily sat upright, wondering what kind of school she had walked into.

"Yes, the lessons. You're here to learn aren't you?"

Karisma handed Lily a clay pot where a thick heavy stew was steaming inside. The broth smelled like cinnamon and pumpkin Lily thought, but it only consisted of seaweed-looking leaves. Lily dipped the spoon into the bowl and scooped a large serving to her mouth. The flavor was exactly as she imagined it—sweet cinnamon-flavored pumpkin soup. But the image of the broth was nothing in contrast to the aroma it displayed and it confused Lily, being that what she saw and what she tasted did not match up.

"What is it that you are going to teach me?" Lily asked, curiously looking around the treehouse room as she swallowed the soup.

"Well, you want to travel around Sa Neo, correct?"

Lily nodded.

"Then, my first gift to you is to tedimeta."

"To tedimeta?"

"Yes, it is how we teleport amongst these lands," Karisma said as she blew the steam gently from her bowl, lifting it to her pointy nose to smell before taking a sip. "To be able to do this, you must understand the elements behind it."

"Okay, I'm listening," Lily said, as she spooned another giant scoop into her mouth. The texture of the broth felt slimy and strange, but the flavor, oh the flavor was beyond delectable.

"When all the possessions of life are removed, we are left with a black vortex full of vibrating energy," Karisma said slowly as the colors in the room lowered to a dimming red. "When you travel through these dimensions, you are exactly that, just a light vibrating through the energetic field of black nothingness. And because your body is a reflection of your mind, it travels with you."

Karisma picked up a piece of powdered glitter that sat inside a jar on a wooden table against the wall. She squeezed the sparkly pieces between her fingers and threw it up into the air, high above the girls' heads close to the dark wooden ceiling. The glitter twirled around in a tornado spiral, until it gradually made its way back down into the jar, perfectly and completely compact, with no dust spilling either side.

"I'm not sure I understand," Lily replied timidly, spooning the last of the leafy stew into her mouth. Only this time, she knew that the leaves were going to create the mouthwatering flavor of ravishing pumpkin soup, and so the sight of the stew excited her, for she remembered the scent and flavor it possessed; knowing it was to share the same taste on her tongue.

"Sometimes you don't need to understand, you just need to believe." Karisma smiled as she placed the empty bowls of stew on a wooden shelf, and she returned holding two milky blue colored crystals. She handed one to Lily.

"Before you tedimeta, imagine a line that joins the inner corners of your two eyes," Karisma said as a colored line of smoke drew from her fingertips along Lily's forehead. "And then at each edge of your eye, draw a triangle point where these two lines meet; this is the third eye. Now close your eyes." Lily closed her eyes, imagining a third eye in the center of her forehead as she was told. She felt as though all her energy was joining together, greeting and meeting each other at this one spot in her mind. "Now think about the color of the crystal that you are holding in your hand right now, so think about the color blue. Envision this light coming from above and into this third eye. Watch as it vibrates and moves in patterns, expanding and shrinking constantly."

The imagery that Karisma described reminded Lily of what she had seen when she first entered the world of Sa Neo. She was excited to see the same portrait and she held her eyes tightly as she was told, but no matter how hard she tried, she could not see the geometric shapes or patterns. She looked back to Karisma disheartened.

"It's okay, Lily, it will come. Have faith." Karisma patted Lily's hand reassuringly. She smiled warmly with her red pupil eyes. The edges of her retina blazed like fire, darker on the edges and cooler toward the center. Lily felt empowered from looking at them, as though Karisma was passing on positive vibrations through just her eyes alone. "Take a deep breath and try again," she told her.

Lily sat still with her eyes closed, waiting for all the clutter inside her head to stop. Colors of black and red swirled around in patches, but after several breaths in accordance with Karisma's guidelines, they finally calmed down. The swirls of light continued to move but they now stretched out into a long thin line. The line came closer, and she felt herself roll over it, and rotate inside it. Next, she felt buzzing in her fingers, a tingling that moved up and down her arm, while heat pulsated within the palm of her hands. And then, a shaking sort of motion moved her sight rapidly from left to the right and right to left, very quickly. So quickly, that it wasn't a movement but more so, a reaction to some form of vibration. It reminded her of the unseen quiver in the air that occurs when a musical note is chimed.

The vibration continued to move down her spine, all over her body. It was so powerful she felt it stretch outside of her body, then back inside her skin. And when she opened her eyes, she was no longer sitting in the comfortable chair at the bottom of the tree in Karisma's living room, but instead, on a rocky shore full of the same blue stones that she held in her hand, with Karisma opposite her, smiling gaily.

"You did it!" Karisma exclaimed proudly, and she waved her hands in the air presenting the coastline. "Welcome to Deia."

The shores were covered in rectangle slices of blue flat rock. And the clouds above looked like fluffy splotches of white cotton. They swam in the sky, moving slowly around, allowing the sunlight to wedge through with mighty arms. The ocean water had no waves, just soft calm rivers flowing along in a stream, moving with the crisp breeze that filled the air. The landscape was very bare, and the rocks outstretched for miles.

"Why are we here?" Lily asked puzzled, confused as to how one moment she was inside the comfy tree house and the next, freezing cold on a rock.

Shut up, shut up you silly girl. Don't ask such stupid questions.

Lily shook her head quickly, trying to shake the hateful voices inside. Karisma looked to Lily suspiciously, noticing the strangeness in her character, and she raised her hand over her throat as she spoke.

"I was showing you how to tedimeta, remember? Are you okay Lily?"

Nothing, nothing, don't talk. Leave me alone. Shut up. Shut up you stupid stupid . . .

Lily shook her head violently this time, covering her eyes and ears, trying to conceal the dark voice inside yet again.

"Lily, talk to me!" Karisma shouted.

Lily looked back to the red-headed lady, her mind lightly frazzled from such a demanding tone inside. It spoke so loudly she was unsure as to who was actually talking.

"Lily, I know what is happening," Karisma whispered in a hushed voice. "The mind can play terrible tricks on you here."

She's lying, she's a liar. Don't listen to her. You are nothing, nothing, you hear me.

"Lily, you must follow my actions quickly. We need to create a sphere of protection around you. The influence of this land can be too strong if you are not prepared. Oh dear me, perhaps we have jumped too quickly."

You stupid woman, you don't know what you are doing.

"Lily, ignore your thoughts. They are not real, do you hear me?

Lily, they are not real!" Karisma took Lily's arms and rattled them hurriedly, and she spoke loudly, in an attempt to suffocate the other voices.

Don't listen to her. She is a liar. She is a peasant. Look at her rags of clothes. She is nothing.

"Lily, trust the energy you felt when you first met me. Hold on to those loving thoughts." Karisma tried again, her eyes now blazing with red flames and they flickered around her pupils sharply. "Now, stand up with me and put your tongue to the roof of your mouth and hum loudly, very loudly!"

Lily stood upright with Karisma and hummed with her tongue to her mouth. From the soothing tone of her own vibration, the voices inside were drummed out like Karisma had foretold. And her head was overtaken with an intoxicating quiver of sound. Lily breathed deeply, able to hear Karisma clearly now.

"Now that you are relaxed, I want you to imagine your body is feeling very heavy. Feel the base of your feet sink deeply into the ground," Karisma instructed, speaking with a stern, yet soft voice. "Visualize yourself as a tree and that your veins are the roots, pushing down into the soil below. Feel those roots dig deeper and deeper, Lily. You are connecting with the land you are standing on. The universe is supporting and loving you, right back up through those roots."

Lily closed her eyes and felt her weight sink evenly between her two feet. Her shoulders relaxed and her arms drooped down. She wondered if she had actually melted into the ground, she felt so heavy.

"Now envision that the top of your head holds a halo of white light above. Let the light float down slowly from the top of your head, stretching over your shoulders, cleansing your heart. It falls past your stomach, along your legs to your feet and into the ground." Lily could not only see the white light around her body, she could feel herself become extraordinarily light, and strangely untouchable. "As the light touches the land it will meet the roots in the soil. Imagine this light bouncing back up to reach your head, encasing your whole body in a protective sphere of constant rotating white light. It creates a never-ending circle, from the top of your head, down through to the ground and back around. This bubble will shield any great sorcerers magic that may come your way. Now put your tongue to the roof of your mouth once more and hum."

Lily envisioned the images as she was told, and the voices inside her head silenced. And although she projected the idea from the inside, it was the outside world that had changed. She was awakening to a different way of thinking, and it helped her realize the impact her beliefs had on her world and how easily she held the power to shatter through all logical realities. She opened her eyes once more to Karisma, standing next to her in a bold stance. Her fiery red hair blew fiercely in the wind, and they stood together on the blue kyanite pebbles on the shores of Deia. The soft sound of the waves crashing engulfed peace in Lily's ears, and she felt calm once more, staring to the outstretched colors of infinite sky and ocean.

"What just happened to me?"

"The energy in the land can sometimes do that to you. The land of Deia is ideal for learning, teaching, and open communication. But the polarity of this land, is miscommunication which too often is the cause of negative thoughts," Karisma explained, placing her hand over Lily's forehead as though checking Lily's temperature. She nodded and released her grip, suggesting she was in the clear.

"But the voices. I have heard them before. I thought they had left me when I came to Sa Neo, but they didn't. And they spoke such hatred; about me and about you."

Lily shuddered in remembrance, even though the memory of what had happened felt so distant, so surreal. Almost as though the devilish words never really existed in the first place.

"The voices are your inner thoughts. We will always have thoughts. It is what makes us unique and separate to all other animals," Karisma said as she held Lily's hand in comfort. "Although our thoughts can be cruel sometimes, it's important to understand that you do not have to believe them, you have a choice every day."

Karisma pulled out a small bottle that was tucked into her pockets, close to the waist of her skirt. She leant closer to the sea and filled the bottle up to the top, so that the ocean was captured in that moment of time, inside the glass. And as Karisma held the bottle up to the sunlight, the two watched as beautiful glittering grains of blue crystals separated from the water, falling down to the bottom of the glass like shooting stars in the night sky.

"They felt so real though, the negative voices. Do you hear them too?"

"We all do. You need to use your power to determine what you want to listen to. And discard all negative thoughts. Accept that they are not real and try to forget. Perhaps this is enough teaching for today. Let me bring you back home to rest."

Karisma took the blue stone from Lily's hand and replaced it with a red garnet crystal. The change of crystals against her skin seemed to vibrate oddly. The red in the garnet helped her feel even more grounded than the exercise they had just completed. It was as though it was the final piece in holding her together, as though it had cemented her into the ground, roots and all.

"Now, we are to tedimeta back home to Otor, envision red light in your third eye this time."

Karisma guided Lily through the same technique, only this time, Lily could clear her mind that little bit quicker. The swirling emotion and overpowering sense of colors that trickled through Lily's head were not as fearsome as last time, and she was able to relax that little bit easier. And when she opened her eyes, they were sitting back inside of Karisma's comfortable home with silent stillness all around, only now the outside sky had started to grow a little bit darker.

"Karisma, that land truly frightened me, why was that?" Lily asked, still quite worried.

"It was my fault, you were not ready to go there yet," Karisma said as she stood and lit various glass-framed candles around the room. "I had chosen Deia because it is the land of communication, a perfect environment for you to learn in. But unfortunately, if you are not at peace with yourself or feel insecure with the power that you hold, you could have a troubled journey here."

Karisma lifted up the rainfall of leaves from the ceiling canopy, so that any covered windows could open up, allowing the last of the natural light to fill the empty spaces in the room.

"I didn't know that I had any power?" Lily looked at her hands steadily, wondering what kind of gift she possessed. Karisma smirked and reached high into a pot plant. She walked over to Lily and placed a tiny seed inside of Lily's hand. Lily could feel the seed heat up as it began to stir, and it rolled back and forth steadily along the love line that was engraved into her palm.

"We all have limitless power; it can be as magnificent as you want it to be," Karisma said. As the seed broke open like a cracked egg, the tiny green sprout pushed itself through to the light. And Lily watched in awe, as the sprout moved up higher, stopping just before her eyes, forming into a flower bud. But then it stopped. Without thinking, Lily blew on the bud gently. Gradually, one by one, the sepal opened up, revealing an intricate design of oval shaped purple petals tie-dyed with yellow tips. The heart of the flower had long soft black and red eyelashes, and they opened wide, as though staring admiringly at their mother.

"How do I find this power?" Lily asked, inhaling the scent of the flower, letting her mind dance for a split moment to another place from the musky sensation.

"You always have it available, it never disappears and it is strengthened through loving yourself."

Lily wanted to roll her eyes at the suggestion of loving herself again. It wasn't to be rude, but she felt as though the concept was too hard for her to understand, and all she wanted was to dismiss it; but here it was again, haunting her until she listened.

"How do I do that?" Lily asked, willing to try and learn.

"By standing by your decision and trusting that your life is exactly as it is meant to be."

"I thought I already do though?"

Karisma shook her head solemnly. "You don't trust your heart," she said, and the flower closed back up, as though shriveling from the pain of being unloved. It retreated back into its bud, and reversed the flow, shrinking down into a tiny seed.

"How did you know?" Lily asked sadly, empathizing with the pain that the flower had felt.

"Because my heart is telling me. You don't know yourself, and knowing yourself is the first step toward loving yourself."

The idea of loving herself, let alone knowing herself, seemed further away than Lily could grasp, and it frustrated her, being faced with the same problem over and over again. It was screaming at her to listen, but she was deaf to such cries.

"How do I do that? Know myself, that is?" Lily wondered as she thought about whether or not she really knew herself. She had never asked herself that question before. And she even went further inside, asking herself if the reason she was deemed unusual or sometimes 'crazy' to some was because she didn't love herself enough. The voice inside repeated her thoughts back to her, mirroring her questions with a question, and giving no answer, as her answer.

"Knowing yourself starts from the inside. You need to spend some time alone really listening to your thoughts and remove anything that is not pure or serving love," Karisma said as she took the seed from Lily and placed it over her chest. She exhaled. A magnificent bouquet of dark red Black Beauty flowers grew between the slithers of Karisma's fingers. She handed them to Lily. "And accept yourself, flaws and all. Commend your strengths and acknowledge your weaknesses."

Lily shifted uneasily as she took the bouquet of black beauty flowers from Karisma. The concept of loving herself was still too difficult to understand and she inhaled the scent of the flowers lovingly, in an attempt to distract her mind.

"Tell me how you love the flowers," Karisma asked as she sensed Lily's uneasiness.

Lily nodded as she stared at the deep shades of red that seemed to evolve into darker shades of rouge.

"Flowers make me feel so calm, and my thoughts circulate on how much I love them. I love the color, the smell, the texture . . ." Lily's words drifted as she spoke and she touched on the petals gently. "Does being around nature help me love myself? Because I am thinking of love?"

Karisma smiled, and fetched a crystal vase from a wooden shelf against the wall. "Yes, it certainly does," she agreed, filling the vase with water from the hole in the ceiling. "Nature helps bring you into the moment, and encourages you to appreciate all the beauty in the world. But think about how you just described your love for this flower. Dissect the love of yourself in the same way," she continued as she arranged the roses into the vase and placed them on a table next to Lily.

The girls were interrupted by a tapping on the window; it was a beautiful green butterfly fairy, with diamond spots of pink on her wings. The butterfly carried a tiny rose quartz crystal and a miniature envelope sealed with a silvery green stamp. Karisma opened the window gleefully.

"Oh thank you sweetheart, we have been waiting for this."

The butterfly fluttered its wings quickly in response and dropped the delivery into Karisma's hand.

"Can I offer you some ginger tea?" Karisma asked sweetly, motioning for the butterfly to follow her.

The butterfly fairy circled away, showing that she needed to get back. *How odd*, Lily thought, *I can understand what the butterfly is saying.*

"You are almost ready," Karisma announced, reading the letter inside the envelope.

"Almost ready for what?"

"For initiation into the world of Sa Neo. Jade, the Queen of Tehar has summoned you to be one of us."

Karisma smiled with satisfaction at the delivery of the news; it was confirmation that she was right to have acted upon her premonition to help the girl. But the idea of meeting new people started to worry Lily, as initiation sounded like she would be judged while prominently placed on display amongst others or something of a similar notion.

"Do you think I can pass initiation?" Lily asked, as she started to doubt herself as usual.

Karisma stood up and gathered several crystals from a small clay pot on the table. She walked to the far corners of the room, and kissed each crystal as she placed it on the ground.

"Well, I think the more important question is, do you want to pass it?"

Lily didn't need much time to think about the answer. She was excited to be a part of the Sa Neo culture. Everything so far had already been truly marvelous. It felt like an organic progression of things to come.

"Yes, I do," Lily replied confidently.

"Then so it shall be." Karisma smiled, clicking two crystals together as though clapping in applause.

"But, I don't know the answers."

Karisma placed the last two crystals on either side of Lily's chair and cupped Lily's face between her warm palms, the way that Father used to do to her when he wanted her to listen.

"You hold the answer to every question you could ever ask," she soothed, her eyes gleaming with the reflection of the soft moonbeams that were now shining through the window.

"That's impossible," Lily retorted. "I don't know everything."

Karisma smiled sympathetically as she went back to the clay pot to collect more crystals, and placed them around the room, this time in a circle.

"You do. You have chosen these questions. You have chosen these people and situations to come into your life, in order to teach you something. Something that will in turn perhaps help you bring forth a deeper understanding."

Lily listened intently as she fiddled with the cushions she was sitting on, admiring the red velvet piping that encased the pillow. She massaged her thumb into the edge, feeling the textures from hard to soft and understanding the necessity of each opposite having needed to exist in order for the other to be defined. And even though Karisma was telling her that she knew all the answers, she still had many questions circulating within her mind, clawing to the edge just waiting to be asked.

"A deeper understanding of what though?" she questioned timidly.

Karisma stopped her crystal grid-making and sat back down next to Lily. She wanted her to know that their conversation was important, despite her constant movement around the room.

"Everything you are experiencing is here to bring forth a deeper understanding of life."

"Ohhh." Lily nodded, her mouth open slightly wide, not ready to close back up. She was too busy thinking about her life and how difficult it was to understand what that meant. She reflected back to her questioning with Jacques, how she had desired to have a purpose for her journey, and yet he said to just let it be. She now wanted to ask her questions to everyone, to gather the information, and make her own assumptions. Take control of the answer to her question, she decided.

"What is life?" She asked confidently.

Karisma smiled with acknowledgement as she looked out through the window to the now dark-lit sky. A shooting star blazed across from right to left, falling down from above as if chasing the formation of a rainbow in the most perfect alignment ever seen. And for several moments Karisma's eyes twinkled vibrantly, as though the stars in the universe were guiding information to her; or perhaps, Karisma knew the answers, like she had said all along, and the star was in fact applauding her graciously, encouraging her to divulge the secret amongst the world.

"To have a heart that beats, that is what life is," she stated as the twinkle in her eyes sparkled again. "Or one could define it as the time frame through which we evolve and change dramatically. Call it what you want, for you are the creator. It is you directing your own evolution." She paused, as a rainfall of stars flooded across the evening sky behind her. And the two gazed together, watching the shower of blazing meteoroids explode amongst the darkness. "It can be as wonderful as you want it to be, or it can be depressingly miserable." She shrugged her shoulders with no judgment. "The choice is yours."

Lily felt the twinkle from Karisma's eyes dive deep within her own. And the information danced around like a spark of fire inside her heart. It ignited a light inside of Lily, and like twin flames, they held hands tightly, twirling together, rejoicing for such a profound idea of passionate love driving everything. But then the darkness began to creep in. Lily could feel it brewing from the far corners of her mind, and the light began to be suffocated. Lily was able to recognize her fear and she willingly asked for more strength.

"Karisma, what if I only ever see darkness in my life?" Lily's voice trembled with terror, instantly forgetting the advice that had just been delivered.

"You must trust that the light will illuminate one day," Karisma soothed, as Lily could feel the light inside start to breathe again. "Try to feel at peace knowing that it is necessary for us to endure the darkness. For we must create a contrasting backdrop for the light to shine so brightly against."

As Karisma spoke, the lights in the room all extinguished except for one that was a glowing frame around Lily. She illuminated fiercely in the darkness. "Do not be shamed by your scars, my girl; for to see clarity in the world you must grow strength through your being. No great fighter ever stood tall without a used sword and shield." She paused as the two sat in silence. "I think this is enough for today, let us sleep. I want you to be well- rested for tomorrow."

Karisma reached for a candle to provide additional light as she created a bed on the sofa where Lily was sitting. It was complete with soft cushions and cuddly blankets. She opened the window up slightly, allowing a cool draft to seep in from the night air. Lastly, she poured strong-smelling ginger tea into an antique gold and finely painted red flower-tipped cup on a wooden table, with a small book in case Lily felt like reading.

"You have no obligation to sleep here Lily, and I understand if you wish to continue on your journey. But please know that you are welcome into my home at anytime."

"Thank you Karisma, I truly appreciate it."

"I am just happy to share my knowledge with you, Lily. It has been a pleasure to meet you and I hope you are still here with me in the morning. Good night."

Karisma closed the door and left Lily alone in the room to sleep by herself.

As Lily snuggled into bed she looked outside the window. The moon glowed with intensity, a reflective mirror of cool crimson red. And on either side of the perfectly round sphere was a sliced half-moon to the right, and a sliced half-moon to the left. There was not one, not two, but three moons in the sky. It was certainly something that Lily had never actually seen before, although she knew such a phenomenon could exist. The wispy clouds crawled quickly across the sky, creating a speckled veil as it covered the moons. And in the small gaps between the clouds of when the moons shone through, they seemed to all glow vibrantly in harmony, reflecting the beauty that the daylight sun had provided, for those who had missed the day. *The night sky, although dark, held so much more beauty than the day,* Lily thought. For one could stare for hours on end, falling deeper and deeper into the peaceful balance of light to dark and dark to light.

The forest around Karisma's house was an enticing playground calling Lily's name. She couldn't sleep now; she was far too excited to see what else there was. She wanted to meet the animals, the insects, the plants and the trees. But ultimately, she couldn't sleep because she kept thinking about seeing Crysanthe again, and she fantasized about what it would be like to watch the dance of Neo. Without further thought, she leapt from the bed, and with hushed footsteps she scurried across the floor, making her way back to the red crystal beach on the land of Otor.

CHAPTER FIVE

THE DANCE OF NEO

Lily stood still on the beach of Otor with the red garnet crystals beneath her feet. The smooth bubbles raced up over her toes and tickled her ankles while she held the ouroboros necklace in her left hand and the seashell in her right. From afar, the waves in the ocean seemed all over the place—a chaotic mess of rough sea and endless water colliding into one another. But upon closer inspection she could see evolving patterns forming as single circles transformed into doubles and then tripled and rippled out into millions and millions of tiny circles. One elongated conjoined pattern, breathing life from the center of the horizon, moving forward from one point to another, back again and directly through to her.

She closed her eyes tightly and imagined the electrical wire from the middle of her forehead projecting out, streaming a line of light straight into the water, diving deep below to find Crysanthe wherever she was. Lily whispered into the wind *'come to the shore of Otor'*. And she visualized Crysanthe's sweet face as she repeated the words once more, a total of four times in her head. *Crysanthe! Come to the shore of Otor, come to the shore of Otor, come to the shore of Otor.*

She opened her eyes, but Crysanthe was not in sight.

Lily continued to stare, waiting for the mermaid to appear.

Nothing. Perhaps she was doing it wrong. Again she tried. Dangling the necklace into the water, she envisioned the line of communication open to Crysanthe once more. She sang with her heart through the wire and along the current, down the ocean path, but she did not appear. And so Lily tossed the seashell into the ocean, surrendering to the idea that perhaps she had imagined it after all. And at that final moment when she felt she had nothing left to give, was the moment Crysanthe appeared, shining vibrantly and elegantly, with the biggest smile upon her face.

"Oh Lily, I am so happy that you called me again. I heard you the first time! Do not worry, it takes me awhile to swim this far over."

Crysanthe hovered in the water, only a stone's throw away from where Lily stood and she handed her the seashell back again. Her body was covered in shimmering crystals that exploded in beautiful patterns across her skin. The glittering sparkles lit up her silvery complexion in colorful fireworks, and throughout her white hair you could see tiny specks of rainbow crystals braided through. Her ouroboros was tied around the top of her head like a crown, hanging delicately in between her violet eyes.

"What do you think of the colorful mishmash on my skin? I let the children dress me today as part of their arts and crafts at school. It's a true masterpiece, do you agree?" She smiled as she pointed to the drawings on her body and Lily nodded in response, feeling her smile automatically light up as she shared happiness for what Crysanthe had experienced.

"It's beautiful! And the colors sparkle in a way that I have never seen before. How is that so?"

"It's because the world is magical Lily!" She giggled, as rainbow bubbles escaped her mouth again. "Anything can completely change in a split second, look!" Crysanthe picked up a handful of water in her hands and Lily watched while it transformed into slivers of red glittery sand and seeped through her fingers back into the ocean, returning to its natural form.

"Wow, that is beautiful!"

"It's only salt in the water. It just depends on how you look at it," Crysanthe said as she wriggled around on the point of her tail, and the water droplets on her skin changed into solid matter again. She dusted off the colored salts from her body and sprinkled the particles in the air, allowing the wind to blow them high across the sky.

"Whatever you want to see, you will see."

"I want to see everything!" Lily shrieked.

"Then so it shall be," Crysanthe agreed. "Now, tell me, did you meet Karisma? What is she like?" Crysanthe played with her hair as she spoke to Lily, pulling out the crystals and skimming them over the water's edge.

"Yes, I have spent all day with Karisma. She is so lovely and kind. She is teaching me her knowledge and she says I have great powers inside of me, just waiting to be unleashed," Lily explained, and as she did she realized that the more she repeated the idea of her talents, the more achievable they appeared to be.

"Lily, I agree with Karisma completely, for I too have had the same intuition about you. And it is for these reasons that I want your attendance at the Dance of Neo tonight."

Lily smiled with her teeth as she listened to the compliments from her new friend. Having never had any friends before, she did not know what to expect, or what was right. But she felt complete love and gratitude from the mermaid and all from just being herself; she knew this must have been what true friendship meant.

"Will you put me under the same spell as last time?" Lily asked nervously, reliving the terror she had originally felt from not being free.

"We have two options. I can freeze you as before, and you can observe silently. Or I can teach you how to grow fins and swim underneath the ocean with me, by your side. And together, we will dance for Neo. Dance to celebrate the happiness and goodness in this world. Are you one with me?" Crysanthe held her hand out for Lily to join her in the water as the waves rose and crashed down tremendously behind the beautiful mermaid queen.

"To be one of you? But how is it possible?" Lily queried, although she tip-toed farther into the water just the same.

"Anything is possible, if you believe it to be so. This time, I will give you the gift of air. Do you know how to swim?"

"Yes."

"Then look into my eyes and have no fear."

Lily stared once again into the violet eyes of Crysanthe. The inner circles swirled around in a nauseating motion making her feel dizzy. The vortex completely overtook Lily's mind and once again she was struck into a motionless trance, stiff inside a statue form. It felt very similar to before, and like last time, she too was now hovering above water. But as Crysanthe lowered Lily down into the water, her feet transformed into a fish tail. Her dress lifted above her head, and floated up as Lily sank deeper and deeper into the water. The feeling of salt water on her skin, which was now her fins, felt liberating, comforting, and lubricating. And with ease she swam, gliding her arms through the water easily, like flying through air. She moved her back fluidly with her hips, swimming through the currents like a dolphin.

Together they swam, hand in hand, while Crysanthe guided Lily to explore her home. The idea of breathing underwater felt strange to Lily in her thoughts, but when she didn't think about it, she naturally flowed in harmony. A school of fish dressed in brilliant colors of yellow and purple swam beside Lily, moving around in a protective arrow. Lily felt strangely connected to the swimming fish, she felt like she was a part of something bigger than just herself, like she belonged in the oceanic world. More and more fish came closer to the mermaids, curiously staring and wondering if they were to be prey or the other way around.

The girls swam deeper below the dark black waters, and Lily held Crysanthe's hand tightly, careful not to get lost. As her eyes adjusted to the darkness she was able to see the florescent lights of the fish moving around clearly. The jellyfish were her favorite to witness, with their opening umbrellas of sparkling circles and mosaics. The texture of the jellyfish looked squishy and soft to touch; she was mesmerized by the size and delicate nature of such a creature. Giant eels wiggled through, some over ten miles long, they seemed to stretch out forever lighting the path. Once again the darkness began to part, as Lily swam over the coral forest, watching below as it swayed in harmony, as though it were dancing to a tune that streamed vibrations through the ocean.

"How do you not get scared of the big fish? Like that one, with giant claw-like teeth and beady looking eyes?" Lily asked, as the giant fish lost interest and swam away.

"Zavier says that they feel fear. And that fear only becomes real if you believe it to be so."

"So if I don't believe that they will harm me, they won't?" Lily asked as another strange- looking fish with huge claws in its mouth swam closer to the girls.

"Yes, they are more scared of you than you are of them. They don't want to hurt you, but if you start thinking they will, they will believe it too, and next thing you know you will be bitten."

"Zavier is smart. It's the same kind of thing my papa says to me about snakes—they only attack if they feel like you are cornering them with no way out. They don't want to be near you anymore than you want to be near them!"

Lily hadn't thought about Father in awhile. She wondered if she held the same power of being able to communicate telepathically to him, like she did with Crysanthe. She called to him through her mind, envisioning his face and she told him, *I am safe Papa!* At that moment she spotted a giant crab and a baby cuddling each other. She felt like it was a sign that Father heard her voice.

The girls finally stopped at a large opening to a cave that was covered in seashells.

"Welcome to the Cave of Zeka," Crysanthe said as she swam through the entrance, motioning for Lily to follow.

The walls of the caves were covered in drawings, and they reminded Lily of ancient scriptures inside the pyramids of Egypt. She stared with admiration at the great many stories that were told through the etchings. The tunnel of the cave was shaped as though a large sphere had snowballed through a giant mountain, opening up a portal for the mermaids to swim through. The layout was a giant cross, at each end air, water, fire, or nature was written and drawn to mark the opening. In the center of the cross, was a giant circular room, colored in a deep rustic red brown, with soft patches of slimy moss growing throughout that looked like little square seats for students to sit on while staring at the artwork on the walls. Directly above the sphere room was a giant ball of light, which Lily had learned from Crysanthe was called Neo, and it shone through the tunnel, illuminating each end of the caves at all times, no matter what time of day it was. Crysanthe held Lily's hand and sat her down at the center point of the tunnel, so that the two of them could examine the scriptures together.

The symbols made no sense to Lily, yet they looked so familiar from her daily life back home—a triangle inside a circle, and a star portrayed as a three-dimensional-drawing with pointing arrows and symbols all around it. It carried forward, with a dot, and then two dots and then a line and further more a shape of additional circles, flowering out from the center. It reminded Lily of the pattern she had seen at the floor of her home that day when she traveled beneath the house to Sa Neo, although she couldn't be certain.

"Do you know what any of it means?"

"Not so much," Crysanthe confessed. "Zavier understands it more than I do, and every time he explains it my mind just wanders. I like simplicity." She giggled, then continued, "But this means the seed, and this is the flower, and together they create life. Here, look."

Crysanthe picked up a large chunk of clear crystal quartz and she smashed it on the edge of a rock, rubbing her hand over the broken edge of the quartz, she showed Lily the inside of the crystal. "See, the pattern is the same inside the crystal. It's everywhere if you start looking for it!"

"Wow!"

The inside of the crystal had a fine intricate pattern with a spiderweb-like design, and it glowed with florescent colors as Crysanthe spoke about it, showing Lily the truth.

"And here, this is the dance of Neo," Crysanthe said as she pointed proudly to the drawing of several mermaids holding hands around a giant sphere. Sentences and verses circled around the center of the sphere, and arrows underneath pointed the way, suggesting the direction and position of the mermaids.

"So, I say the words inside the center here, and everyone is to hold hands, one facing in and one facing out. We turn around clockwise four times and switch positions, and then back around the opposite way."

Lily nodded with understanding.

"Do you want to know what the peculiar thing about this is, though?"

Lily's eyes widened.

"No one is actually swimming, or moving, we are just pulled in one direction, and then the other. It's a force beneath us, above us, and inside us. We don't know how or why it happens, but we just move with it."

Lily gazed at the drawing, probing for answers, yet accepting that such a mysterious process could evolve.

"Do you think it will matter if I am included when I am not a real mermaid?" Lily asked, not wanting to interfere, yet feeling it necessary to be included in such an important occasion.

"Lily, you hold our ultimate life symbol around your neck," Crysanthe reassured as she pointed to a giant ouroboros drawn in white on the far wall. "It would be our honor to include you in our dance."

"Why do you do the dance of Neo?" Lily asked, looking at the beautiful sketches of the mermaids gleefully holding hands.

"Because it makes us happy to share something together. We do the dance of Neo every day."

"Every day?"

"Every day!" Crysanthe giggled again and shuffled her tail with excitement as she continued, "something unexplainable happens when we do it; the fire glows brighter, the warmth of Neo is stronger, we feel closer as a community as well. It's like the whole ocean benefits from it—the coral, the sharks, the dolphins, everyone. Perhaps it affects you there on land too, we wouldn't know."

"I will try and find the answer for you tomorrow," Lily promised, as she wondered how she could measure what success meant.

"Come, we should hurry." Crysanthe waved Lily to follow as she swam off quickly, her giant silver tail battering through the water creating a trail of bubbles behind.

Together the mermaids swam up to where several mermaids were crowded around. Lily could recognize Zavier from last time. He was sitting on a seashell throne playing a game with checkered colored squares and carved out shapes. It reminded Lily of chess. His features were quite distinct, with long shaggy hair and a marvelous crystal that hung loosely around his neck. Aside from Lily recognizing this from his exterior, he immediately swam over to Crysanthe as soon as she came into his sight.

"Oh Crysanthe, you look absolutely beautiful," Zavier praised as they swam closer together.

"Silly Zavier, you saw me only a little while ago! Surely I can't look any different than before!" she teased, moving her body away from him as though letting him chase her slightly.

"Yes my love, but I can see the spark in your eyes of your findings. I know this girl is making quite an impact on you. And although I was against it at first, seeing the way it makes you happy, well, it makes me love you even more. I want to remind you how grateful I am that you have chosen to share your life with me."

Zavier spoke his words with integrity, not caring who was around to overhear, just as long as his beloved was listening. And even then, Crysanthe looked away coyly, as if she was undeserving of his affection. But he held her hand tightly, showing that he was not going anywhere until she acknowledged his presence.

"My love, we have company," she said and smiled as she stroked his hand on top of her hand. In one look she spoke words back to him that only he could understand.

Lily observed eagerly. She had never seen such a beautiful display of equally balanced male and female energy. There was an undeniable spark between the two, and it gleamed like stardust swirling above their heads, soundly encasing them both in a shell together, as though they were untouchable as one. And as a result of the love that Zavier professed in words and gestures, Crysanthe was like a flower in a vase, observed and drizzled with love, giving her no other option than to bloom in such trust that he allowed.

"Come merpeople, it's time to start the dance of Neo!" Zavier motioned for the dance to commence.

"Lily, stand here next to me and hold my hand," instructed Crysanthe, as they joined the group of mermaids already in position, holding hands around the giant ball of fire.

It must have been at least a hundred mermaids gathered around the Neo, in one great big line, not too close, careful not to burn. It looked exactly like the picture in the cave Lily thought. And on the ground to the side there was an orchestra of mermaids, casually lined up with giant shells for drumming, tightened seaweed for guitar strings, and Zavier at the head, instructing the music to play.

The dance began.

The swishing sound of moving tails echoed in vibration and Lily felt the movement from the person next to her beat right through her heart, and the synchronic motion liberated Lily right to her very core.

Without thinking, she smiled.

The dance continued for several turns as Crysanthe had explained. Each time the mermaids changed direction a huge explosion from Neo burst through the sea. Sometimes up top, sometimes below, but never harming any of the mermaids. And the atmosphere in the ocean felt different; there were patches of warmth and overflowing streams of bubbles seeped between the mermaids as they moved. Particles of light and weighted textures exploded through the backdrop of blackness. The light from Neo extruded veracious flames of fireworks, satisfying the sense of sight equally with the touch of warmth. And the colors and vibrations of the dance energized Lily; making the blood in her veins circulate in a fast motion, her heartbeat strummed faster with excitement and all she could think about was doing it again and again!

When the dance was over, the family of mermaids laughed, and they gathered together to share a huge feast. A giant tumble ball of seaweed spun in the center like the flaming ball of Neo, and on top sat a beautifully decadent seashell table throne. The mermaids each took turns in pulling off the seaweed-like string, and chewed on the delicacy as they chattered about their day.

"Do you like the seashell table? Zavier made it himself," Crysanthe gushed proudly talking about her partner's creation, and she pointed to the fine artwork of crushed seashells and stone.

"It's beautiful!" Lily exclaimed. "Everything here is amazing. Why is it that I feel everything so deeply in Neosa?"

"I know what you mean Lily, I feel that our underwater world communicates to you in other ways."

"Surely we have the same kind of beauty on land too, though? Why do I not see it the same way?"

"Perhaps it is because there are too many distractions around you. Look, here." Crysanthe pointed to the water behind her. "There is nothing but a blank canvas of ocean and fish. In the land you are distracted by the beauty of the sky, the pictures of the clouds and the fire of the sun to begin with, then there are smells, and there are so many colors contrasting to the flowers, the grass, the dirt. It is impossible to focus on just one. But if you can manage to do it on land as you do here below, it is all the same, just a vast floating landscape of dancing energy."

Lily gazed at the ocean with an insatiable thirst. She felt radiantly alive floating in the water, weightlessly. And she smiled with happiness, finally feeling the gratification of her uncontrollable urge to explore the water world in her daily life. There was something bigger to be found! And she sat in undisturbed bliss for several minutes until the scene dramatically ended, as a baby mermaid was carried through by an older male and handed directly to Crysanthe.

"Crysanthe, we need your help! Cloudia has choked on

something, something that does not belong in the sea. She cannot breathe, can you help her?"

Crysanthe quickly took hold of the little mermaid girl, who looked no more than four. Cloudia's facial expression was sweetly calm, and her eyes were closed. But the color of her skin was a dark shade of violet, and her arms were hanging disconnected from her torso. In a split second, the harmony was overtaken with complete silence in the ocean, an unsettling feeling of everyone staring at a lifeless body.

Crysanthe placed her hand on the merchild's forehead and closed her eyes as she sweetly hummed a soothing lullaby. And Lily could feel that any pain or trouble that was still left in the body was gone. *Perhaps Crysanthe performed an act to soothe the crowd around her,* Lily thought. For it was evident that there was no life left inside the vessel of the body.

Crysanthe motioned for the body to be taken away and turned to Zavier for condolence, but he wasn't giving any kind of sympathy, and he turned to the crowd of mermaids, offering his voice to calm them.

"The displacement of one body in this world can disrupt the peace in thousands of others standing by. It is how we chose to interpret this situation that will determine our future. Let us listen to the teaching of Cloudia and be wary of anything that is thrown into the ocean that does not belong here. We must work harder to clean our waters."

Crysanthe moved to Zavier and handed the body over, taking the ouroboros into her hand. She looked into his eyes, searching for comfort but Zavier looked back to Crysanthe and spoke sternly. "I am not blaming you Crysanthe, nor am I telling you not to interact with Lily, but we should have realized that Cloudia was missing from our ceremony. But no, we were too busy entertaining our new guest, we forgot what was important."

But Crysanthe wasn't alarmed; she paused and fired her words back at him, holding Cloudia's ouroboros tightly between her hands.

"Zavier, listen to me," she reasoned. "Death is a gift to teach us impermanence. You have never looked at death as being anything other than rebirth, why is it bad now?"

"I am not saying this is bad. But no one has died from our negligence. And things are changing in a different way than they have ever changed before."

Zavier's forehead creased with dark lines as he spoke with anger in his voice and the crowd of mermaids silenced as they listened to the quarrel.

"Well it is times like these that we need to remember most of all that change is forever good, it's always for the better. It is never a bad thing," Crysanthe said as she felt the anger rub off from Zavier while he listened, and she turned to the crowd of mermaids to continue, "come all, let us go to the Cave of Zeka and seek the rebirth of this mermaid."

The group of mermaids all followed Crysanthe back to the cave of Zeka, where the scriptures of history were engraved. They stopped at the far edge closest to the flaming Neo where the seaweed grew high. The mermaids all gasped with open eyes as they looked to each other excitedly, and Lily watched as the sadness of death was positively replaced with the anticipation of hope. Crysanthe moved forward from the crowd and swept away the tall seaweed, pulling out one large glowing golden egg.

"When one cycle finishes a new one begins, and we become a child once more, to continue learning. Let this new life transform for the better."

"Transform for the better," the crowd chanted in response.

She cocooned the egg with both hands as it slowly began to crack. A little hand pushed out first, then another, and in one quick motion, a tail whipped back and forth, cracking the entire egg, as a handsome little merboy opened his eyes for the very first time.

"Lily, would you please name this baby?" Crysanthe asked, while a puzzled Zavier stood by.

Lily looked over to Crysanthe, surprised to be asked such an honorable request from her new friend. Under normal circumstances her nerves would have overtaken her stomach with anxiety from having been made to not only speak in front of a large audience but also to innovate an idea on demand; however, for some reason she was okay. It felt completely natural and absolutely right.

"Crysanthe, this is a huge honor. I am beyond grateful to be given this opportunity," Lily accepted, speaking with a clear voice, ensuring all around were able to hear.

"The opportunity is yours to take. I believe it is a true blessing that you have come here to meet us. We welcome you into our family and look forward to hearing the name you choose for our new boy."

Lily thought hard. She held the merchild in her arms and stared at his beautiful dark blue eyes. She whispered to her mother for help, opening up her mind to allow a name to speak through clearly. *Indigo.*

"I would like to name him, Indigo."

The merchild flapped his tail upon hearing his name, and his long black eyelashes blinked delicately as they crossed over one another. His eyes were a dark blue indigo, and they stared through Lily, into her eyes, and beyond. She felt strangely connected to him, more so than anyone else she had ever met.

"And so it shall be. He suits his name perfectly and we thank you."

"Thank you," chanted all the merpeople as they bowed their heads to Lily.

Crysanthe cradled the merchild in her arm and placed the base of her palm over his forehead. She closed her eyes and breathed slowly, humming gently as she rocked the babe softly. Lily looked around and saw that all the other merpeople were humming and swaying lightly the same, so she followed as well.

"Welcome to Neosa, Indigo. May your life be as bright as Neo, and may the love inside of you shower in abundance upon all of those who are blessed to come your way."

"Welcome Indigo," repeated the mermaids as they all bowed down once more, holding hands and rejoicing at the beautiful addition to their family.

"I would like you to be his guardian angel. Will you accept?" Crysanthe asked, brushing the soft black hair from the baby's face.

Yes, said a voice inside of Lily.

"Yes," she replied out loud.

"May you give me your left hand, please, Lily?"

Crysanthe took Lily's hand and crossed it over Indigo's small palm. She took the ouroboros off the crown on her head and held it on top of his hand, then she wrapped the chain around the two, bonding each hand gently together.

"With this chain I unite you together, creating an open line of communication, able to speak fluidly with ease between one another."

Crysanthe picked up an oyster shell from the bottom of the oceanic ground and blew lightly to the edge. Very slowly, the clasp of the shell opened, proudly displaying two perfect black pearls inside.

"Lily, may I have your necklace, please?" Crysanthe requested, as she used her dainty hands to remove the ouroboros from around Lily's neck.

She handed Lily's ouroboros to Zavier, who effortlessly removed a white crystal from one of the serpent's eyes. He then replaced it with a black pearl, and matched Indigo's ouroboros as well—one eye with a black pearl from the ocean, and the other, a white crystal that was in Lily's original necklace. Creating two unique, matching necklaces for both Lily and Indigo.

"You are now forever connected together. Whenever you wish to contact each other, it will be through these black pearl eyes. A simple whisper of your name will ignite the connection. From Indigo to Lily, or Lily to Indigo." Crysanthe finished her sentence and smiled to Lily, nodding with appreciation, handing the black and white eyed serpent necklace back. Lily tightened the chain around her neck and it clicked securely, as if it had always meant to fall that way.

"Come, it is time for me to take you back to shore."

The girls swam back above to the red-pebbled shore of Otor as the sun was beginning to rise. A milky pink sky bloomed across the sea, and the red crystals on the beach were glistening, still holding a reflection of love from the moonlight. Lily's dress had not only washed up on shore, but was hanging perfectly over the branch of a tree, crisp and dry. Crysanthe took both of Lily's hands and twined her fingers in between. She kissed both hands gently, and blew kisses on their fingertips. When she unraveled their fingers, Lily's legs had unraveled too, and the mermaid tail slipped off like a snake skin, drifting away to sea.

"How did you feel seeing Cloudia's life move into another form today?" Crysanthe asked, as she helped Lily walk back to shore, making sure she was strong in her legs.

"It was strange. I'm not quite sure what to think," Lily replied honestly, buttoning up the top of her white lace dress. "What about you? Do you wish it didn't happen?"

"I don't think like that, Lily. Wishing something to be different. We cannot change the course of life."

"I know," Lily replied as an image of her mother flashed into her mind and she lowered her head, heavy with grief. She hadn't cried for her mother in a long time, however, every now and again she would really miss her.

She walked back closer to the water, and pulled her mind over to Crysanthe, eager to change the subject to stop any tears that may arise.

"How does it feel to know that you are the owner of this whole ocean?" Lily waved her hand across the line of the horizon slowly, as she too took in the weight of its beauty.

"I could ask you the same question. I am no different than you," Crysanthe replied, looking over her shoulder into the distance.

"But these waters are yours. You control them."

"I am no master, and the waters are not my possession. Join me in loving them." She smiled, nodding to Lily with reassurance. "Be thankful that we are alive and able to witness such pure pleasure that satisfies all of our senses. We can see, hear, smell, touch, and taste. We are meant to share this together."

The two paused in silence as they listened to the soft waves crashing by Lily's feet. The drumming noise of water lapping onto the crystal pebbles mirrored the sound of trees whispering in the forest behind them. And together they stared at the brightening sky against the dark-lit ocean, the simplistic contrast of dark and light. The blurred line between one shade to the other extended far beyond what the eye could see, and yet they didn't need to see it to know that it existed. They believed it to be so. It was defining infinity. And yet in the moment of staring at nothingness they were creating something so much more. Something that could only be felt by truly loving both sides equally, knowing that it relied on the other in order for itself to be able to exist. And she was grateful to be able to share that moment with Crysanthe. For it was in this tiny moment of space that she was able to see all the love that surrounded her clearly. The moment of clarity only lasted for a second, and although the same flame cannot be lit twice, a burn to the skin has the ability to scar for an eternity.

CHAPTER SIX

THE MASTER VOLCANO

The sound of birds singing together in harmony outside the window awoke Lily first. She nuzzled her head back into the pillow and imagined their conversation. The male called out to the female, and the female flirted back. *I wonder what they are saying,* she thought. The smell of hot ginger tea drifted through the doors, and it was then that she opened her eyes to welcome the new day. The room looked different in the morning; the entire ceiling was covered in leaves, long overhanging vines in different shapes and sizes. Nuzzling into one another, crossing over like a large canopy of giant spiderwebs. Lily felt so comfortable lying at Karisma's house, it was as though she could have been lying in her own bedroom. She was in complete peace. The pillows and covers had cushioned her with warmth all night, cocooning her to provide a safe place for her to dream. Lily pushed the sheets off the bed and stood upright. It was only now that she realized she had been dressed in her lace nightgown for over a day.

Karisma knocked on the door softly, waiting for Lily to invite her in. She opened the door holding a tray with hot tea and wore a dark red silk crochet dress. The dress hung low to the ground and had large pieces of twisted fringing around the waist. The gold and garnet ring still faceted on her ring finger, prominently standing alone as her only piece of jewelry.

"How did you sleep?" she asked as she walked through, placing the tray on a wooden shelf that protruded out from the large trunk. The rawness of the wood looked as though the tree had a hand and was eager to hold it, the roots curved around like a bowl, and the tray locked easily into place.

"Soundly," Lily replied as she sat up. "Have you been awake long?"

"A few hours. I went into town to teach the children how to grow vegetables so that they never become hungry," she said as she lifted the silk drapes, letting the morning sunlight pour through and tickle the leaves that hung like a rainforest canopy upon the ceiling.

"You are a teacher?" Lily asked, sitting upright, eager to feel the warm sun on her face.

"We are all teachers. I have learned from you also." Karisma smiled as she poured the tea from a meticulously hand-crafted ceramic teapot, painted with red flowers. The steam from the cup boiled over lavishly and the aroma of sweet ginger tickled Lily's nose.

"What have I taught you?" Lily asked as she took the warm teacup from Karisma.

"That you never know what or who could knock at your door. And that is why my door is always open." Karisma pointed to the door and it creaked open to prove her point. Lily smiled at the synchrony, although something inside was tugging at Lily to understand more. How was Karisma so generous when no one else ever was to her? She didn't need to talk or act in a certain way; it was an agreement from the moment they met. *How is it that someone could be so kind?* she wondered, as her thoughts changed quickly, and her brow creased with confusion.

"What is the matter Lily?" Karisma asked and blinked her eyelashes slowly as she observed Lily. Her lashes moved with such effortless ease, they reminded Lily of butterfly wings fluttering, prompting a desire for her to see another butterfly soon.

"I am wondering why you are helping me?" Lily asked curiously, taking another sip of the ginger tea, allowing the scent to pleasure her senses once more.

Karisma smiled with a sympathetic grin, and she shook her head lightly as to dismiss Lily's inadequacy of accepting help.

"I am being told inside that this is what I am meant to do, and I do not question that voice. For she is the greatest master of them all, she is me." Karisma stood as she referred to herself, giving herself the respect and love that Lily wished to give to herself also. She picked up a silver watering can from the windowsill, and held it up to the ceiling where a small hole was visible. She twirled her finger around the inside of the hole as a small stream of water dribbled through, filling up the metal can.

"I wish I could learn to listen to that voice," Lily confessed as she strummed her finger on the shiny teacup.

"Of course you can and I will help you." Karisma smiled showing perfectly aligned teeth, and she proceeded to water the plants around the room. She moved gracefully, tipping the water high and low. Her skirt sashayed behind her. It twirled around as though she were a belly dancer, clinking the watering can against the pot plants creating music to sway her hips to.

"But I have many voices inside of me. How do I know which is the right one?" Lily took a sip of her tea and sighed with confusion. She had spent a long time trying to silence the voices in her head, and here she was being told that she should listen.

"When you love yourself, the right voice will stand forth, and you will know," Karisma assured. "Now please, have some more tea to awaken your belly, and then let's go outside and see what the day will bring!"

Lily took another sip and stretched out her arms as she stood up and made the bed. Karisma helped as they folded the blankets and moved the cushions to a vacant seat by the window.

"Thank you so much, you have been so kind, I don't know how I can repay you."

"Your words alone are enough. I am very pleased to have you as my guest, so thank you for staying."

Karisma's rouge cheekbones pushed high near her eyes as her

smile broadened across her face. She walked to the wooden cabinet by the entry of the room and took out a piece of plain red fabric, no bigger than the size of her hand.

"What is it?"

"Something different to wear today, if you want?" Karisma replied easily, handing Lily the fabric.

Lily looked puzzled. It wasn't a dress, or a shirt, or anything to wear.

"How do I . . . ?"

"Think of what you want and it will be."

"But how do I have the ability to do something like that?"

"Because our thoughts create our reality. You hold the potential to be the best creator that you can be. Shall we try?"

Lily looked at Karisma's dress and thought how nice it was with the crochet, but perhaps it was a little too womanly for her. She pictured the same dress but with longer sleeves, and a little bit shorter, more of a smock style. No sooner had she completed the image of a dress in her head but the piece of fabric in her hand fattened. It plumped up and out, changing shape quite dramatically, and when Lily opened the cloth, it was no longer a small square piece of fabric, but a beautiful lace dress. It was precisely the style that she had imaged. Except prettier!

"Oh Karisma, this is gorgeous! But . . . how?"

"This is your gift Lily. Whatever you think will come true. You cannot change other people though, so do not try to. It is up to them to want to change."

Lily listened to the advice as Karisma escorted Lily to an outside shower that was fenced with tall rosemary leaf bushes. Above her head, the water streamed along a bamboo branch, exploding droplets of fresh rainwater upon Lily's skin. The birds outside sang harmoniously, as the sun warmed the land tenderly, and the sweet-smelling aroma of rosemary drifted up Lily's nose while the water powdered down on her body gently.

After a long cleansing shower, Lily proceeded to get dressed into her new red gown. She buttoned the back up tightly and brushed her silky brown hair. Karisma was waiting for Lily in the backyard of the giant tree, holding a basket full of berries, singing as she reached up high to pick the delectable fruit. The garden was in no way perfectly organized in rows or lines; rather it was a jungle of mix-matched fruit and vegetables overgrowing through the meadows as a continuation of the forest. Karisma stood under a mulberry tree that had stained red on the floor from where the berries fell. She wore no shoes and let the blood from the juices mark her feet where she stood.

"Lily, will you help me gather some fruit for our breakfast?" Karisma asked as she saw Lily approach in her fresh attire.

Lily nodded gleefully and skipped over to Karisma to help pick the berries from the tree. A rush of birds flew overhead, and Lily could feel the presence of someone else near her. It wasn't the animals or lizards or insects watching; she knew the feeling of nature. There was someone else and she looked behind her back to see.

"Come forth, Isabella. To what do we owe the honor of this visit?"

Karisma spoke loudly to a beautiful young woman walking through the field behind where Lily was standing. She had a great rosy smile, with white crooked teeth shining through, and strawberry blonde hair. And her dress was a simple red cotton smock, with lots of layers like a tiered cupcake, hanging loosely over her delicate frame.

"Good morning Karisma! I'm here to bring you some good news!" replied the sun-kissed lady as she walked closer to the girls.

"Then let it not rest with you Isabella, please do share. And may I introduce you to my dear friend here, Lily."

Lily blushed at being called a friend of the beautiful empress, even though she was beginning to believe that she deserved such a title. The age gap between them seemed irrelevant—their bodies were merely an exterior that did not interfere with the mutual connection they shared; a love to teach and to be taught. Isabella pulled out a strong perfumed blood red rose from her basket as she walked closer to the girls under the mulberry tree.

"Ah, so it is true, you have a beautiful young girl here with you."

"News has traveled fast?" Karisma asked interested, however with little emotion, as she did not seem surprised.

"It is impossible to keep anything a secret here, you know that!" Isabella laughed cheerily, as the layers of her dress bounced in the wind.

"I hope that everyone is behaving themselves with the news of Lily's attendance in our world," Karisma replied, and she narrowed her eyes to Isabella sternly.

"Of course! We have all heard of such beauty and divine innocence. Please forgive me, however, I too wanted to see if it was true. And this rose, I picked it for you in the hopes that it was."

The rose floated in the air from Isabella's hand to Lily's, and she accepted the rose graciously, lifting it to her nose to smell. The sweet aroma of perfumed musk seeped through the pores of the petals, and her mind drifted away to a time when she was a little girl, playing in her old cubby house back home. She stood still for a moment, lost in thought.

"Thank you so much," Lily replied as she moved shyly toward the girl, curtseying down as she bowed her head.

"Please tell us Isabella, what news do you have?" Karisma asked curiously.

"Certainly," Isabella replied as she walked over to Karisma and pulled out from her basket a large black crystal and handed it over.

"The master volcano has erupted in such plentiful mass, that of which I have never witnessed before! I thought you would like to come and see it for yourself."

Lily felt strange when Isabella told the story of the volcano, and her immediate thoughts were to question whether the volcano and the dance of Neo were connected. She wanted to find out more but couldn't divulge her secret relationship with the mermaids, remembering Jacques' words of advice.

"Oh that is splendid news Isabella! Please continue."

"The volcano has outstretched further than I have ever seen. It has expanded across the Detre Valley, almost reaching the Wisteria

Tree! And the crystals that it has produced are a miracle from below. Here, feel the power of this piece of volcanic dust alone."

Isabella held up a small glass jar full of volcanic dust that had a sparkling aura around it. And inside, the dust swirled around slowly in a vortex, playfully moving together.

"Here, Lily. Please accept this gift from me."

"You are most kind, Isabella," Lily replied as she opened the palm of her hand to receive the magical dust.

But Lily shrieked loudly as the glass touched her hand. It burnt her skin in a stabbing motion, forcing her to drop the bottle on the floor immediately, and in slow motion she watched as it smashed into tiny pieces, the black dust dispersing into the ground below.

"Merv ru hego yoss rad ke rot fymm li!" Karisma spoke loudly and forcefully as she pointed to Isabella, creating a golden cage around her body. Instantly, as she did, the girl transformed into a deathly-frail toad-like creature, hunched over with a balding head and popping brown boils all over her skin.

"How dare you! I welcome you into my home, and you try to poison my guest? An innocent girl who has not caused you any harm, any pain or discomfort. Why?" Karisma yelled as she twirled the cage around with the power of her finger. Lily stood speechless, unsure of where to move, if to move, and she nursed her scalded hand.

"Please forgive me, Your Majesty. There are whispers through the trees that this girl possesses dark magic. We have been told she is to be our leader. She brought me here herself." The voice of the witch sounded remarkably like the voice in Lily's head that she heard on the shores of Deia. *Could she have been with her the whole time?*

"SILENCE! Tell me, who else knows about the girl?"

"We all know. Everyone does. You know that." The toad-like creature cackled with a rough deep voice and her eyebrows rose up toward Karisma, as though the two were in on a secret.

Lily felt her heart beat fast. She was nervous. Very nervous. No longer did she feel like an innocent little girl wandering alone in a brand new world, but her whole universe had just been flipped dramatically and everything she once knew to be true did not seem real at all.

"Karisma?" Lily whispered as she felt tears well up inside. But there was no voice in her mind telling her to run. She felt frozen into the ground, forced to witness and watch it play out.

"Come here angel, do not fear," Karisma said as she turned to Lily and gestured for her to move back inside the house.

Lily began to walk but stopped and looked behind her shoulder at the caged beast. It was sitting hunched over, staring at the ground. As Lily gave it attention, it began to perk up, knowing it was being watched, and it squeezed its bony arms through the cracks of the gold jail, signaling for Lily to come back. Lily was hypnotized in her own footsteps and was magnetically drawn toward the cage.

"No Lily, come with me," Karisma pleaded, not using any magic to force her away. "Do not give it any attention, continue on your own path, and walk with me."

Lily felt a wire-like cord pulling her stomach back toward the cage. And when she turned to look once more, the beast had turned into the innocent Isabella—so beautiful and mysterious, holding her hand out to Lily.

"Yes," Lily heard the voice inside again. *"Come and rescue me. Listen to my voice,"* it said. *"Pull the petals off the rose and sprinkle them to the ground to release the spell."*

Lily looked to the rose in her hand, and started to pick the petals off one by one. Karisma watched her silently, not interrupting.

When the last petal had dropped to the ground, the cage disintegrated into the air, and the beast leapt forward, charging at Lily. The fear inside of Lily bolted through her veins and she cowered down to the ground, burying her head while Karisma pointed to the beast again, freezing the animal in mid-air.

"Go back to where you came from," Karisma yelled, swirling the dust from the ground up around the beast and sucking it into the sky, removing it from sight.

"Why didn't you stop me from pulling the petals when you knew it would release the cage?"

"Because it was your intention to do so. I am not to change you, you know that. Those were the words in our first lesson, remember? I had to let you discover the truth for yourself."

"Where did she come from?"

"She comes from you, we all do."

The words of Karisma resonated soundly with Lily. *She comes from you, we all do.* They repeated themselves in her ear, swinging back and forth as they vibrated through her head. *She comes from you, we all do.* It chimed so loudly that it disoriented Lily; the words stretched out into long sounds, and she was unable to decipher the meaning anymore.

Karisma had continued to talk, inattentive of Lily's reaction. And her mouth continued to move, but the sound was delayed. And although Lily was still frozen on the words from before, the conversation waited until Lily was ready to continue, as though the words were hovering, waiting for Lily to tune in. And in fast forward motion, Karisma's words continued to speak, even though her lips were sealed.

"So Lily, yes it is true. Darkness exists inside us all. But do not fear this darkness inside of you, for without it, light cannot exist."

Her words reminded Lily of Crysanthe, of Jacques, and the horizon. And she felt dizzy, wondering if Karisma had been with her all along, listening to her thoughts. Nothing made sense, she felt faint, she needed something to eat, it had been too long.

"Come Lily, let us go inside and share a meal and talk it through."

Karisma held Lily's hand and guided her back inside. Although the turn of events made Lily question Karisma's intentions, she could not deny that she felt safe inside the house. As Lily walked back through the door at the base of the tree, she felt content, relaxed, and happy.

It wasn't until now as Karisma guided Lily through the different corridors that she realized just how huge the tree house actually was. Each root of the giant tree lead to a different room. Some of the roots went on for miles. Karisma explained that they connected into many other passages, so that she could visit other folks who chose to live underground too. The girls walked uphill and downhill, crossing over and under, and eventually they arrived at the kitchen, where two glass goblet-style bowls sat on a wooden bench. The layout of the room was molded into a circular spiral with cut-out holes that supported the necessary components of a kitchen. The pantry was an open flat wall, which held different jars full of odd spices, powders, and oils. Large square blocks were carved out naturally in the wood, and here the spaces held plates, bowls and cutlery. It was like a museum that honored the display of food, enforcing the creation of eating to be inspiring. Lily sat down on the wooden chair and watched as Karisma explained the breakfast.

"I am preparing an acai bowl for breakfast, complete with maqui berries, golden berries, goji berries, camu camu, and baobab!"

Karisma dazzled her finger around and as she said the name of each fruit, the corresponding jar from the wall flew off and popped itself open, allowing Karisma to sprinkle a handful into the bowls.

"Now, crumble some walnuts to feed the brain. Here, would you like?" she continued.

Lily stared at the bowl full of strange shapes and sizes of berries and nuts that had miraculously fallen so casually into place, painting the bowl beautifully like a painting. The only item that looked familiar was the walnuts and it was only now that she realized how much they resembled the image of a brain. *How funny,* she thought. And although it was all very healthy in contrast to what she usually ate, had her father handed it to her she would have stuck up her nose, but here she decided to expand her palate and she thanked her host kindly.

"I have no idea what any of that is but it sounds delicious!"

The fresh berries burst inside of Lily's mouth, oozing a vibrant flavor that swirled all over her taste buds. And the variety of textures in the berries and nuts that crumbled between her teeth satisfied her every craving. She was quick to eat the entire bowl, and absolutely loved every minute of it. Knowing where the fruit had come from had made the berries taste sweeter; in fact, it was one of the best breakfasts Lily had ever had. She thanked Karisma politely once more and reminded herself of how rewarding it was to try new things. She took Karisma's bowl as well as her own and washed them gently in the basin that was full of soapy water.

"Now sweet Lily, would you like to accompany me to the Master Volcano?" Karisma asked rhetorically, rising from her seat and walking to the door. She picked up four cloth bags that were hanging on a nail, handing Lily two, and carrying the others.

"I would like to, although I think I am too scared to walk through the forest," Lily replied nervously, accepting the cloth bags and following her all the same.

"Why?" Karisma smiled as she asked, knowing perfectly well that Lily was being ridiculous.

"Because if others know I am here wouldn't they want to cause harm to me too?"

Lily stood at the edge of the door, withholding herself from walking through. But Karisma just shook her head and laughed, tossing her red hair furiously in the wind.

"Fear is only real if you think it is," she soothed, her red hair radiating brilliantly from the sunlight. "This problem is only imaginary. Let it go. No longer breathe life into this thought." She delivered the ends of her sentences sternly and continued to walk, knowing that Lily would follow her into the garden. She stopped just before the entrance into the dense forest, and turned back to check on Lily.

"You are right Karisma, I apologize. Let's go visit the Master Volcano!" Lily held the cloth bags in hand as she ran through the garden, swerving around the edible plants throughout the overgrown jungle. The herbs reached up almost to her waist, and she could smell each aroma thoroughly as she passed them by. Mint, coriander, sweet basil leaves,—the fragrances wafted alongside her all the way to the entrance of the forest where Karisma was waiting.

"The pleasure is all mine, and you have beautiful manners Lily," she said, and nodded, swinging the cloth bags back and forth in her left hand. "Your mother would be very proud." She picked up a long wooden stick in her right hand, using it to lift the branches up high so that the two were able to walk under the canopy of trees.

Lily bowed her head down to show respect for her mother. And for the first time in a long time, she felt the desire to confide in Karisma about the lack of relationship that had existed. Although, they walked through the forest in silence for several minutes before she was ready to initiate the subject.

"Karisma, I never knew my mother. She died when I was born." Lily attempted to speak the words clearly, knowing that she had welcomed the discussion of her misfortune to be addressed by the queen. But her voice quivered, and she combed her hair through her fingers as she looked to the small pink paper flowers on the ground to help deter the tears from surfacing.

Karisma stopped in their path and placed her hand on Lily's shoulder, making sure that she had Lily's attention before she spoke. "I'm sorry to hear that Lily."

The words were simple but perfectly comforting, and it was the release Lily had always hoped for, but was too scared to try in case she was disappointed. When most people found out they would react in a way that made her feel like she ought to be lost without such a figure in her life, and would try to overcompensate with suggestions of how it must be. Or some would just be uncomfortable with the subject, reacting with 'are you serious?' Implying that she would ever joke about something as serious as that. But Karisma's reply of empathy was all she needed, and she felt open to explore her grief in a different light.

"Karisma, you say that we choose our reality, why would I have chosen to miss my mother every day of my life?" The tears had welled up to the surface, she could feel the blood push up to her cheeks and rise up to her eyes, ready to stream over. "Because she is not with me, I feel inadequate, and much of my problems seems to stem from this cause."

A single tear released itself from Lily's left eye. It didn't even touch her face, for her lashes had pushed it out as she blinked. When it dropped onto the ground it stayed intact, like a rainbow-colored bubble sitting safely on the surface of the dirt. The weight of the tear must have created a noise only noticeable to the creatures of the forest, and within seconds a family of little ants scampered around and drank greedily from it.

"In addition to accepting yourself, you must accept your life for what it is." Karisma stopped with Lily as the two watched the ants crawl over each other, suckling the water from Lily's tear, and Karisma rubbed Lily's shoulders lovingly, patting her to move along. "There are no problems, it's all about how you look at it. Your lack of a mother has allowed the relationship with your father to take an alternative form. Embrace the differences in life Lily, for you are fortunate to be growing up with an unusual outlook on what having a family is. It's not just about the mother and the father and brothers and sisters, it's about the bond of love between the two of you."

Karisma reached down and picked a handful of small red flowers from the ground, she handed Lily two and kept one for herself. She held the tiny flower up to her pointy nose to inhale the fragrance. Lily mirrored her actions, smelling the fruits of the flower that was able to miraculously intoxicate her nose with an incredible scent. The urge to cry had stopped, and her cheeks blended back into a creamy complexion.

The girls continued to walk, and Lily kept on thinking about her relationship with her father.

"What if sometimes I don't feel like he is on my side?" Lily asked as she stared intently at the flower's stigma, a dark purple with lilac tips.

"He always is, in ways you can't really imagine until you have children yourself. But even if what you say is true, maybe it's happening so you can learn to stand strong on your own?"

"Maybe," Lily replied, as she strummed the soft petals against her cheek and listened intently, enjoying the comfort of fragrance, touch, and words in one.

"Lily, your life is created for your benefit. Even if you don't understand why something is, trust that it is meant to be."

Lily stared at the ground of polished red dust they were walking upon; she found she was able to absorb the knowledge easier when she looked away, there were fewer distractions, fewer of her own thoughts overtaking the other voice. *My life is created for my benefit,* she repeated in her head. And although there was still confusion embedded in her thoughts from times past, Lily finally felt the courage to accept the idea that the circumstance of her life was right for her, and exactly what she needed to experience. She smiled with happiness, thinking about how lucky she was to have met such an inspirational woman.

"I am so appreciative of your kindness Karisma. I have difficulty opening up about my mother, and talking to you has restored my faith to give more people a chance," Lily confirmed, although she realized that speaking her thoughts out loud solidified the idea to herself more so.

"Of course, not everyone you meet is going to be kind to you Lily, but remember it is their own demons they are dealing with, not yours. And these people are just as great teachers as those who are kind."

Karisma lifted the stick underneath a large banana leaf above, and tipped the base closest to the branch. A stream of water gushed from above, and it tipped to a concave crystal slab of rock below. Two small raccoons with pink fur and orange painted faces dipped their paws into the dish and drank the water. They appeared to take no notice of the girls, and nuzzled their noses into one another, playfully.

"You have helped changed my whole outlook on fear, honestly. What can I do to thank you?" Lily paused, wondering what it was that she could give Karisma in exchange.

She looked to the ground where they were walking. The pebbled footpath of rough and polished crystals surrounded the two in a synchronized grid-like form all around. It reminded Lily of the crystal creation Karisma had made earlier in the house before she slept, in perfect synchrony. Not only were the crystals in a grid, but they also lit up as she looked at each one, creating a pattern similar to that of which she saw the night she crept underneath the house. The plants on the ground grew in uneven patches all over the place. There were different shapes of leaves, different colors of green, the majority with flowers, but the shapes of leaves looked more like stars than traditional oval-shaped leaves. It all seemed supernatural to Lily, but to Karisma it was normal. Even though Karisma saw such incredible beauty repeatedly she was still utterly and completely infatuated with all the fauna and flora constantly around her. The way she touched and smelled each plant, it was as if she cuddled and spoke to them, telling her admiration and desire to look after them. Lily felt bad to break off a part of their being, especially after they had been so kind to purify the air around them. But then she remembered how Karisma gave her flowers, and the words from Crysanthe flashed into Lily's head, how in every death there is rebirth. And so Lily picked the most beautiful flower she could see in sight, a purple, red and white-headed passion flower, and she handed it to Karisma.

"Thank you sweetheart, but you keep it, add it to your carry bag," she kindly declined as she stepped over a great big root from a tree that had protruded from the ground. "All I want in return is for you to be happy. In Sa Neo, this is how we define unconditional love. It is to give love abundantly with absolutely no hidden agenda or even desire for the love to be returned."

Karisma stopped and walked over to where a strangler fig had entwined its roots around the base of a giant tree trunk. She weaved her arms in between the vines and stopped to hug the inside host. She breathed deeply for several seconds, and rested her forehead against the bark, whispering love and kissing the skin.

"I never knew that kind of love existed with anyone other than my father, and even then I believed he had an obligation because we were related," Lily joked. She put the flower into her cloth bag, but not before smelling it one more time, allowing the aroma to intoxicate her senses.

"No one has an obligation to anyone, to love is a choice we make in every moment," Karisma replied, feeling the veins of the strangler tree and asking it to be gentle. "And as for unconditional love, it can exist with everyone if you chose it to. But again you must be wary that people can abuse that kindness, like what we saw with Isabella this morning."

The image of Isabella turning into a sickly toad was ingrained into Lily's mind, and the fear felt real once again. She frightened herself, but before she let the fear overtake her body, Lily told herself to let it go. And miraculously, it felt like a huge weight lifted effortlessly off her shoulders. Lily smiled.

The road started to turn into a steep incline and the morning sun shone from behind the mountain up ahead and created a splendid backdrop to display the silhouettes of the trees and animals in the distance. Up ahead nestled between the base of two large trees stood a large arrangement of folded leaves and branches that looked like a gigantic nest. Karisma and Lily examined the opening carefully, however there was nothing there except for a marvelous white feather which had protruded from the nest proudly. The feather was elongated with a wide oval, and at the edges to the top laid wispy long strings. Karisma pulled the feather out and handed it to Lily, telling her to keep it for later. Lily obeyed willingly, and she folded over the delicate tips before placing it inside carefully.

"The bird here has abandoned her nest, for we are getting closer to the volcano, can you feel the change in the air?"

"Yes, and the ground feels warmer too, is that strange?"

"Not at all, where do you think the volcanic lava erupts from? The core, Lily. Everything starts from the inside; it's the root of the matter, remember?"

Lily nodded as she noticed the trees around them becoming more sparse. They not only had died from the fire exploding, but the thickness in the air would have suffocated them too. And only a few more footsteps further along, the landscape was completely dry, with large chunks of rubble scattered along the ground. In the distance the girls could see the base of the volcano. It stood proudly on the edge of the cliff, with crashing water spinning violently below. A stream of black colored water covered the ground upon which they walked, and it calmed the ashes above into an almost mud-like consistency. Karisma held the base of her dress as she walked through, displaying thinly cut-out silver shoes tied up with string around her calves in a gladiator-type fashion.

Lily looked up to the top-most point of the volcano. The volcanic lava was gradually oozing out, thick and bubbly, in a golden fire of orange-red with a piercing outline of black soot. Thick smoke sifted through the air directly above the tip, and the smell of burning ashes filled Lily's senses. In between the black smoke and blazing fire, she could see a single flame of white light dancing solo. High above the red flames it flickered in the air, finding pleasure from being tortured by the coals beneath its feet. It was both calming and inviting. Lily gazed uninterrupted in a trancelike state for several minutes. She felt bewitched by the dancing white light and ached to escape her body. She would fly across the volcanic dust, high up through the mountain and touch it. But there was nothing to touch; it was only heat.

"Lily, come and collect the obsidian crystals with me." Karisma interrupted Lily's levitation and pulled her back to her body. Karisma was now standing amongst the muddy soot and dirt, holding up a large black rock to indicate what she was to look for. "When volcanic lava comes into contact with the water it turns to a glassy stone," Karisma said as she passed the black rock to Lily, "it is still called a crystal, however some crystals take hundreds, sometimes thousands of years to form. This crystal solidifies instantly, when the fire and water come into contact. For this reason, it is extremely powerful so you must be careful when using it."

Lily looked at the texture of black crystal and slid her finger across it slowly. The lustrous texture of the stone looked slippery and gave the illusion of being dangerously sharp.

"What kind of power does it possess?" Lily asked, stroking the shiny stone, feeling a strange vibration from the freshly formed crystal as she did so.

"It is able to attract, absorb, and remove negative energy. For this reason you must cleanse it regularly to neutralize it," Karisma replied, picking up some more pieces of the stone, placing them inside her satchel.

"Cleanse crystals? I never knew you did that?"

"Just like you and me, crystals absorb energy too. So, it is important to regularly clear the energy that has been absorbed."

Lily reached down to the dusty soot and spiraled her fingers through the mud. It oozed with pressure, filling the gaps in between her fingers. Tiny grains of dirt prickled through, but it felt nice, the contrast of smooth and rough. She fiddled around until she touched something hard, and she yanked it out, displaying a large chunk of black obsidian crystal.

"How do you cleanse crystals?" she asked, holding up the muddy rock.

"The same way that we wash ourselves, with water," Karisma said as she rinsed her hands with a small amount of clear water that was dribbling through the stream. "The salt water has the most beneficial nutrients and minerals that you need for your body. Think about how refreshed you feel after a swim in the ocean. This is how we cleanse the crystals too, although the crystals like to bathe in the moonlight as well."

Lily placed the muddy crystal inside her satchel bag and repeated the action again. She collected eight in total and giggled to herself, thinking of washing and lining them all up to soak in the moonlight.

"You're right Karisma, I always feel so amazing after the ocean. I never knew why," she replied, remembering how reenergized and clear-headed she felt after a swim at the beach. "I wish I could live near the water all the time."

"Well if you can't make it to the ocean, have a relaxing bath every now and again. Light a candle for your eyes, some oil for your nose, and just let your skin soak. You will feel so cleansed and refreshed."

Karisma foretold the instructions in a daydream-like state, and Lily could see that she was imagining herself relaxing in a beautiful hot bath. She shook her head and looked around to the volcanic dust, realizing where she was, she collected a few more crystals with Lily and then they began their journey back home.

Behind their backs the girls could still feel the warmth from the powerful structure for quite some time as they walked back through the forest. It dominated the air above, the ground below, yet as seen with the crystals water was able to trump it, freezing it completely within seconds. *There is always something that can stop life from breeding,* Lily thought.

After quite some time, Karisma steered the two off path, and they climbed over large tree trunks that overlapped each other, not stopping until they reached an open field of long grass that framed many flowering trees. A brilliant wide stream of water flowed to the edge where the grass grew high up to the girls' knees. A family of deer was drinking the water on the other side of the riverbank and they stared as the girls washed their hands and crystals.

The mud peeled off effortlessly in the water, and even though it seemed like there was a great deal of thick mud to clean through, as soon as it touched the stream, it dissolved, disappearing as though the darkness never existed in the first place.

"Let's sit over there," Karisma said as they packed up their clean crystals inside the spare bags, and she pointed to a gigantic wisteria tree which towered over, creating a large patch of shady grass. A circle of garnet crystals protruded unevenly from the ground in a large circle. Karisma and Lily sat down together in the center, cross-legged, facing each other.

"When you asked me about cleansing the crystals earlier, I thought perhaps we should have a lesson about them," Karisma suggested as she tipped her bag out, displaying her crystals. "So, please choose a small crystal from your satchel that speaks to you the most."

Lily reached into her bag and chose the smallest crystal there was. She looked deeply into the blackness intensely. The raw nature in how it formed felt electrifying and immediately she was addicted to the dark beauty.

"Look at it carefully and hold it tightly between your hands, sharing the warmth from your body. This is how you begin a connection," Karisma explained. "Now place the crystal in your mouth, on top of your tongue, careful not to swallow! Try to clear your mind and let any messages, thoughts, or words come through to you."

Lily placed the stone inside of her mouth to try and connect with the piece of land, but her mind kept yelling that there was a foreign object in her mouth. The harsh coldness of the stone was a fiery contrast against the warmth in her body.

"Breathe through it Lily, you can do it," Karisma encouraged as she continued to guide Lily with a soft voice.

Lily took deep breaths and persevered to clear her mind. She pushed her tongue to the roof of her mouth and cocooned the crystal in between. The crystal adjusted to the temperature of her body, it seemed as though it had surrendered. That's when she felt it—a pulsating vibration of energy soaring from the center of her mouth outwards. Sharp lightning which pushed around and around, straight up through to her brain. She felt like if she held it inside for any longer that she would explode. Lily spat the rock out quickly, suffocated with dizziness.

"I can't handle it. The motion was too intense." Lily threw herself back onto the ground, and rested her head on the grass. The sweet-smelling flowers hung low in clusters on the branches of the wisteria tree and they moved gently with every breeze. But even despite the picturesque view, Lily still felt like she had failed, and she sulked quietly to herself.

"It's okay Lily, I understand," Karisma reassured her, patting her on her knee. "The moment before you spat out the rock, what were you thinking?"

"That I couldn't handle it anymore. It made me feel nauseous."

"But it's just an object, how can it make you feel nauseous? It wasn't doing anything to you. It was your imagination, it was your thoughts that were getting the better of you."

"I felt like if I had left it any longer, it could do something, something bad to me." Lily relived the motion she had felt moments before. It felt so real. She could distinctly remember the texture of the stone, how cold it felt inside her body. She felt nauseous again and wriggled her tongue around in her mouth over her teeth to be sure it wasn't there again.

"Nothing will harm you unless you let it. Yes, it can be hard to accept things sometimes, especially when it consumes your mind and your thoughts. But you just need to rise above it. Learn to separate your thoughts from your reality."

As Karisma spoke, a great red-belly black snake slithered along near where they were sitting. It rubbed its skin against the edges of the crystal circle, as though it were scratching an itch, and a layer of skin peeled off. It happened too quickly for Lily to be alarmed, and the fear inside her had no time to brew.

"How do you mean? Aren't my thoughts my reality?" Lily fiddled with the edge of her red lace dress as she questioned Karisma again, pressing the fabric between her fingers to comfort her. She liked to focus on the stitching when she wanted to listen carefully to what someone was saying. It deterred her mind from side-tracking, although she didn't seem to have that problem in this world.

"Your reality is the repercussion of your thoughts. It's how you interpret your circumstances that determines the way your thoughts will play out. Any incident can be bad or good; it depends on what you choose."

Lily sat up and stared at Karisma, confused. Sure, she could understand that if she imagined the crystals to be, say sucking candy or something delicious she could tolerate the object, but . . . And just as she thought of it, the crystals transformed into the most decadent looking cubes of caramel-striped treats she had ever seen. The edges of the square had crystalized tips and they had a lovely stripe down the middle that looked like creamy chocolate. She blinked twice and they had changed back into the black obsidian crystals again. She picked one up just to be sure. They weighed heavy—a mix of smooth and roughness to touch. Lily moved the crystal back into her mouth, but just moments before she placed it inside, it turned into the caramel-looking treat again. Inside her mouth, the crystal felt like it was exploding inside of her. She spat it out again.

"I can't do it! I had no idea crystals had such power."

"You can," Karisma spoke sternly. "Let's look at it this way. It is just an object, and it is only thoughts. They are two separate identities. Your rejection to the object, which is your thoughts, is your reality. You are ultimately rejecting change, but there is nothing to be feared from change. Just surrender to it."

Lily listened to Karisma's words of wisdom but somehow they hinted at her to apply them to other aspects of her life, not just the exercise they were trying to conquer. She had often rejected change in her life (the new house), making it difficult for those around her (her father), but most importantly, (herself). If it wasn't for moving to the new house she would never had discovered such a world existed. She would never have been able to meet such interesting characters, or more importantly, understand what it meant to know herself. Everything that she was experiencing was confronting her with situations and circumstances that were helping to shape her into a woman, and for the first time, she was grateful for all the hardship, all the fear that kept pushing her to seek clarity and happiness.

Karisma stood up and picked some furry leaves from a plant that was growing nearby. In one hand, she pulled out a thin crystal rock and held it over it, ensuring the sunlight above was directly present. She blew gently on the leaves and slowly it started to smoke, emitting a pleasant aroma of eucalyptus. Karisma stood up and circled around Lily. She held it high and lowered it again, all the while humming a sweet-sounding lullaby. Lily closed her eyes and breathed deeply, enjoying the smell of burning incense and the sound of wildlife all around. She could hear the stream trickling over little pockets of bunched up rocks, the insects buzzed as they were talking to one another and the birds chirped, singing with praise for yet another beautiful day. She wondered for a moment how was it that she could feel so at home, yet was lost in another world, far, far away.

"I think you are beginning to see the way things work around here," Karisma spoke, as she extinguished the smoking leaf. "Aside from teleporting to another land, we can also become invisible."

"How do we become invisible?"

"We move our consciousness to an alternate universe."

Karisma picked up the snakeskin that had been shed and patted her fingers over the skin gently. She wrinkled her nose as though deep in thought and handed it to Lily.

"Is that what happened when I came into this world? I teleported to an alternate universe?" Lily asked as Karisma picked up four black obsidian crystals and placed them evenly around the circle.

"Lily, you never arrived, you've been here all along."

A twinkle in Karisma's eyes flashed with a red fire gleam and she sat back down opposite Lily. She smiled with amusement to herself as she combed her hair back behind her ears, displaying the ruby ring on her finger.

"Are you ready?"

Lily nodded.

"For the spell of invisibility we must hold two crystals, one in each hand," Karisma said as she folded two black obsidian crystals into Lily's palms as well as her own. "And we close our eyes and allow the darkness to overtake our body. Feel the weight of the shadows fall on your shoulders, and understand that black is merely the absence of light."

Lily could feel a cool breeze blow through the curls in her hair as she inhaled deeply and closed her eyes. The smell of incense was still lingering, although the sound of nature was blending into a long, humming noise.

"Keep the mind strong," she continued. "Watch it consume you but do not allow it inside. Now, listen and repeat this sentence with me, three times."

"Sa Neo I, lo las, we, rah tend, kis, es, nid."

"Sa Neo I, lo las, we, rah tend, kis, es, nid."

"Sa Neo I, lo las, we, rah tend, kis, es, nid."

Lily repeated the words mechanically. They did not sound separate to her anymore and instead extracted from her mouth in a long extended song. The vibration of sound echoed through her body from the crown of her head down through to her feet, and it bounced back up again, like an internal light that was playfully jumping from one end to the other. It shook her greatly to the core, and she felt like she looked like the tongue of a bell, the vibration resonating long after the music had finished.

"Open your eyes."

Lily lifted her eyelids in a daze, hearing the familiarity of Karisma speaking to her, yet unable to see anyone around. The trees, grass, and the circle of crystals were still visible, but when Lily looked down, her body had disappeared as well.

"It worked!" Lily shrieked with excitement, although her voice came through distorted.

"Yes, fantastic Lily!" She could hear Karisma's voice directly opposite her. "Now, to remove the darkness, saturate your thoughts with light. Envision something that you love and allow your body to warm up to that love. Believe you deserve it. See love, and pure white light, imagine it all around you."

Lily thought of Father back home. But this time she saw her mother too. And she imagined her father holding her mother and her mother holding her baby, Lily. It was a story that Father used to tell Lily as she fell asleep. How the three of them would hold each other in harmony, saying no words to each other, just sitting together in silence, loving one another just as they are.

And slowly, she faintly saw the outline of her own body, and the tiny particles of vibrating energy came into play, and there she was once more, in her body. But before she opened her eyes, she had a vision.

She was staring at a giant crystal ball fountain, full to the brim of water, and wishing for it to break. She felt trapped staring at the enclosure, struggling to be free. Yet she was not inside, nor could see anything. She just felt fear.

"You performed that beautifully, Lily, I am very impressed,"

Karisma's voice interrupted the vision and Lily opened her eyes.

"Thank you," she replied, still disoriented from the confined feeling of what she had seen. The image of the fountain had disappeared but the memory how she felt had lived on, not to be forgotten.

"Karisma . . ." Lily looked down shyly, eager to share her innermost thoughts, but terrified of being rejected by her friend.

She had often seen visions like this before, sometimes people, faces, or situations. She would often be able to recognize the people, however they had changed dramatically to what she knew them as, and so she asked herself whether they really were the same person. But this vision was a feeling, an emotion. That idea was new to her. She was terrified to speak of it, but her heart told her to trust.

"Sometimes I see things," she confided.

Lily waited for Karisma to laugh, but she didn't. There was no judgment in her eyes, or smirk beneath her smile, and instead, Lily felt like she was genuinely interested.

"What kind of things?" she asked, raising her eyebrows gently.

"Like, just now after we were invisible, I saw a giant crystal ball fountain and I felt trapped." Lily could feel her distress overtake her senses once more, and although she knew she was in the open field surrounded with nature, she felt her throat tighten, and her body freeze. She looked to the sky for reassurance, remembering it wasn't real.

"The crystal ball fountain sounds like Jade's castle," Karisma said. "But feeling trapped . . . perhaps you are unsure you are able to leave? But Lily, you can leave Jade's whenever you like. You are never trapped anywhere. Understand?"

Karisma shook Lily by the knees, as though embedding the information into her head. Lily hadn't been nervous to visit Jade. After all, everyone she had met so far in Sa Neo had been so lovely and friendly. But, something was telling her to be cautious.

"Yes, I understand. But Karisma . . ." Her words faded away again. This time she wasn't scared of the unknown, it was more so knowing when to trust herself.

"How do I know when it's the right time to leave?"

Karisma packed up the crystals in her bag, as Lily mimicked her actions.

"Your heart will tell you what the answer is," Karisma replied, directing the two back on the path to her home. "And if you cannot decide, then don't decide. It is simply not the right time to make that decision."

CHAPTER SEVEN

JADE & THE LAND OF TEHAR

Lily had been summoned and she needed to go. It was important for her to arrive at the land of Tehar by herself, she was told. *You have entered this world on your own, and you must learn to journey on your own,* she heard a voice inside her say. She left Karisma's nest of safety for the unknown on the verge of the night, but there was no fear inside of her. Something was guiding her, and something was protecting her. Maybe it was her new connection with her crystals, and she could feel their energy encourage her. Or perhaps it was the lessons and teachings she had learned from Karisma. Lily could still hear her voice, and feel her gentle, motherly nature as she walked along the red-pebbled path. On the ground the marble swirls illuminated underneath her footsteps. They could sense the pressure of her foot well before it touched the surface, reminding her of her entry into this magical place. And she wondered how her father was, hoping he wasn't worried where she was. *I am safe Papa!* she whispered into the air.

With each step of the way Lily reflected on the world of Sa Neo that she had encountered so far. Jacques, who embraced his fun-loving zest for life; Karisma, who was more of a mother figure than she had ever had before; and Crysanthe, a true angel of whom she bonded with completely on her own. She wondered if her new friends thought about her too.

To the shining water she found herself once more. The beaming moons and glowing stars whispered soft hellos as they followed her dance, shining brightly, drawing her closer to the garnet sparkling shore. The sea shimmered in a monochrome of red hues, clearly defining the ever-changing patterns as the water melted into the sky, marking the horizon. This was the first time that she would be teleporting to another land by herself. She needed to believe in herself; no one else would ever give as much strength as she could. There was no turning back now. She sat down, cross-legged with her back straight up and tall. She closed her eyes, imagining the crown of her head touching the sky.

Never before had she sat cross-legged on the ground and felt so grand. She felt as though she were the connecting force between the ground and the sky, as though a light shone through from the heavens above. It pulsated through her, and united her with the ground. She was preparing her mind and her body to tedimeta.

The sound of waves crashing consumed her ears with a therapeutic buzzing noise. She cleared her mind and envisioned a light pouring out from the top of her head that spun turbulently around like a vortex. The sound and imagery of tiny particles circling sounded like white noise, and it threw her mind into mush. It was so overpowering she couldn't think, she was just still. She watched the theater of bright lights and sound play out in front of her with no questioning. Her eyes began to move higher and higher inside her head, so far up that she almost felt dizzy and quite nauseous. Too chaotic the movements grew, she had to open her eyes, with fear of falling over. But when her eyes opened, she realized she was there. It had happened. She was on the green-pebbled shores of Tehar.

The dark green crystals were dense with color, and they looked like a raindrop of thick green paint, splattered on the ground with dark convoluted swirls continuously twirling. The temperature felt significantly cooler and she only just now realized that she needed something warmer to wear. Just as she thought about needing warmer clothes, the fabric of her dress grew in thickness, and she now wore a woolen dress to cover her milky skin. The layout of Tehar beach was more tropical in contrast to Otor. It had low dipping palm and coconut trees, which lined the edge of where the water greeted the forest.

Lily turned to her right and followed the palm trees as they grew in density. She had no idea why she turned right instead of left—she hadn't been told to, but she knew better by now than to question those decisions that came without thinking. And before she knew it, she was standing in front of a large open field with a square sign saying, 'Queen Jade's Palace' written in thick green malachite crystals.

The field was covered in a mossy green grain-like sand, carefully laid out as though it had been crumbled down to finite pieces and shaken over the ground. *Individually the particles of sand were almost insignificant, but altogether, they held the power to suffocate,* Lily thought.

In the center of the field sat a large crystal ball fountain. Although the elegant structure looked nothing like Lily's ouroboros necklace, she had the urge to connect the two together somehow. The way the water trickled delicately over the sphere, down to the ground, and back around, it circled inside and out, over and over again, never-ending— like the ouroboros.

The palace behind was a typically formed castle, with large towers at each end, and a rectangular base. It was painted in a very faint pink with glistening green diamond-shaped crystals covered from top to bottom, it tied in nicely with the colors of the sign. Jade's castle was exactly how Lily imagined a queen to live; her gardens were immaculately pruned, perfectly kept with an unbelievable display of pink and green-colored flowers. It was an extensive display of flora and fauna in exotic breeds of endless shapes and sizes that grew short and tall along the towers. Each color varied in shades and textures, scaling from soft pale pinky-white to a fiery magenta red. There was pink/orange, a pink/yellow, and as strange as it would be to see, there was a pink and blue flower, and the strangest of them all, a dark black rose with violent hot pink streaks shaped like a tiger's face which guarded the entry door.

The pristine presentation of the castle and surrounding grounds were the complete opposite of Karisma's humble way of life, and Lily felt a pang of nerves swimming around in her tummy, cautious to be included in such royal affairs. Lucky she had been invited, or Lily would have felt quite intimidated and probably would have turned around and been on her way home by now. But she had grown older in the last few days from conversing with the Sa Neo folk, and now it seemed as though any suggestion of worries faded quickly from her mind, forgotten without a trace.

As she paced closer to the castle gates, she could hear beautiful music drift through the walls from the other side of the grounds, from behind the castle, or perhaps it was from the front, depending on how you looked at it. The music was a merry humming of what sounded like a ukulele or some form of string guitar. It reminded Lily that she also once played a musical instrument when she was a child, and loved it so. But when she was nine, a little boy teased her for playing it, and the flute now stood in a sealed-up box, somewhere in their storage. Upon hearing the musical notes once again, Lily could predict exactly each chord as though it were only yesterday.

As she poked one eye around the corner of the castle she was immediately bedazzled from such a sight. Gigantic chandeliers swung around from the trees above, glittering down like a rainbow waterfall above the women and men who dined below. A ukulele guitar was being played by a short dwarf girl. She had pixie pointed ears and swayed with her music, keeping the beat with a tapping foot as a small crowd danced joyously in front. A circle-shaped picnic blanket encased with crystal tassels held children squealing and playing, while eating yummy treats on little round plates. Behind the children's playground, sat upside down pyramid tables and matching smaller triangle seats that were full of men and women dining merrily. Lily thought her peeking eye was subtle, but it seemed to have caught the attention of a gnome who was standing guard in the garden to her left.

"Can I help you there?" said the gnome as he marched up to Lily, wearing a matching one-piece suit in a dark forest green with pale pink woolen gloves. His proud display of uniform and polite tone gave Lily the impression that he took his job very seriously.

"I'm looking for Queen Jade," Lily replied, her voice a bit rocky from a nervous twitch kicking in.

"Well don't be frightened there, come with me," the gnome said as he waddled his head and leapt out of the garden, charging forth, ensuring that Lily followed.

For a little man he walked quite briskly, and just as well, for as they walked through the center of the party the crowd all stopped and stared. The gnome took no notice and continued to march proudly toward the tallest lady in the room. *Queen Jade.* The queen's pale pink hair matched the color of the castle, and she wore it fastened high in a tight French twist bun, secured with a green crystal butterfly clip. She was dressed in a dark emerald green fine lace stitch dress with a high collared neck and little cap sleeves. A chain of gold rings that joined to a bracelet continued up along the arm to the elbow and created a beautiful gold pattern that looked like chained gloves. It glistened in the sun with miniature crystals.

"Your Highness, this lovely little lady is here for you." He bowed and swerved his arm as he presented Lily, who promptly curtseyed and smiled to the queen while doing so.

The lady studied Lily up and down before showing any emotion on her face. It was an intimidating moment, and Lily's immediate reaction was to think that the queen was doing it on purpose, trying to scare her. But then recollections of her and Jacques' encounter came through and she decided to think loving thoughts in replacement of fear.

"I believe you sent for me? I am Lily." She introduced herself, smiling candidly.

And it was an infectious smile, for the queen grinned too as she replied with extreme animation.

"Oh darling! Well now aren't you just the most beautiful girl I have ever seen!" She paused, smiling yet still perusing Lily's exterior from her head to the ground. "I shall like having you beside me as my princess," she concluded, nodding and looking over Lily's shoulder to see if the crowd was watching.

And it was. She grinned to herself smugly, opening her big olive eyes and fixating her magenta pink pupils onto Lily. Her eyelashes were painted with a thick green paint, and were long and tall. *A butterfly could land on them,* Lily thought. And just as Lily created such an idea, what should happen, but a little pale pink butterfly landed on the queen's eyelashes!

"Oh shoo you little witch!" Jade said while she furiously tried to push the butterfly away quickly. "Oh the horrid children are always playing jokes on me!" She squirmed once more, attempting to catch the butterfly with her bony fingers and long pointy nails.

She was a funny sight. Long thin arms with pointy claw fingers, thin legs, and a horrid fat belly shaped like an apple. And although Jade had done nothing wrong to Lily, there was something off in the air, and it made her hesitant to get close; but then at the same time, she couldn't help but feel strangely attracted to the queen. The idea of being a princess, surrounded with royals and riches to do as she pleased, and perhaps make changes for the greater good, sounded pleasurably inviting.

"Your dress is really beautiful, Your Majesty," Lily replied as she bowed down to the dress as though it were a piece of art.

Queen Jade twirled around to show the dress off, allowing the bottom piece of fabric to fly behind her like a tail, reminding Lily of a wedding dress she had once seen.

"Oh get up here you, no need to bow down, it's just a dress you know." The queen fluttered her eyelashes and waved her hand away pretending as though Lily's admiration was unnecessary, and in the same motion, she leant forward to Lily, holding her hand up as if to whisper a secret but yelling it quite loud so that everyone around her could hear.

"The lace is actually hand woven by the old ladies on the hill by the well to the west. They have nothing to do with their time so I thought it would be nice to give them a little project, to make the queen's lace! And their eyesight is quite poor being old, so they use their hands to feel the weave, making their attention to detail beyond perfection! Look, look at it, look up close! Here! Here!" Jade pulled the trail of lace from under her skirt and shoved it under Lily's nose for a closer look.

Jade was right, the attention to detail was remarkable. Not a stitch missed, and the pattern was quite unpredictable, yet it made perfect symmetry. In between each of the lace squares was a line of beautifully embroidered soft green crystals. The crystals started off light around the top of her chest and as the dress reached to the ground, the crystals became darker, creating a dramatic impact as it swished across the floor.

"Do the ladies create lace for anyone else here?" Lily asked, realizing that Queen Jade enjoyed talking about herself.

"My dear, as if! They barely can keep up with my commands!" she chuckled again. "I meant to say, they are too busy. I don't want to over-exhaust them, you know how it is." She quickly covered up her selfish error, and finished the sentence pretending as though Lily knew what she was talking about. Lily went along with the story, noticing that the crowd was reluctant to die down and she wanted to make a good impression. Although, she did feel quite strange as she pretended to agree.

"Of course, it would be hard work to create such a beautiful masterpiece."

This pleased Jades ears, and she stroked her own jeweled glove as she continued to converse with the girl.

"You understand the quality of fabric in fashion Lily, you really are already like my own daughter. In fact, trusting that all goes well with the initiation tonight, which I do not see how it would not," Jade winked at a neighboring lady, suggesting that perhaps the initiation would not go to plan, "I will have a special dress made for you." She flickered her fingers with excitement. "Yes, I will have a dress and you will wear this at tomorrow's ceremony where we may welcome you into our hearts."

Upon her announcement Jade snapped her fingers ferociously

and a small pixie girl ran to her side. The pixie took notes hurriedly while Jade whispered in her ear and pointed to Lily, coiling her finger over certain aspects of Lily's body. The pixie maid then rushed over to Lily, measuring her waist, hips and length, very quickly, and very awkwardly. Lily did not feel comfortable. But she didn't want to offend the powerful empress and thanked her kindly.

"Queen Jade you are too kind, how can I repay you?" Lily expected the same response as Karisma, well perhaps not expected, but more so desired. But instead, Jade gave her rules in return.

"Always be a good girl and do what you are told."

For some reason Jade's conditions didn't feel quite right to Lily, but she ignored the feeling and instead she decided that she also wanted to be a good girl. She would listen and take instructions, if it meant she was able to get something in return, for example, a princess title, then she was willing to compromise her happiness.

"Let's not get ahead of ourselves here, Lily. You may not pass initiation." Jade's eyes changed dramatically, the dark olive bled into the pink pupils forcefully as she chuckled to herself and lifted her chin up slightly so she towered above. Lily could feel hatred inside Jades words.

"What happens if I do not pass initiation, Your Majesty?" Lily looked to the ground as she asked the question, realizing that she had not bothered to question such an idea before, not until Jade bluntly suggested that perhaps she would not in fact pass.

"Are you asking me what happened to the last girl who crossed over our shores, absorbed all our secrets within our lands and when the time came for initiation, she tried to overpower me? What happened to her? Is that what you are asking?"

The musical dwarf ceased playing her ukulele guitar, and the patrons all zoned in on the queen's conversation. Even the children were quiet. Jade raised her eyebrows as she replied and turned around fast, letting the skirt trail lift under the wind and thump back down. It walloped down hard on the floor, squashing a baby green frog that was jumping across the path. Jade ignored the sound of crushing bones and continued to walk, curling her finger to imply that Lily was to follow. Not only did Lily follow, but the crowd followed too, several steps behind. For it was suggested that all were to attend the announcement of what would happen to anyone who would try to overpower the queen.

Jade stopped in front of a giant tree on her right, which towered over the garden magnificently. A proud display of outstretched arms, lush dark green leaves and beautiful soft pink flowers decorated the gigantic tree. Jade pointed her long green claw to the bottom of the trunk for Lily to focus her attention on. The trunk stood thick and large, with a hollow circle inside, yet plaited thick roots framed the outside. And within the opening, Lily could see a sad timid butterfly fairy perched on a nub of wood. It had green antenna-like legs and pale pink wings, decorated with green spots.

She appeared unable to leave the tree. Despite the boundless air visible to the naked eye, there was something holding her in, and the butterfly fairy barely moved under a weight of undefined sadness. There was an imaginary barrier that stopped her from spreading her wings completely, and flying away. Something held her back.

"Let her be a lesson to us all," Jade said firmly to the crowd. She paused, and bent down to engage in Lily's eyesight.

"Lily, do you think I enjoy misery? Do you think that feeling such paaaaaain and saaadness comes easy to me?" Jade scratched the side of her neck with her dark claw nails as she pulled on her lace collar in discomfort.

"No, Your Majesty."

Lily felt uncomfortable, wishing she never brought up the issue of not passing initiation. But at the same time, she felt overpoweringly drawn to the tree. She wanted to go and talk to the butterfly, to find out what she did wrong that made her not pass. She wanted to know. *Perhaps just ask?* She heard the voice inside her head. But she was thrown with her thoughts in this new land with these new creatures. Could she be as open as she was with Karisma? *Yes.*

"Queen Jade, may I ask what it was that did not allow her to pass?"

Jade stood up tall and lifted her head as she looked down at Lily; and she narrowed her eyes along her nose as if smelling the air.

"No, you may not!" Jade replied assertively and laughed in a loud roar that sounded more like broken glass scratching against a cement rock. *There was no kindness in her laughter.* "But what I will tell you. The color of your stone will determine your future."

The color of your stone. What does that even mean? Lily thought, thinking back to her ouroboros necklace, and the crystal stones. She swallowed hard and listened to a deafening crinkle in her ears, trying to buy some time as to what to ask next.

"Is there anything I can do in preparation?"

"Are you telling me what you need to do?" Jade barked back aggressively.

"No, Your Majesty," Lily replied timidly. She was quickly learning that the land of Tehar was a lot trickier to master than Otor. And she looked down to the ground again, casually lifting her eyes up to see if any of the crowd was watching. They all still were. Although Lily could see that no one felt joy when Jade talked down to her, they appeared to be just as scared as to how to react.

"I didn't think so. Speak to me only after I speak to you first. That is how you will please me."

The words echoed in Lily's ear. *What an awful way to live life. To only speak when someone else tells you that you can do so. Is being treated this way even worth the royalty?* If she were to refuse initiation now, it would be considered offensive behavior to the queen, and although she felt sad to have been subjected to these kinds of people, something inside of her kept telling her to keep moving forward. And it forced her to feel hope that perhaps one day it would all make sense. Terrified to startle the witch once more, she bowed her head in agreement.

"That's better. Now child, listen carefully, for I will not repeat my words. You are to go out to the woods and find something tangible to represent the following four elements—air, fire, water, and nature. No item can be duplicated. Understand?"

The details of Jade's requests were blunt and short. She gave no indication or suggestions as to what something tangible could be, and Lily felt doomed before she had even started. She thought of Karisma's words, *always question everything.*

"Can I have some jars please, to capture things like water, or air? Or can you suggest anything else?" Lily replied confidently, thinking her response was smart and that she had used her brain to think ahead of what she would need.

"You want some jars to capture water or air? Oh you are ridiculous child. Absolutely not, no more questions. Oh, one more thing, you need something to symbolize transformation, so it's five things. Now off you go, be back before sunset, or consider yourself failed!"

Jade shooed Lily away with the same manner that she had brushed the butterflies who teased her eyelashes earlier. She was automatically dismissed. One moment she was the most important person to be alive and the next, she was swept to the bushes, to walk amongst the unknown by herself yet again.

Lily left the party and walked through the thick heavy forest. It was full of scattered trees, just spaced out enough for the sun to burn her head above. *Five things,* she thought. *Air, fire, water, nature and transformation—five things.* She continued to explore further east and soon the nature overlapped the sky, with thicker leaves, heavier trees, more dense, dark and tropical. The rainforest had intensified. The canopy of trees was so close that their leaves crashed into one another, whispering secrets into the wind. With limitless boundaries of only the sky up above, the trees were free to grow into extraordinary shapes and sizes, some so tall that Lily couldn't even see where they ended. As she saw the changes of the plants, she noticed the temperature change as well; no more cool and dry, there was a moist aroma of warmth and the sound of life bustling. Animals and insects buzzed loudly, dancing magic around her feet, encouraging the direction of her path. She was once again completely alone and she waited for the moment to miss her father and life back home, but she didn't. She felt destined to be standing in that very moment, searching for an answer that might not even exist. She had accepted the situation for what it was and felt determined to succeed.

Getting lost amongst the gardens was always one of Lily's most favorite things to do. No matter how alone she felt, she always believed in herself to be as one with nature, where she ultimately belonged. Lily didn't just love the pretty flowers, she loved the bees and insects that found their way into the center, she liked to calculate how much pollen that flower would have given to reproduce, and how many times a day such an event would happen. She liked to think about the process involved, how the pollen would be collected and how the flower expanded so quickly with the assistance of another. She loved how everything related to one another, helping each other evolve. She felt safe in her natural environment, supported somehow.

She was distracted by a familiar scent of rich vanilla infused with lemon and spices. As she turned her face to catch up with the inhalation of her nose, a tree full of soft pink magnolia flowers stood before her. The magnolia was one of Lily's favorite flowers with its distinct fragrance, and she reminisced about her old house where she was lucky enough to have her own magnolia tree in her backyard. Hypnotized by the memory of her childhood, she wandered over to the tree and then realized that she had found her first product to symbolize nature, the flower of a magnolia tree.

The magnolia tree was strong, and the stems connecting the flowers were thick. They were so high it was too difficult to reach them on her own. But she lacked the confidence to use any form of magic to obtain one all by herself, without the help of Karisma. What if she would fail? Even though there was no one around to see, she speculated that someone could have spied on her and gone back and told Jade that perhaps she wasn't worthy for initiation. Oh no, she couldn't risk it. But then again, she had fulfilled every other task that she had ever tried, so why would this be any different?

She looked up above. The flower seemed even further away than when she last looked at it.

Have confidence! You can do it! she heard the voice inside of her sing. But something stopped her, and held her back. She was too scared; too scared of failing.

She looked up and stared at the flower. It didn't move; it didn't budge. And why should it? She wasn't doing anything different. She had the intention, the desire, but no action and she walked away, not even going to give it a try. She walked past the tree into another field to look for a flower that was on the ground, even though she felt such strong magic from the magnolias. As she walked, she hung her head low, disappointed in herself for being so weak. She picked a pink peony flower nearby, as equally beautiful of course, and it solved the mission to represent nature, but she couldn't help but feel a pang of regret, for not giving it a go and trying.

Nature, done. Next, air. Lily looked around again. *What to do for air,* she thought. And she sat down on a soft patch of dandelion flowers to think about her choices.

Nothing, not a thing! What to do, what to do . . . What do we use air for? To breathe. To fly? Who flies . . . birds. And how can we capture birds? No, capturing a bird is wrong. But is it, when it is a part of initiation? Could I cage one and then allow it to be released? But what if Jade hurts the bird? Would she sacrifice it?

She battled the idea in her head. And she looked above to a beautiful green and pink parrot sitting in a branch of the tree, just singing to itself, not hurting anyone. She hadn't thought of anything else, and it seemed so easy. But as she thought about the process involved, she could foresee the little bird screaming in pain, for being confined to a small caged space that it had never been in before. She couldn't deny that she would be hurting another. *Surely that cannot be the right thing to do if I was hurting another?* And after much deliberation she simply decided that capturing the bird would be wrong and that she just needed to figure out another symbol for air.

As the idea vanished, the bird flew away too, as though it knew the thoughts that Lily had envisioned. While the bird spread its wings to escape, a colorful feather floated down far away, too far for her to get. But it didn't matter, for she already had a feather. It was a gift from Karisma the day they went to the volcano. And a flower too, she realized. She smiled as the corners of her mouth rose up to touch her cheeks. She had been carrying both elements all along already.

Nature—flower; air—feather. Water . . .
I need to be more original than capturing water, she sighed.

Nevertheless, she wandered to the ocean, and looked to her surroundings for inspiration once more. But she couldn't see anything to help. How disappointing! She thought to her science class at school, all the different experiments they would do with water. Oh, if only she had paid more attention! Lily wandered over to the large slab cliffs of green tourmaline crystal. She sat on the edge of the stone, tempted to call out to Crysanthe for help. But alas, she wanted to solve this problem on her own. She had gone this far to hide the identity of the mermaids and the only word of warning that she received on this land was to keep the secret sacred. *Do not tell anyone!* Jacques had said. She looked out to the ocean, sitting on the edge, wondering how long she had been gone and how glorious it was to feel as though time did not exist. In her moment-to-moment that she encountered, she could spend as long as she liked just breathing that happiness in. The sun was starting to set and she knew she was meant to be back before nightfall. Still, she had three more items to find, but her mind was boggled for the answers and she started to tell herself that maybe the initiation wasn't right for her.

I'll simply say, Jade—I was unable to complete the task due to . . . but she couldn't think of a reason that was good enough. Lily wanted to participate so badly, she realized that was it. She wanted to do it. And she stood up, ready to march back out to the wilderness, but her hand slipped down on the rock, forcing her to lose her balance. She slid all the way down to her elbows. Upon standing she looked to her arm and noticed the tiny dust particle residue that came with it. She poked out her tongue and licked her hand. *Salt.* And it came flashing back to her, in snippets of a memory, her science class with

Mr. Johns, where salt water evaporated over heat, and what was left? Salt! Could this symbolize water? *Yes!*

Air—feather; nature—flower; water–salt; fire . . .

Fire sounds so hard . . . how can I find something for fire other than fire itself? Perhaps burnt ashes? So predictable again!

Lily opened her pouch to place the folded leaf of sea salt away and as she did so, the crystals all glistened under the sun, she felt like perhaps they knew they were near the ocean. She proceeded to wash them carefully. The black crystals shone unusually bright this day. Was it because they were the newest of her collection? Or did they have something more to say? She thought back to what Karisma had said. *The obsidian crystal forms when molten lava touches water. The rock would represent fire! Perfect! Now, the last one—transformation.*

The ouroboros necklace flashed into Lily's mind; how it symbolized eternity to the mermaids. *In order for one to be eternal, one must embrace change, and accept all types of transformation,* she thought. And she began to play with her thoughts yet again. She imagined all the other witches gasp as she handed over the symbol to Jade, and she even saw Queen Jade herself bow down to her, telling everyone how Lily was clearly the most powerful girl in all the land. She would then be given a crown, and the castle, and have everything that she ever wanted.

This little dream of hers felt so real, Lily couldn't help but even imagine words and conversations and feelings that could have taken place. But alas, she knew it was just a daydream, and that even if it could be possible, she would have to reveal the truth about the mermaids, and potentially cause danger to her one true friend. And she foretold in her mind that to hurt her friend would bitter any sweetness of success. But her voice in her head started to talk louder, and it convinced her that she could show them the necklace, telling them it was from her home. If they were to take a vote, she quickly calculated due to the number of people she had seen in the garden that it would be in her favor, but then again, what if they were too scared to go against Queen Jade? *No, that would be unethical of the town folk,* she rationalized to herself. And she turned around to walk back to the castle, satisfied with her choice of showing the ouroboros for transformation.

As she walked, the idea continued to battle back and forth in her head. And she questioned whether she was doing it for the right reasons . . . to succeed at the initiation task, or to try and outsmart Jade? She looked back inside her crochet pouch. Sandalwood oil, a little key, the small envelope that said 'I love you', the snakeskin . . . *wait the snakeskin! The snakeskin sheds its skin as it outgrows it, transforming into a new snake . . . beautiful!* She had done it! She had done it!

Air—feather; nature—flower; water—salt; fire—obsidian crystal; transformation— snake skin.

Lily skipped back to the castle, eager to arrive before the sun had set. A pointy-eared pixie was already standing at the door, waiting for Lily's return and she politely instructed her to have a bath in preparation. Lily followed the pixie to a large tiled bathroom, with a great big circular bathtub. The water was warm, and bubbled over in soft purrs. It was covered with pink rose petals and sweet-smelling rose oil. The pixie left Lily to relax on her own, and Lily soaked her limbs in the bathtub lavishly. When her feet had wrinkled up with extra skin, she climbed out of the steaming tub and dressed herself in a dark green robe that was hanging ready for her to wear. She stood in front of the gold-framed mirror, admiring herself in the cloak. But she could not recognize herself. No longer was she a young girl with plaited hair and shy eyes, she now felt herself looking like an adult, with wild loose hair, and confidence in her stare. She combed her hair thoroughly, embracing each stroke. She plaited two pieces of hair around the crown of her head, and weaved through it tiny pink flowers that were resting on the basin. Her face was soft but she felt wiser, more comfortable in her skin. She had managed to complete the task at hand and felt stronger for doing so. One last look at herself in the mirror, and she told herself, *be brave.*

Jade was already standing with four other girls when Lily arrived. They all wore identical dark green robes, and held no expression on their faces. The eldest of them carried a large wand that smelled of white sage and had been ignited for several minutes prior to Lily's arrival. She stood at the front of the pack, and twirled the flame up high, allowing the smoke to dance in circles and cleanse the air. Two other girls stood on either side of Lily, and the third was behind, holding a giant rose quartz crystal sphere.

"How did you get on today? Were you successful?" Jade asked in a conniving manner. Her eyes narrowed down along the point of her nose once again with an intimidating stare. Lily could tell what Jade was doing, and she knew she needed to pretend that she was underneath the powerful figure. It reminded her of the quarrels she used to have with her teachers, always struggling to give them authority, knowing that sometimes they weren't necessarily wiser than herself. But her father's words would always repeat in her ear to overcome the situation with kindness.

"In all honesty, Your Highness, I struggled from the very beginning," Lily spoke humbly. "I chose a flower to represent nature but I could not cut it down from the tree, the roots were too strong. So I picked up a peony from the ground. Unfortunately, it has been walked over a few times, I think."

"So all you needed was a flower, like these on your head?" Jade raised her eyebrows looking unimpressed and smirked with another girl while pointing out Lily's stupidity. Lily touched the flowers in her hair. Soft petals suckled against her fingertips and the plaited vines wrapped through her hair strongly. She looked down to the floor embarrassed.

"And all the remaining symbols, were you able to find them?"

"Yes, Your Majesty." Lily curtseyed in response, nodding proudly, not daring to speak of her findings again until asked.

Queen Jade looked to her peers and raised her eyebrows, tightening her lips together as though she were displeased.

"One more rule, I forgot to tell you. You cannot use something that came from an animal. We always get some stupid girl wanting to give a caterpillar cocoon for the animal transformation. Ugh, pathetic!"

Nothing from another animal? That eliminated two of the five symbols—transformation and air! How unfair! *She wants me to fail!*

"That's quite an important rule you should have told me Jade," Lily replied with a bit of poise. She was fuming inside, panicking that she would fail. But just knowing that Jade would have favored the defeat, gave Lily ammunition to carry forward.

"Surely this small rule would be no match for a smart young girl like yourself sweet daaarling Lily?"

Jade spoke in such a patronizing way that Lily couldn't help but feel hatred. Her body temperature rose as all the blood rushed up to the crown of her head. She thought of her father's advice; take a deep breath. She had two choices and she prayed for the courage to make the right one. *I can do this.*

"Okay Lily, we need to start, please show me air."

Lily stared Jade in the eyes, still angry, still hurt. It was hard for Lily to concentrate on anything else. But she vowed not to give up, and she opened her purse to see if there was anything that she could give instead. Lying on top of the pouch was the glass bottle that held the rosemary oil from Jacques. The scent traced through the air, unforeseen, could this pass? It was worth a try. And she handed over the bottle of oil in exchange for air.

"Thank you Lily, I accept this. And what do you have for water?" Jade replied with no emotion, as she ticked the list off mechanically.

Lily didn't have a moment to feel relieved and she handed over a folded leaf that held the salt flake residue from the beach.

"It is the salt from the water on the crystal rocks by the ocean," Lily explained as Jade slowly opened up the leaf and picked up tiny specs of salt dust between her fingers.

"Of course I know what salt is Lily," Jade replied disgruntled flicking the salt between her fingers. "Anyway, I accept. Fire?"

Lily pulled out the obsidian crystal. The particular crystal that she chose was especially magical; it looked like a wave caught in a crystal formation. Jade took the rock and handed it to the lady on her right.

"Interesting choice Lily, I don't think anyone has provided this before. Visiting Karisma has been quite beneficial to you, obviously. And, nature?"

Lily handed Jade the peony flower in her bag. The petals around the center pushed out with grace, standing strong.

"Thank you," Jade said as she handed nature to the girl to the left. "Lastly, what do you have for transformation?"

Lily's heart beat fast. She reached inside her pouch, feeling for something to be able to use. The idea of showing her ouroboros for transformation clicked through her mind. But no, she couldn't show the secret of the mermaids, especially to Jade. Not only that, but Jade would force her to give it up completely. She was close to surrendering and looked down shamed, ready to give in and accept defeat.

"Well, young Lily?"

"I . . . I . . ." Lily fumbled in her bag once more. But, she could not find anything. And she knelt to the ground in preparation to be disqualified. But there, right in front of Lily's knees, a small seed on the ground called out to her. It was colored a pale pink with speckled green and no bigger than the size of her fingernail. She handed it to Jade.

"This seed creates the fruit of life, and is therefore transformation. For one cannot live without the ability to change," Lily stated as she handed the seed over, unsure as to where the words had actually come from.

Jade appeared taken back for a moment, and she surprisingly appraised Lily where credit was due.

"I am impressed Lily. You have supplied strong symbols for our initiation."

Perhaps she is not as horrid as expected, Lily thought.

"Thank you," Lily replied kindly, curtsying to show her respect.

In Jade's hands she held a thick wooden shaft wand. The bottom of the stick was a blistering black red coal. It looked frail and as though it should break off, but there was something deeper beyond what the eye could see. With the burnt rubble end, she drew a circle around where Lily stood. The charcoal pieces scratched off while doing so, embedding the ground with not only a grove into the dirt but a layer of black dots. The dots hovered just above the ground, swirling as though encasing Lily from moving.

"We must keep our secret places sacred and therefore you must be blindfolded. Do you trust that I will cause you no harm?"

Lily looked to Jade. A blaze of red streaks had flooded the whites of her eyes, pushing the green pupils to dart toward Lily's like spears. But she did not feel anger or hatred from the queen. There was something higher, Jade was possessed by something blind to the naked eye. And a fuzzy white light surrounded the edge of Jade's hands. *There was goodness in her still,* Lily thought.

"I give my eyes to you," Lily muttered as she closed her eyes and nodded her head down, succumbing to her knees before the queen.

With her arms by her side, Lily felt someone from behind wrap a soft silk scarf around her eyes securely. It smelled like eucalyptus, and she immediately felt relaxed.

"Please stand Lily and allow the elders to walk you to our place of meeting."

A small warm hand held Lily's right, and she felt a cool wrinkly hand hold onto her left. The three walked forward without being pulled; it reminded her of the dance of Neo, drifting side to side, just allowing the tide to flow. And although she could not see, she could feel the girls around her continuing to guide her along the path. She listened to the sound of their feet shuffling along the ground, pitter-pattering lightly, and her mind played out to guess the exact distance of where everyone was standing.

Jade would be in front, and someone on both sides, and perhaps one person behind. The fleet would be in a diamond shape layout, directed by the head of an arrow. With Jade charging ahead, step by step, across the crystal dirt land of Tehar. Together they marched, up what began as a slight increase that quickly turned into a steep hill, and they shuffled their feet along the glittery road. The night sky felt farther away than usual, as though the trees were hovered in closely, covering their heads. They towered together as they walked along a narrow pathway, and then, they stopped. They had arrived.

"Locem wo te Initiation," Jade said as the edge of the cloth peeled back from Lily's eyes and she stared with awe at the magical landscape.

Gigantic slabs of colored crystals decorated the ground and they erupted with lightening inside, sparking energy from the core of the planet as though wanting to break free from the mold. Lily could feel the explosion through her feet and into her body, causing the vibration to resonate loudly through every ounce of her being. The powerful motion both excited and scared Lily at once and she felt an overwhelming feeling of lightness overtaking her mind. It prompted her to feel truly magical in her own essence, realizing that for her to be able to feel this emotion so deeply was truly beautiful in itself.

The ceremonial space towered on the edge of a high mountain cliff, the highest Lily had ever seen. It stretched high above a river of water that smashed rapidly against the reef below. And a rainfall fell on either side of the sacred space, trickling down slowly and calmly, a contrasting noise to the fierce roar beneath their feet. A full moon shone directly above, and watched down on the girls, with the two additional moons on either side, supporting each other, all three spaced out in harmony. In the center of the sacred ground was a circle of burning coal, and on top lay a large crystal slab of clear quartz. The quartz was sliced in such a way that it pointed in an even cross, directing the fire toward north, south, east and west.

"Unclothe her!" Jade ordered, as two girls either side of Lily began to unbutton her robe.

No one had ever seen her naked before, not since she was a baby. The pressure of initiation felt too much to bear, and she felt nervous, very nervous. For a split moment, Lily thought about escaping, forgetting everything and everyone around her and giving up. She imagined herself diving off the platform, into the sharp currents below. Here she imagined that she would call on the mermaids and live forever in peace. But fear set in, and she wondered if her body would shatter on the reef, cut up like glass before she even reached the water to where the mermaids lived, and perhaps no one would ever know that she had lived at all. Was that a risk worth taking? She thought . . . she would be abandoning her life and not trusting it. It would mean she did not love herself. And it was the first time that she truly understood Karisma and Jacques' words of self-love. To allow her life to evolve the way it was meant to. And with a deep exhalation, she surrendered, and allowed the girls to undress her completely. Her innocent body, pure in the moonlight, the most open she had ever been.

The ouroboros! Lily could hear Jacques whisper in her ear, *keep the existence of the mermaids secret.* She shivered, terrified that she had accidentally revealed her necklace to them. But no one stirred. No one even looked at her neck. To the others, it did not exist for they had never seen it before.

"Lie down on the crystal bed, Lily," Jade commanded, as the sound of drums began to beat loudly. Lily mechanically crawled onto the platform and lay down as requested.

Boom cha ba ba, boom cha ba ba, boom cha ba ba, boom.
Silence.

The sounds of drumming engulfed Lily's ears. The crystal platform was cool to touch, yet the warmth grew quickly beneath the weight of her skin. The flames from the fire licked the edge of the crystal platform upon which Lily laid. She could feel the heat rise savagely around her body, shooting electricity from the core of the earth. It reminded her of the volcano. She imagined the eruption of molten lava ooze through the crust of the earth and spill onto the ground around her. The sheer imagery she created in her mind forced her heart to beat faster. And the feeling of anticipation mixed with excitement and terror overrode her senses. She didn't know what she was feeling. All her emotions seemed to roll into one conjoined vibration.

Boom cha ba ba, boom cha ba ba, boom cha ba ba, boom.

Silence.

The girls spun around where Lily lay, and in rhythmic chants, their bodies moved. Their shadows molded into another form, in clusters of floating clouds and speckles of stardust, or perhaps they had become the shadows of their former selves as they rose above their bodies. Mirroring the girls above flew a circle of birds, flying around in a clockwise position. Encircling the ceremony below, protecting Lily, or perhaps they were others who had transformed, watching the ceremony, eager to see what mystery would outplay.

Boom cha ba ba, boom cha ba ba, boom cha ba ba, boom.

Silence.

"Ma I, lei fe, ce mi beo, vio le, ka pi se, si ee, ni who," Jade said.

"Sa Neo," The girls all replied in a hushed voice.

Jade motioned for the girls to each bring forth the gifts from Lily. One by one they presented the pieces.

"Life begins with air," Jade said as she tipped the oil into the palm of her hands and placed them on the base of Lily's feet. "Take a deep breath and meet me here." She slithered the oil on thickly and massaged the tips of Lily's fingers; her knuckles were pressed the way Papa would do to distract her mind. Lily exhaled deeply as though releasing her thoughts, and Jade held Lily's crown of her head, humming loudly while doing so.

Boom cha ba ba, boom cha ba ba, boom cha ba ba, boom.

Silence.

"SA NEO," the girls yelled loudly.

Jade opened the folded leaf and poured the sea salt into her hands. She sprinkled the dust over Lily's naked body, and then rubbed down hard, exfoliating dead cells off her skin. The residue flew away with the wind, cleansing Lily's body of anything that she no longer needed.

"Our bodies are made of water. Let our water never run dry."

"SA NEO," the girls replied.

Boom cha, boom cha, boom cha, boom.

Silence.

Jade placed the obsidian crystal on Lily's neck. Lily closed her eyes, feeling the weight of the crystal connect and sink deeply within herself. She felt a strange tingling sensation on her body where it lay, as though the power of the rock was seeping into her blood stream, fueling her veins. The blood pumped around her body quickly, and she could see her veins in her body as though they were on the outside of her skin. They had risen up high, entangled tubes full of dark red and deep purples. They appeared in synchronization with the beating of the drums and then, they disappeared as quickly as the sound evaporated from the air.

Boom cha, boom cha, boom cha, boom.
Silence.

"The fire is lit within your passion, let it burn forever in your eyes."

"SA NEO," the girls replied.

Boom cha, boom cha, boom cha, boom.
Silence.

Jade crushed the flower within her hands. Tearing each petal off roughly and savagely. She threw the components high in the air like confetti over Lily's body and they slowly dropped down like kisses of a rainfall, each drop in tune with the beating drum, now strumming louder with momentum.

"With this flower, I feed the strength of nature into your vessel."

"SA NEO," the girls chanted.

Boom cha, boom cha, boom cha.
Silence.

Jade held the seed above Lily's chest and placed it in between her rib cage. She pressed it down hard, forcing Lily to breathe out noisily. And from the pain that Lily felt from the seed being pushed, she automatically mirrored the action inside with her own emotions, releasing with her exhale any built up anger or sorrow that she had once held onto.

"Plant this seed inside your heart and let love grow out into the world around you."

"SA NEO!" the girls chanted.

Boom cha boom cha boom cha.

"You have been given the gift of life Lily."

"SA NEO!" the girls chanted.

"Louder," Jade commanded as the drumming grew in vibration, and the girls chanting of Sa Neo echoed through the night air, whispering along the journey of the winds.

Boom cha boom cha boom cha.

"SA NEO!"

"AGAIN!" she screamed.

Boom cha boom cha boom cha.

Silence.

Lily closed her eyes tightly and watched as patterns of white and yellow swirled together into new shapes and sizes. She felt herself float above her body and she opened her eyes, realizing she had done exactly that—detached herself as a separate entity. She watched the ceremony from high above, floating afar, connected to her body by a long gold rope. The burning flames fenced her body and they joined together directly above in a pyramid. She could still feel the heat, it was pleasurable, and forced her body to shiver with a moment of ecstasy as an overwhelming joy immersed her body.

Such a strange feeling, to appear detached, yet not entirely from your body, she thought. *To see yourself so clearly, yet so separate from all you have ever known. There is a life outside of myself, yet it begins from inside of myself.*

Click clack.

The sound of two giant crystals smashing together pierced through the air loudly disrupting Lily's levitation, bringing her back down to the ground.

Click clack click clack.

The vibration grew as Lily felt multitudes of the crystals clinking together, as though more people were joining the circle.

Click clack click clack click clack click clack click clack click clack.

The girls moved around hurriedly, until the stones smashing together rang out in a long conjoined beat, connecting altogether in one harmonizing tune.

Through her closed eyes she could see the light of the stone, and Lily felt as though each stone hovered above her, ringing the sound out on its own. The light of the stone had faded except for the noise, which still existed, and it held a shape above her body. A pure stream of sound and white light spun violently, in a tornado-type fashion all around Lily, but despite the chaos, the peace held strong. And Lily was calm, feeling her body stretch out with new shapes, and new skin, and a new vibrational frequency. The energy from the crystals had entered into her body and the powerful forces were being ignited inside her heart.

"Silence!" Jade commanded, as the beating ceased all at the same time and she draped a lavender-smelling silk cloth on Lily's face. "You may open your eyes."

The smell of lavender calmed Lily completely and when she opened her eyes, the fire had extinguished. She felt at peace.

The sky was the same deep green as before but this time it felt more alive. The moons looked brighter, the clouds felt closer. She felt like she was floating in the middle of the sky. The senses in her body were running on overdrive. She could feel the wind softly purr over every piece of hair on her body in precise detail. Something in her hand brought her back down to the ground. And when she opened it, there on her finger sat a purple amethyst crystal ring.

It is a gift from the land, she was told. The voice inside her was growing stronger; it was ready to roar, but she still had more to learn before she was to speak openly about such matters. The observations that she absorbed with such silence were taking over her mind, and she was learning, learning so much from her surroundings whether she chose to or not. These surroundings were teaching her. And the lessons that she was learning were invaluable, irreplaceable, and only she alone could witness them. They weren't to be shared; they weren't to be spoken about. For the power she now possessed, the gifted ring was to symbolize it all, and it would be envied from all of those she would meet, but even still, they would respect the wish of the ring to be with her, to sit on her finger so proudly, so closely. The ring had molded its shape around her finger, it was magically fastened, so that no one could break it off, they would have to slice her fingers in order to try and remove the purple amethyst stone ring. It was beautiful, raw and pure, with sharp thunderbolt lightning strikes throughout, reminding her that it had been created under the night sky.

"To complete this initiation of welcoming you to Sa Neo, you must bathe in the Sacred Valley of Lucidity. Follow me."

Still in her open nakedness, with the moons high in the sky, Lily followed the tribe to the sacred valley where she was told she would be bathing. She stood on the edge of the still waters with dark tourmaline crystal rolled in oblong shapes all around on the ground. Slowly, Lily walked into the christened water, feeling the cool shudder of bubbles release a chilling sensation around her ankles. The chill moved from the base of the feet, along the back of her knees, up past her thighs and along the edge of her spine, until it reached the crown of her head, and although she had not submerged herself in the water completely, she could feel the potential of what was to come, and it excited her. Her eyes sparkled beneath the thrice-beaming moonlights, hungry for more. If this were a taste of what living in this land was like, perhaps she would like it more than she thought. It was wonderful to feel the empowerment of the women around her, supporting her, and comforting her choices. Slowly, she walked. The water now reaching just above her shoulders, it was the moment she would completely surrender and come back up as one of them. The initiation would be complete.

"You are alone. You were born on your own and will die on your own, exactly as you are. No one is here to save you."

Jade forcefully threw both her arms out to either side of her body and above her shoulders. She drew her arms in together and pointed directly ahead.

"Rew ae Sa Neo!"

Jade spread her fingers above and drew a faint outline of pale pink colored smoke through her claw-pointed fingertips and she repeated this again. In the sky above, a swarm of six bright rainbow-colored birds flew around in a clockwise circle. They swooped down low above each of the girls' heads almost touching and then back up high. Each bird performed the exact same movement. Flying gracefully up and down, up and down, around and around. Lily stood with her head just above the water, waiting for the signal from

Jade to leave the still waters. The longer she stayed beneath the water world, the stronger the movement of currents underneath.

Jade turned away from Lily, pulled out a small cube of fabric from her pocket and dangled it in front of her face. She threw the fabric up above her head and allowed it to float down to the ground, never once turning to Lily again. And the words she spoke were muffled in the wind, away from Lily, making it impossible to understand what was being said. And when the voice was finished, she heard one last time, 'Sa Neo' being chanted in the night sky as each of the girls followed one by one behind Jade.

Gradually, the shadows of the girls slowly dispersed into the dark forest, as did the trail of birds above. And all that was left was Lily floating in the water, cocooned in a nest of the family she wished to be a part of. Her immediate thought was not in fear of getting home, or finding clothing, for she was already home, anywhere and everywhere she walked was her home. And while she floated in the water, dancing beneath the stars, no one cared what she was wearing or to whom it was that she belonged. She was accepted as just herself, and the world danced around her, praising her body and giving gratitude for her heart that beat a song of love that sang out into the universe for all who would listen.

CHAPTER EIGHT

A DAY WITH SILVA

Lily saw herself lying beneath a net made of gold, but it wasn't a protective net; it burnt her skin and weighed heavy on her petite frame. She heard Jade cackle in the background, but she couldn't see anything, nothing but the golden net over her face and body. And she sank deeply into the ground, pushed down from the weight of the net crushing into her bones. It was difficult to breathe. The sheer shock of it all made Lily toss and turn and she knocked herself awake. Lily was having a dream, or was it a vision? She didn't know the difference. She had barely slept the night of the initiation. Her mind was too energetic, too eager to go and play with her new-found powers. There was nothing to keep her asleep, although she had no idea what the time was, but the moon was beaming high in the sky, and dawn still looked to be a few hours away. Too scared to go back to sleep, she rose. Whisking the sheets to the end of the bed, she stood up straight. Taking her little crochet pouch that she had barely worn, she dressed herself in a dark green long-sleeve hooded dress. Through the giant hallway she crept, down the stairs, out to the garden, where the naked beach shone brightly ahead and the sound of the water kissing the pebbles with each crashing breath sang loudly in Lily's ears. She walked to the far right of the ocean, a place where she could hide behind large rocks and feel safe to perform the ritual of calling upon Crysanthe once more.

"You are on a different beach!" Crysanthe exclaimed, as she hovered above the green waters on the shores of Tehar. Her hair was messy and ragged, and she wore a loose necklace full of chunky seashells around her neck. Her crown, once again, placed sturdily on her head.

"Yes! This land is called Tehar," Lily announced proudly. "Queen Jade invited me so that I could be initiated to Sa Neo."

The mermaid's violet eyes widened with excitement, and she propped herself onto a giant slab of tourmaline rock, closer to Lily in order to listen to the story.

"Oh Crysanthe, I was so nervous. If I did not pass the queen suggested that my life would have been sacrificed," Lily explained, recalling the turn of events clearly in her mind.

"Sacrificed to who?"

"I don't know exactly. I guess I would be sacrificed to their beliefs?"

Lily only now realized that the idea of sacrifice seemed unreasonable. Surely she would not have been taken prisoner for not agreeing with someone, although the temper in Jade's voice did sound crazy, and people can be drunk with too much power.

"Their beliefs don't need your sacrifice. Forcing authority onto another will not change anything. How can witches be so stupid yet so powerful at the same time?"

Lily chuckled at Crysanthe's outspoken emotion. She was very heated in the moment, and her silvery skin emitted a layer of steam under the moonlight.

"Well it's okay, because I passed!" Lily reassured her, trying to calm the mermaid down.

Crysanthe giggled to herself for her outburst, and she dusted the steam off her skin as though the heat was peeling a layer off.

"So what happened during the initiation?"

"Crysanthe it was magical! I have never experienced anything like it. To be a part of something higher than myself, and to have control over something too big to comprehend. I felt like I levitated above my body and watched the ceremony from afar, and the girl on the table was not me. I mean, I was not her. But if that were true then where did I go?"

As Lily recalled the events that had played out, it gave her a chance to actually process it properly, to float above her body and yet still be attached with just a cord. When she explained the way she felt and the emotions that had arisen during that time, it was as though she was reliving the experience once more, only this time it felt more alive, and the truth of her reality felt more real. Maybe it was because she was sharing it with someone.

"I was given this ring, look. I don't know how it was placed on my finger, but when I opened my eyes, here it was. And I was told that it is to both create and protect."

Lily held her hand out to show Crysanthe the ring. The splinters in the amethyst stone appeared to have changed, and they now swirled around like milky clouds. The silver that held the stone together had softened into her skin, and it felt completely natural on her hand.

"Have you tried to use it?"

"No, I'm too scared. But I do have a present I had wanted to give you!"

Lily reached into her pouch and pulled out a piece of obsidian crystal from the volcano on Otor. "This stone is produced when you dance to Neo! The heat rises through the center core and erupts up here on land. Your dance creates heat in the atmosphere," Lily explained with enthusiasm for solving one of Crysanthe's questions.

"It does?"

Lily nodded and handed over the piece of black obsidian. Crysanthe closed her eyes and twitched slightly as she held the black crystal. Lily could sense that she could also feel the immediate power it possessed, and she knew instantly that she had done the right thing by giving the stone to the mermaid.

"Everything starts from the inside, out," Lily replied factually. "And there is something else . . ."

"What?" Crysanthe's entire face lit up at the idea of her being thought of outside of the water and she listened eagerly to her friend. "This world is called Sa Neo, and whenever Jade would talk, the girls would reply—'Sa Neo'. Neo—like your Neo. But if the mermaids never met anyone on land, how did they both call the world they live in, Neo? It's a little bit more than just a coincidence, don't you think?"

"Oh seashells!" Crysanthe sighed a big gasp of air, and looked out to the horizon of splashing waters. She held a confused frown on her brow, and pouted her lips expressing both frustration and excitement to uncover the truth.

"And another thing . . ." Lily whispered to Crysanthe, so only the two could hear.

"What?" she whispered back, combing her hair from her face and leaning in closer.

"The ceremony was in a circle, and inside the circle were four points, and at those points a girl stood holding the items that represented air, water, fire and nature."

Lily described the placement of the girls during the ceremony to precision, using stones on the ground to explain visually. Crysanthe knew what she was implying.

"You mean, like inside the Cave of Zeka? The drawings?" The waves behind Crysanthe grew with strength as the two connected their worlds together. The water roared, splashing down hard, as though clapping with applause.

"EXACTLY! If mermaids never had feet, how did they know such a place existed to be able to draw it?"

Crysanthe nodded as she wondered the same question. "What do you think this all means?"

Lily stared back at the beautiful creature, feeling so happy to be asked for advice from someone so powerful. The differences between them faded with just one look, and she felt friendship and safety in anything that was said.

"That we are all connected somehow," Lily said and smiled back at her friend, knowing that there is something unimaginable connecting them all together, something so big that neither of them could fully grasp it.

"Wowwww!" Crysanthe dove from the rock into the ocean and twirled through the air, jumping up and down out of the water with excitement like a dolphin. Her tail gleamed with rainbow scales under the beaming moonlight and she hovered back up to meet Lily.

"This is amazing Lily! I can't wait to tell Zavier that I was right to pursue my desire to understand your world better."

"I'm glad you did too."

The girls smiled with mutual understanding, and they said goodbye, knowing that it would not be long before they would see each other again. Lily crept back along the forest path, past the giant crystal ball fountain and along the castle corridor back into her room.

She managed to sleep perhaps one hour, and awoke to the dead quiet silence that pierced through Jade's home. The walls of her bedroom were large and quite empty, and strange paintings that didn't really make sense were scattered at random heights. Lily couldn't figure out if the people in the images were trying to scare her, or perhaps they just hated their life. Why choose to show images of people in sorrow? *Does Jade show her power through fear?* Lily thought.

The bed sheets were fresh-smelling, but the sense of home like Karisma's touch was not to be found. The room felt as though it had been cleaned and the sheets changed every day. Lily could almost feel the sweat of the lady who was forced to clean over and over again when there wasn't anything dirty. The room was being cleaned just because Jade could tell someone to do it so. *So then isn't she giving someone a job? But jobs don't exist in this land, so no, not really. Let the person who cleans, clean for the love of cleaning.*

Lily had a conversation in her head again. Staying with Jade certainly puzzled her. She liked the aspect of space and had the availability of anything she wanted at her fingertips, but it was at the cost of feeling uncomfortable. The room was so perfectly clean and stark that Lily was nervous to disrupt the white walls. She laid in bed some while longer until the sun peeked its head through the window. Lily had given in to the fact that she could not sleep anymore and so she opened the door from her room to a small pixie girl who was standing outside, ready to take her to the bathroom. And although the spa bath that she had was made of soothing pink rose petals and refreshing eucalyptus oil, she was being watched at all times. She was told it was for the purpose of helping to make her life 'at ease' but it didn't make her feel very relaxed at all, and she wished to just be alone.

Her outfit for the day was chosen for her by Jade, and was quite similar to the style of dress that Lily had seen Jade wear the day before. The idea of elderly ladies doing nothing else but make the hand stitched lace didn't make her feel any better, and she wondered what working conditions the ladies were making them in and she hoped they were being looked after properly.

The pixie motioned for Lily to follow her into the back garden where Jade was standing near a giant table of food, with a crowd of little pixie girls all around. Jade casually fluttered her eyelashes toward Lily's direction as she entered the room; but she didn't ask her how she was or how she had slept, and instead began the conversation by boasting about herself.

"Basically, I have all the delicacies from all the lands around the world," Jade said as she twirled around and showcased the table, picking up the treats. "We have olives eyes, a true little gem of a tart they are. Pink marshmallow froth, (the most divine tea in the entire world). People travel far and wide to get their petite little claws on such a tea my girl! Consider yourself lucky that you are even able to sip on such a stew!" Jade said as she threw the stew toward Lily to take. It tipped over the edge of a teacup and burnt her hands slightly. "And just look at these snowflakes! Have you seen anything more beautiful? Queen Violetta gave them to me. It's rumored they are off a duck's back." She held up a jar in the sunlight that was full of the most intricately cut-out flakes that Lily had ever seen. "She's the most powerful empress in all the universe you know. She gave me these snowflakes! They are off a duck's back. I mean can you believe it? She. Gave. Me. THE. S-N-O-W-F-L-A-K-E-S off a duck's back? I know! IIIIIII KNOW!"

Jade squeezed Lily's hand with excited delight and held up ever so proudly the small square glass jar full of milky white snowflakes, each unique with perfect design of an eight-pointed star, with a faint rainbow color flashing in all directions.

"Now try them all, eat as much as you like, they are my gift to you! Just do me a favor, don't tell the others. I pretend I don't play favorites, oh but child I do, I do!"

Queen Jade scrunched up the side of her face and squinted with one eye to Lily. Her face was so ghastly and terribly unattractive that Lily could only imagine that she was attempting to wink at her. Lily smiled with no teeth, forcing her cheekbones to protrude loudly, and her eyes opened wide, to attempt an equal level excitement and not to offend the queen.

"Now girl, which do you want to try first?"

Overwhelmed with curiosity, Lily stared at the giant table full of treats. The wooden table was carved around a tree in the center, and each branch balanced a square crystal plate full of individual goodies. A different pixie-like fairy with pointy ears and long silky gold hair stood at the side of the table. She had a timid-looking face, a bit scared of what was going to happen. But she was harmless, and Lily wanted her to know that she was safe.

"Hello, what is your name?" Lily asked politely to the well-dressed pixie maid.

"Silvia," she replied nervously.

The fairy pixie wore an apron with a matching hat and balanced a thin rectangle silver plate in her arm, awaiting Lily's instructions on how to fill it up. Each of the delicacies had a hand written note saying 'made with love' and the name of the dish. Lily stared with excitement at all the elaborately designed sweets in front of her, and she picked the pieces out carefully.

"Can I please try the 'vanilla chia seed pudding', and perhaps the 'strawberry lime coconut cream parfait'?"

The little pixie nodded in approval and handed Lily the

miniature treats off the trays. The coconut cream parfait spiraled into a pointed cup that twirled around like a cloud inside, decorated with diced strawberries and a light green swirl. The vanilla pudding had wobbly eyes pointing in all directions from the bursting chia seeds.

"Miss Lily, can I suggest the mango moose tart too? Or perhaps the watermelon soup?" Silvia said as she pointed to an orange gooey-centered crusty tart and miniature watermelons stacked up like a pyramid.

"Yes, I would love to, thank you so much."

"You're very welcome, Your Highness," Silvia replied as she added the treats to the tray and bowed down in gratitude.

"But I'm not . . ."

"Oh girl yes you are," Jade interfered as she overheard their conversation. "You have been initiated to be one of us, which means that you are superior to these pixies."

Lily looked at the pixie's face at having been told that they were not equal. She felt pain. Like someone had pushed her down and she was unable to get back up. And in that moment, she saw a flash timeline of the pixie's life. The hardship Silvia had endured throughout her life of never being good enough, of never belonging anywhere. She was an orphan pixie with no mother or father, nor any friends. Lily could see Silvia go home, day after day and walk into her treehouse with no one around her but an empty room. The pixie would fold her apron and hat perfectly on the chair before she sat down to eat with barely any food on the table. Lily looked to Jade and back to the pixie. Jade was already walking to the table expecting Lily to join her. Lily wanted to talk to Silvia and tell her that she didn't think she was any different than her. But she could see Jade staring at Lily out of the corner of her eye and she felt she couldn't. Instead, she asked the pixie what her favorite treats were and decided that she would give them to her later.

Lily sat down with Jade at the largest table in the garden, and three pixies (including Silvia), stood next to Jade, in case something was needed.

"So, tell me. How is Karisma? What was the food like at her tree?" Jade asked shrewdly while she picked a cherry off from the top of a pink sprinkled cupcake.

"Karisma is so lovely, I am so grateful to have met her. And the food was delicious! We got up early and picked fresh berries from her backyard for our breakfast," Lily gushed, thinking about the berries squishing between her toes on the ground. She looked back to Jade, who was staring at Lily with her mouth slightly open, and a furrowed brow.

"You picked your own fruit and vegetables at Karisma's? Made your own breakfast? Sounds horrific!"

Jade scrunched her face up as she shoved a caramel nut into her mouth. She scrunched her lips around as she overloaded on the nuts, crunching down hard.

"I enjoyed it actually," Lily replied, feeling more confident with her new status.

Jade shook her head ferociously as little crackles of nuts spat out across the table. They bounced up and down along the table and landed on Lily's plate.

"Did you just talk back to me?"

Lily was horrified.

"No, Your Majesty. It was very boring, I said. You were right." She lied.

It was one of the very few times in her life that Lily had ever lied, and she felt terribly guilty. But something made her do it. This time it wasn't just to see what would happen, this time she felt her instinct tell her to, the way an animal can feel on the back of their skin that a larger animal is watching them and they need to be on guard. She automatically needed to protect herself for some reason, and even though she didn't know why, she didn't question it. *I am beginning to know myself,* she thought.

"Queen Jade, I am sorry to disturb you," squeaked a quiet voice from behind where Lily was sitting.

It was one of the guard gnomes having come at a perfect time to break the awkward silence. He was standing tall and proud, only just reaching the height of the table.

"You are always disturbing me, but it's fine." Jade said as she slapped her hand on the table. "What do you want?"

Lily looked to the gnome at being spoken down to aggressively. She wanted to say something but had no confidence to do so, and instead just watched the scene play out, cringing in her seat quietly. He seemed to ignore the outburst from Jade and continued with his mission.

"Three things, Your Majesty."

"Good, you are learning. Let's just have two today. Quickly." She clicked her fingers, demanding he speak on her command.

"Very well," the gnome replied as he threaded his gloved fingers in between one another and cleared his throat. "The Toto Farmers in town have asked for your help. Their daughter has gone missing and it is not normal for her to leave and not return."

"Oh people go missing all the time, she will turn up." Jade scooped up some coconut marshmallow with a spoon and shoved it into her mouth as she replied. "Next!"

Neither the gnome nor the pixies blinked an eye as Jade rudely dismissed the request, but Lily felt ashamed for having chosen to sit at the same table as someone who would treat another person in that manner.

"The people of Tehar have asked for your participation in the community ritual to show leadership to the children," the gnome continued.

"Oh, I'm far too busy to participate in community activities. I think that is all for today, please be on your way."

Jade shooed the gnome away. The disappointment on his face was evident, and Lily could see the affect that Jade's reluctancy to help had on the village people. She could imagine his grave face of having to tell them their queen was unable to attend. *How could someone abuse their power like that?* she thought.

"Tell me more about our little hippie girl, Karisma. Are the trees and plants controlling her still? I tell you." She stuck her fork into a sticky covered raspberry and continued. "Letting nature run wild and free like that, it can't be good. I mean, look at how beautiful all this land is." She pointed with a straight palm and fingers toward the garden. "I have trimmed the hedges and flowers, making the design just exquisite, don't you think?" Jade continued to talk to Lily as though nothing had happened, and claimed to have pruned the garden herself!

Lily nodded in response, too scared of fake words escaping her mouth in case her stomach turned again from being false like before. She wanted to talk back and say, *You idiot! All of the plants are synchronic, if you cared to look, instead of looking in the mirror! If each petal on every flower was sliced in half she would see equal sides of the veins blooming through, waiting to be recognized.* But Lily had quickly realized that no matter how hard you try to show someone the truth, they would be blind until they chose to see. Perhaps Jade liked to be in her own little world, and in which case, Lily could be in her own little world too. She decided that she was fed up with this proper way of life, and longed to go back to Crysanthe, to swim under Neosa as a mermaid once more.

"So today Lily, I am going to travel to see Violetta. You can't come with me yet; I will ask her if you can come next time. But feel free to roam around and do whatever you please! Make yourself at home. SILVIA!"

Jade clicked her fingers and pointed to the air, not looking around. She stared at her food and shoved the treats into her mouth again, very unladylike. The golden-haired pixie girl ran quickly to meet Jade, and stood next to the table, bowing her head to show her respect.

"Ah Silvia, there you are. So, I am going to spend the day in Neveah with Violetta and while I am gone, I want you to make sure that anything Lily wants, Lily gets. Do you think you can do that for me?" she asked in a patronizing way, and Lily once again cringed at such a manner.

"Yes, Your Highness, I would be delighted to," Silvia said as she bowed down in agreement.

"Lily, you ask for anything you want okay? It's not everyday that we are lucky enough to have everything that we want, and you know what, you can and you do! Just don't ask Silvia many questions. She's quite stupid."

Lily looked to Silvia at being shunned once more and all the feelings of sadness were transparent in the pixie's eyes. Lily felt like she understood the pixie completely, almost better than she understood herself. She felt like there was a part of her inside of Silvia who just wanted to be loved. And although Jade appeared to have everything she wanted, she was missing key ingredients in her personality, including kindness and compassion. And some things she said or did, just didn't feel right to Lily. She couldn't figure it out exactly, for everything seemed to have an excuse. But if she were to take note, this would go down as a warning sign of something being not quite right.

"So, tell me Lily. What would you like to do today?" Jade asked. But she wasn't even looking at Lily, and Lily didn't feel like she actually cared about the answer, rather she was asking just to make sure she could approve it.

"I'd like to go explore the land? See the animals that you have, the trees, the flowers?" Lily thought quickly. She actually wanted to see what the people were like on the land, if they too were being mistreated, and whether she could help them. But she was too scared to admit the truth.

"Oh please darling, you've seen one animal, you've seen them all!" Jade shooed the idea away with her long claw fingernails in the same manner she shooed away the gnome.

"Um, okay. Well I would love to learn how to play a musical instrument from the band that you have playing here?" Lily asked, as she thought of strumming beautiful notes from a guitar.

"Oh come here now, you don't want to associate with the help! Let the professionals play the music."

How will I ever better my playing if I do not practice? she wanted to ask Jade, but again she held her tongue. She felt like she was expected to know all the answers to everything and if she didn't know it now, she wouldn't know it later. She missed patient Karisma, who not only explained things clearly, but encouraged her to ask questions.

"Are you hungry? How about I get the chef to make you something really special?" Jade offered, raising her arm, ready to yell at another staff member.

"I'm quite full considering that we just ate, although I would love to learn how to actually cook the food we are eating?" Lily asked excitedly, thinking about how she could make the delicious treats for her father back home.

"The chefs are too busy to teach you anything Lily," Jade replied without looking again. *How could they be too busy to teach me yet have time to make food had I been hungry?* Lily thought. She was beginning to feel like anything she asked was not allowed unless it was Jade's idea or under her supervision. She had an idea.

"Queen Jade, perhaps you could come up with a suggestion that would be suitable, for you see, I would very much like to see this land that you rule, to understand the hardship of responsibility you tolerate daily. How do you think the best way to do it would be?"

To this Jade smiled at Lily proudly; finally they were speaking the same language!

"Yes my land is definitely the most beautiful of all the lands here on Sa Neo. Maybe Silvia here can get you an elephant to ride upon and you two can go explore? I would take you myself, but I am just too busy and the townfolk will want to talk to me, and ask advice. It just becomes quite draining." Jade rolled her eyes with boredom as she knocked her plate away, having signaled she had finished her meal.

"I understand your predicament, Your Majesty; it sounds like you are right, and that just Silvia and myself is the ideal solution."

Lily grinned to Silvia to show her secret excitement, but Silvia looked straight ahead, as though she were too scared to indulge in her own thoughts of what it would be like to have an enjoyable day together.

"Silvia, go get an elephant for Lily here," Jade said and snapped her fingers haughtily. "And you two, you must be back before supper. It is crucial that we spend every meal together, do you understand?"

Lily nodded in response and looked to Silvia who was already running away to get the elephant. Meanwhile, Lily could hardly contain her excitement. She was thrilled to not only explore the lands, but to ride a real elephant! She had never done so before. And she was also looking forward to some alone time with Silvia, so she could give her the treats she had been saving for her. Silvia arrived with the elephant that was painted white and had great beautiful patterns painted all over its body. Lily patted the trunk, feeling the squishy layer of scaly skin, and she felt the lively nature of another creature, just as alive and radiant as she was. The girls climbed onto its back where a wooden chair sat, decorated with colorful silk shawls. And they immediately waltzed off deep into the jungle on the land of Tehar.

As soon as they were far away from the castle, Lily opened her bag and handed Silvia a box she had been saving full of the lunchtime sweets.

"Oh m'am, no, no, I mustn't," she replied, turning her shoulder away as such.

"Oh please Silvia, I want you to have them. You deserve them. I am so grateful for all that you have done for me. I want you to know how much I appreciate you," Lily pleaded as she watched Silvia's face lift from a stressed mope into a happy relief, and she gobbled down the coconut chia seed puddings in two swift gulps.

"The pudding really is delicious isn't it? I would very much love to learn how to make it," Lily replied, eager to continue conversation with Silvia, who had warmed up slightly. It was obvious that from the way she had been treated with Jade's emotional hot and cold temper that she was waiting for Lily to turn too. Lily wanted to show her that not everyone was that way and that she did not deserve that treatment.

"Do you think there is something I could give to the chef as a thank-you for all their hard work?"

Silvia nodded, "Up through the rainforest and over the mountains is the infamous Tehar's market. We may find something there for her."

"A market? Oh Silvia that's brilliant, I love markets!" Lily exclaimed as she thought back home to her favorite local market, which was full of dancing music and beautiful crafts. "How do we attain things though?" she asked, puzzled remembering that money did not exist in this land.

"Either through gift or trade."

"What could I trade?"

"Anything . . . anything that you think is important. It could be something entertaining, a poem, a joke, a spell, or perhaps something useful—a crystal or a flower. The harder it is to find, the more valuable it is."

Lily thought about the contents inside her crochet satchel. Only a few items weren't from Sa Neo, and the others had quite strong sentimental value that she didn't want to give up. So she suggested picking some flowers along the way to which Silvia happily obliged.

They stopped upon the first meadow they encountered, full of brightly colored shades of pink tulips. Lily collected several flowers while Silvia patted the elephant. She could overhear Silvia's sweet voice singing to the creature while she was waiting. But Silvia stopped singing when Lily came closer.

"Silvia, don't stop singing, you have such a beautiful voice," Lily exclaimed while they piled back onto the elephant.

Silvia turned away coyly, unsure of how to accept the compliment.

"Where is the song from? Did you learn it from the band at the castle?"

"I don't remember, I have just always known it."

"Perhaps your parents used to sing it to you when you were younger?" Lily tried again, but the wall between them was no closer to falling down, and Silvia shrugged her shoulders in response, unwilling to talk about her personal life.

They continued along the path of crumbled green tourmaline pebble stones as little monkeys sat in the branches watching the girls go by. Lily felt like she could talk to them. There was some kind of language that they were able to communicate together. She wasn't sure what it was, but for some reason she felt an understanding of mutual respect.

Lily kept trying to warm Silvia up to her, and finally, about half-way through their trip, Silvia opened up. It was evident that she loved to talk, and enjoyed telling Lily all about the land that they resided on. It wasn't until the pixie explained that she was never taught how to tedimeta, that Lily realized how lucky she was to have traveled already to two different lands, and have the warmth of love opened up to her by both Jacques and Karisma. Lily wanted to teach Silvia how to tedimeta, and introduce her to Karisma. *But is it my place to change someone's life for them? And furthermore, did Silvia want to live differently?* Lily thought. Lily wanted to tell Silvia how to tedimeta, but something stopped her. She couldn't figure out why, but as Jacques had said, don't question it. If she is unsure about the decision, it is not the right time to make it.

"I heard that your initiation created sparkles in the sky up above, Miss Lily? I overheard the other sorcerers talk about it. They said it was truly a magical ceremony, like no other they had ever experienced. They like you better than Jade. They think you are more intelligent and have a bigger heart." Silvia confided in Lily timidly, and she tightened the reigns over the elephant to distract her eyes to receive praise from her compliment.

"They said that?" Lily asked confused, not reading it as a compliment. "But our hearts are the same. I think we just differ in our thoughts. Perhaps Jade allows her thoughts to control her heart and not the other way around."

Lily didn't know where the words had even come from, but they reminded her of the conversation she had with Jacques before she left him last. And she thought of how strange it was that such ideas she originally did not understand were now embedded into her mind without her consent.

"Miss Lily, they wish for you to reign the land Tehar. Would you?" Silvia turned to Lily sternly and spoke her words as though she had an army of village folk behind her, just waiting for the answer to their prayers. And although Lily marveled in the idea of helping those in need, she, herself had her own problems to figure out. *Maybe when I love myself enough I will be able to help others,* she thought. But alas, she did not want to appear weak to her peers, and she pretended she was unable to rule for other reasons.

"I am honored for you to speak such words to me; but I fear I am too young to take on such serious matters, and I have my home to go back to. I cannot leave my father."

"I understand," Silvia replied, staring to her hands to avoid eye contact. "I wish I had a family," she continued solemnly.

"Oh but you do! Your friendship with the other pixies, can't they be your family? And what about the animals in the forest? They need someone to talk to, to show love to. The land can be your family, no?"

Lily allowed her arms to float up gracefully as she spoke kind words in an attempt to cushion Silvia's pain of feeling so terribly alone. She pointed out the flora and fauna that surrounded them both, the beautiful elephant upon which they sat, and the endless wonders that breezed through the sky, dazzling around them both just waiting to be recognized.

"You are so wise."

Lily chuckled at the irony. If only Silvia knew what kind of mental problems her world back home thought she had, and after awhile, she had believed them too. What was it about this land that made her think differently? She held no anxiety of tomorrow, or any regret of what had happened in the past. She just focused on the moment they were sharing right now, and trying to make the most of whatever came her way. And as of right now, she was sitting on an elephant's back, next to a pixie fairy, traveling through a beautiful luscious forest, on her way to a wonderful market.

The elephant grooved slowly as the girls felt every part of its body sway into the ground and push back up. They waltzed over the mountaintop as the heat from the sun burned warmth to their heads. As they rode up higher, the trees spaced out, until at the very top point of the hill, all they could see was the valley below, and down along a thin pathway, far up ahead, Lily could see a magical circle full of market stalls, performers, colored smoke, and animals all around.

The marketplace was a great field of short green grass and shady trees upon which each little market stall was set up. The smell of freshly baked goodies and sweet perfumed oils wafted through the air, tickling the girls' noses, and an abundance of giggling laughter from children playing, and music singing, calmed the girls' ears.

The market had a relaxed feeling to it. No one was yelling or pushing products on to passersby; they all were enjoying each other's company, chatting openly if one so wished to communicate.

Lily was drawn to a stall owned by an old lady that displayed a beautiful collection of antique silver jewelry. Buried in amongst the riches was a small cedar wooden cubed box which had a fractal pattern drawn in a black ink pen. When Lily opened up the lid of the box, it was not empty or hollow, but pulled out like an accordion with a long piece of paper attached from one end to the other. The pages were blank.

"Ah my dear little sweet pea. For you to have chosen this treasure of humble wood amongst all the jewels and riches on my table, I believe it belonged to you all along,"

the old lady cooed as she shuffled closer to Lily and Silvia. She smelled of nut butter and orange marmalade sandwiches. Her hair was a rich dark green, combed back to a low ponytail, parted in the middle. She wore large hoop earrings, and a scarf tied around her neck.

"What is this?" Lily asked inquisitively as she folded the accordion paper into the cube box once more and handed it to the old lady. The gypsy promptly rubbed the edge of the wood with her wrinkly hand and then returned it to Lily.

"It is the magic scroll of spells," she spoke again with her gentle voice. "Whisper into the box any question upon which you wish to seek, and allow the truth to unravel. But dearest beware, anything you so desire to create, destroy, or manipulate will be yours."

Lily felt slightly nervous and deemed unworthy to be gifted such a potent tool upon the land. She had already seen the strength that others around her possessed, and she too was growing great and powerful as well.

"Why did you give me this incredible gift without anything in exchange?" Lily asked surprised.

The old lady stepped closer to the girls, as though letting them in on a secret. She crouched down slightly, using her warm hand to lift Lily's chin.

"It's because of your eyes that I trust you," she spoke, her voice calm and soothing. "You are not one of us."

Lily knew she was safe yet she felt uneasy and she jolted in her body quickly. Her uniqueness was apparent, although she had spent several nights in Sa Neo. She knew the movements, wore the clothes; she thought she blended in, but it was her eyes that gave her away.

"I did not mean to startle you, sweet pea. I intended no harm. Your eyes are pure. They compel kindness and see the truth. You will not let evil play in front of you, for your eyes are strong. They know the way of life." The old lady spoke as her hands cupped Lily's cheeks. "I want to help you, in any way I can," she continued.

Lily felt her face mold so casually in between the old lady's hands, she didn't want to move. The warmth from her touch and the wrinkly skin cushioned her so comfortably. Lily could feel the old lady searching her eyes for answers, and they stared at one another for several seconds.

"Thank you so much for your gift, but I too wish to give you something in return, in exchange for not only this item, but for your kind words," Lily replied as she softly took the old ladies hands off her cheeks.

"Okay, well perhaps we can exchange another day, I will come and visit you. Where are you staying?"

"I am staying with Queen Jade, in her castle."

The old lady tried to hide her shock but Lily could see it. Lily also felt the lady could have perhaps regretted gifting her the item, but then she remembered that all was as it should be. Lily understood perfectly well the response that was implied, and she tried her best to speak partially to define her intentions.

"I traveled from the land of Otor, and have come to Tehar for initiation. I am still learning, please understand that." Lily smiled as she handed over a small shell from her satchel to give in exchange for the scroll box. The old lady gasped at such a gift, and Lily did not realize the attention that the small shell would have garnered.

"Where did this come from?" the lady asked, turning the beautiful shell over and over again in the palm of her hand.

"Yes, Lily, where did this come from?" Silvia piped in, moving closer to the merchant seller to have a look at the treasure from the ocean.

Lily wanted to confess all and share her knowledge of the oceanic beauty with the people of the land. To tell them about the poetry she had felt when she was floating in the ocean. How the visions of the light from the fish beneath the sea are so obscurely designed that they manage to satisfy the sense of sight with just one flash. But something stopped her, and she had to listen to herself.

"I brought it with me from where I was born, far away from here." Lily spoke truthfully, and thought back to the days when she collected such lovely seashells on the golden sandy beaches back home.

"I had only seen this in my dreams, I did not know it was true!" the old lady exclaimed, staring wondrously at the shell in her hand.

"I think everything in our dreams can be true. Perhaps I was destined to give this to you, so that you believe in it too," Lily said lovingly, understanding just how powerful her words were.

"I am so grateful that you crossed my path sweet pea," the elderly lady replied as the wrinkles on her skin curved upwards with a smile.

"And, I, you."

Lily thanked the stall seller and moved along. She held the small cube in her hand and looked at it again. She whispered quietly, *show me what I need to know.* She pulled open the lid of the box once more and looked at the pages inside. This time, they had writing. Two words: "Mia Veol."

From just those two words, Lily felt strange. There was an unusual sense of relaxation of having being told direction. She knew immediately that holding that box was exactly what she was meant to do, and although she was looking for something for the chef, she was unable to let this box go, and she believed it was a gift for her to keep. She told Silvia she wanted to keep looking.

"Miss Lily, what did the box say?" Silvia asked impatiently, having overseen her whisper quietly.

"Mia Veol."

Silvia's eyes twitched with discomfort. The two words made a strong impact on the pixie fairy, and Lily could tell that she was too scared to voice what it had meant.

"Tell me Silvia, I know you know something."

Silvia looked to the side, down to the ground where the grass had grown in sparse patches. She crouched down, and picked up the small green pebbles, sifting them through her fingers, contemplating her next course of action.

"Silvia, it's okay. What you say to me I will hold as a secret." Lily held her hand up, showing her truce of secrecy.

"Mia Veol is the name of the caged butterfly," Silvia replied very seriously, unable to look Lily in the eyes.

"You mean, Mia is the girl who passed initiation and threatened Jade?"

The image of the beautiful butterfly inside the hollow tree was etched into Lily's mind, along with the sadness that the butterfly held, unable to be forgotten.

"Yes, Miss Lily. But you see, she was no threat, she was just herself." Silvia stood up hurriedly, eager to explain.

"So then how is it rumored that she failed?" Lily asked perplexed, although she remembered how quickly words from the tongue can change as they pass to each person.

"No one knows for certain. They say that when she passed initiation her whole body illuminated with a bright white light around it," Silvia confided, speaking very quietly, and looking over her shoulder to ensure no one was listening. "Her aura was so beautiful that Jade was severely jealous of such mystique. And although she did not want to destroy her beauty, in fear of karmic duties playing out, she decided to capture it for her own pleasure!"

Lily felt a knot in her stomach from hearing such hateful actions, and the thought of spending one more night under the control of a beast such as she, sent prickly splinter shivers all over her body.

"But, Silvia how did she get away with such an awful act? How was justice not served?" Lily replied angrily at the outcome, remembering the eyes of the sad butterfly trapped within the tree.

"Queen Jade is hated and feared throughout the land of Tehar, I think that could be justice enough," Silvia admitted solemnly. Lily could sense that although Silvia did not respect the queen, she still felt sad that someone could attract being hated by others.

"Now, Silvia, you are very wise."

Silvia smiled at Lily for the compliment.

"I think we should go and see Mia when we get back. It will be our secret, promise?" Lily asked, excited at the thought of helping the troubled butterfly.

"I promise."

The girls continued to walk amongst the marketplace, Lily walking first and Silvia pattering quickly behind. The wooden market stalls were displayed in a large sphere, making an outline inside the field where children and animals played inside. Silvia ushered Lily to a large table that had pocketfuls of different spices all over. A handsome bearded middle-aged looking man wearing a felt-tipped hat and shining yellow eyes greeted them.

"Well, hello there ladies! You have both traveled far to come here today I can tell." The gentleman picked up a scoop of sweet cinnamon spice and put it in a bag. "Now, I know that this is what you are looking for." The gentleman handed Lily the bag of cinnamon and smiled with wide-set teeth.

"It is?" asked Lily, surprised at his confidence.

"It is! This is a gift, correct? She likes to make sweets, am I wrong?" He winked his yellow eyes and smiled with freckled dimples.

"You are correct," Lily replied excitedly, although she wondered how the man was so in tune with her own desires.

"Then the voices are too," he said as he slapped on his knee and pointed up to the sky.

Lily chuckled to herself with the irony, nothing sounded crazy to her anymore.

"Thank you. May I give you this crystal in exchange?" Lily replied as she pulled out another obsidian crystal from her bag.

"Thank you, but you know what I would love?" his yellow eyes winked mischievously as he placed his hands together in a prayer. "A story!"

Lily wasn't sure what to tell the handsome young man. She didn't think she knew anything worth sharing.

"What kind of story?" Lily asked nervously. She wasn't good at public speaking, although telling it to a stranger didn't feel too scary.

"Any kind! Something that excites you or maybe it puzzles you?" He edged a bit closer, nodding with encouragement. "It can be anything at all. A poem, a joke?"

Think of a story . . . think of a story . . . But Lily couldn't think! She opened her mouth hoping for something relevant to come out.

"Here, smell some of my spices and see what story stirs up inside you," the kind-eyed man suggested, pointing to all the dusty sacks full of colored grains.

Lily was drawn to a yellow colored spice that reminded her of the merchant's eyes. She took a deep inhale of the mustard smell; it tickled her nose with slightly floral and musky accents. It took her back to an Indian restaurant she had eaten at the night before she moved into her new house with her father. And following her meal that night when she went to sleep, she had the most peculiar dream.

"What does it remind you of Miss Lily?" Silvia asked, standing next to the merchant and staring eagerly.

"It reminds me of my home, and the night before I arrived in Sa Neo, I had a very strange dream." Lily spoke her words carefully, unsure of the reaction that such a story would attract.

"Ah a dream! I am fascinated with dreams. It is the outside world speaking to us. Except that the outside world is our inner world and the voice is you repeating back into yourself."

Silvia looked at Lily, puzzled. And although Lily was just as confused with the words from the merchant, she pretended to understand just the same. The notion of herself interacting within herself reminded her of the ouroboros around her neck, but she wasn't sure why.

"Exactly! So, before I tell you, I will let you know, it was the night before we moved into our new house and I was worried that it was not the right choice. Father and I had quarreled in-depth and I was traumatized over the idea of not only moving to a new home but also going to a new school and meeting new people. I felt like my dream spoke to me about it."

The merchant and Silvia eagerly awaited the delivery of Lily's every word. It appeared she had chosen a good story, even though she, herself, did not realize it at the time.

"What happened next Miss Lily?" Silvia urged impatiently, tugging on the base of Lily's skirt.

"I had a vision of my life, but not of events or people, it was more of a feeling, and it came to me in the dream."

"Ahhh . . ." The old man sighed as he squinted his eyes in acknowledgement, almost grinning as though he too had shared the same vision.

"I was running home from school. But the road kept changing, and the streets grew fierce. Darkness overlapped my lane, and my vision was blurred, yet still I kept running," Lily began as she relived the dream vividly, remembering her longing to get home but unable to with so many obstacles falling in her way. "And although the path was not familiar, and I was utterly overwhelmed with such turmoil; still, I kept running. On and on I continued. Through roads that were flooded with rivers, and along laneways torn apart by rocks. I jumped and I flew and I . . . just . . . kept moving."

Lily drifted off into her dream once more. The running and searching to find her way home overtook her mind, and she wondered if it was a sign. Was she being warned about Sa Neo?

"Weren't you scared Miss Lily?" Silvia's timid voice brought her back to the moment, and she realized that she had left her audience half-fulfilled.

"Oddly, there was no fear inside of me, Silvia. I knew that I ought to be scared. I ought to have been worried that I would not make it home, but I was strangely calm."

"Why Miss Lily? What was it?" Silvia tugged the skirt again to gain her attention, for now a small crowd had gathered near to listen to Lily's story.

"I felt the presence of something higher above watching over me," Lily announced, gauging the reaction of the people as to whether she should divulge more. The crowd continued to look in awe, and so she continued. "Despite my lack of sight, and the road having been terribly impossible to walk, I still held faith that I would make it; knowing that no matter what troubled my way, that I would get to where I needed to go. And when I arrived to the rightful place, the troubled path before seemed just a distant memory, a necessity to have endured. And as I awoke, words filled my mind and they were laughing, saying, 'you know I am always looking after you'."

The spectators at the marketplace clapped their hands loudly, and the yellow-eyed man chuckled, throwing Silvia up high into the air as he laughed.

"Oh my, that was a fine story. I sincerely thank you."

"I, thank you," Lily replied, as she curtseyed, feeling her nerves kick in, ready to leave all the attention. "Now if you please excuse me, I think it is best we are on our way."

"You think or you know?" The merchant asked, raising his bushy eyebrows.

His playful manner reminded her of Jacques.

"I know," she replied, winking back at the jolly spice man.

The whole trip back Lily could not stop thinking about the trapped butterfly, and how it was only by chance that she was lucky enough to have not been caught as well. Her mind was swallowed with the desire of wanting to save her.

"Silvia, will you take me to the caged butterfly?"

"Yes, right away Miss Lily."

The girls got back on the giant elephant and swayed side to side up over the hill and back through the rainforest. As Lily reminisced on the day's events, she stared lovingly at the white flower painting on the elephant's trunk. Silvia noticed Lily's focus and informed her that the painting was a symbol to show that the elephant was sacred, to be used as a means of transportation across the lands, as opposed to roaming the fields. They were well looked after, with an abundance of food, and they could play with the other animals etc., but Lily could feel the pain of the elephant not having its own freedom and it made her sad. She knew Karisma would never have let that happen, and that it wasn't the pixie's fault, for she did not know any better. Lily felt slightly guilty that she was encouraging such behavior, and wanted to get off, and walk alongside it instead. But the fear of the forest bothered her, and she sat silently, battling the voices in her head.

"Silvia, do you think this animal is living a peaceful life in harmony?" Lily questioned the pixie girl, who looked back to her uncomfortably, and fixed up her already bloused sleeves to avoid the question.

"Silvia? Do you think he is at peace with his daily life?" She pestered again, twitching her head.

"I'm sorry, Miss Lily. But I do not know what you mean by the word peace?"

Lily tried to control her shock, realizing the impact of such a reaction would have on the pixie girl. She looked to the forest for strength and explained that she was figuring out the best way to describe the word.

"Peace means without conflict, without violence, confusion, hatred, or sadness. I guess the word is best described by what it is without."

Silvia looked curiously to Lily at the foreign concept.

"I did not know such an idea existed, that life without sadness was possible," Silvia admitted, half smiling, nervous that if she showed too much eagerness to experience such a life that it would result in her not receiving it.

"Anything can be possible Silvia. But maybe, because we describe what peace is by what it is not, perhaps for us to also know what happiness is, we need to know what it is not. And that is why it is necessary for us to endure such sadness."

Silvia looked straight ahead in the direction of the elephant, as she comprehended the depth of Lily's words. And even though Lily was providing the advice for her new friend, in that moment she felt a new appreciation of the hardship and depression that she had been suffering. There was a buzzing desire inside of Lily that wanted to help Silvia see the same change of heart.

"Silvia, tell me about your family. Where are they?"

Silvia shifted uneasily with the question, and she stroked the crackly skin of the elephant, pretending as though it needed her attention. Lily realized she needed to open up a bit first, in order to get Silvia's confidence.

"Silvia, I never knew my mother." It was the first time Lily could say the words without sadness in her heart. Slowly the idea had become just a fact of her life.

"You didn't?"

Lily shook her head.

"I didn't. I grew up feeling like no one would ever understand me, and it always pressured me to wonder, whether she would have."

Lily thought back to herself as a young child, wondering that question over and over again in the play yard of the school, after having been rejected by all of her peers.

"And now?"

"Now, I realize that as long as I understand me, that's all that really matters."

She answered with more confidence than she had ever had when speaking about herself. She realized in that moment it was she who defined her power to others, not the other way around. And as long as she could hold her head up high from her choices and decisions, that's all that really mattered.

The girls looked into the forest together in silence as the elephant continued to sway from side to side. They allowed the influences from their conversation to saturate their thoughts into utter stillness. After several more minutes of waltzing through the forest on the elephants back, Silvia began to hum softly once more.

"Silvia, where are you from? Were you born in Tehar?" Lily asked, hoping that the pixie's trust in her had now been established. "I believe I was born in Salor. Do you know it? It has a yellow citrine pebbled beach."

"You don't know for certain?"

"No, Miss Lily. I just have always had this citrine crystal since I can remember. And this is only found on the beach of Salor." Silvia held out her hand with an open palm and proudly displayed a yellow crystal upon which the sunlight glistened through. "I have a memory of flying to Tehar upon a dragonfly's back when I was very little, but I don't know if it was just a dream."

Lily looked into her crochet pouch and pulled out a similar yellow crystal, one that she had found in the house back home. The crystals were identical and must have had the same origin.

"Silvia, do you think about going home?"

"Every day," Silvia replied, as she halted the elephant near a pond, and jumped down, directing its trunk to reach the water.

"Why don't you?" Lily asked puzzled, wondering how it was possible that Silvia could desire to do something and yet not fulfill it.

"Because I don't know how to get there."

Lily jumped off the elephant too, and stood on the other side of the trunk, patting its nose and feeling the water sift up through, and then moving it to its mouth.

"Would you like me to teach you how to tedimeta?"

Silvia smiled, and then quickly covered her mouth, cautious not to display too much emotion.

"What is it like to tedimeta?" she asked, feeling the wrinkles of the elephant's skin, and patting its giant ears.

"It's incredible . . ." Lily sighed as she looked above to the sky, remembering the feeling of being so light.

How lucky to have been taught such a splendid gift, she thought.

"It does take dedication and practice to clear your mind, but once you can, you can do it effortlessly. And the visions of colors and shadows in evolving patterns overtake your thoughts. They fall into each other, stretching and curving around and around, colliding together as one. And you feel like you are floating in nothingness, a light flickering in complete darkness, and when you open your eyes . . . you have arrived."

Lily blushed as she thought about how happy tedimetaing made her. Aside from the reward of being able to teleport to any place in the world, the fact that she was able to clear her mind so profoundly, so effortlessly, showed how powerful she had become at controlling her own thoughts. And everything around her didn't seem to be such a problem. *There is nothing that cannot be solved,* she thought. Everything was wonderful, everything was amazing. All from simply clearing her mind and allowing the light to enter her thoughts.

The girls tied up the elephant by the watering pond, and sat on the ground together, holding hands and sharing the two crystals. As Lily sat and taught her new pixie friend, she realized how well she had understood the spell, better than she thought she did. It was in that moment of sitting on the floor that she felt herself. Her back stood upright even straighter, and her spine pulled in a little taller. She sat proudly. She realized that she was beginning to know herself from having confidence in the things that she was doing.

"Now, clear your mind, Silvia. Think of the land of Salor, and let's tedimeta there as one."

"Okay Miss Lily," Silvia agreed, holding back the bewilderment she secretly held on her face.

"Close your eyes." The girls did so at the same time and Lily continued to guide them together. "Take deep breaths and listen to your heart beat. Clear your mind." Lily could feel her own deep breaths escape from her lungs. With every inhale she took, she felt goodness in the air, and with every exhale, she released any anger or troubled fears that she had held. She relayed her thoughts to Silvia. "Surrender everything you have ever known to be true. It has nothing to do with this moment. Let it go. Let your mind float into the spaces of darkness, but do not fear. For the light that shines inside of you will triumph over anything that could ever possibly come your way."

A light inside of Lily's mind contrasted fiercely against the darkness, and she watched with grace, as an illuminated blue triangle turned into a diamond and then a star, and then strong geometric patterns moved like rippling waters in different directions. They created a frame-like spider web with miniature squares, expanding from the center and shooting past her line of vision. Lily felt that the vibrations were more intense when the girls held hands together, and she squeezed Silvia's hand as she opened her eyes. Together, the girls were sitting on the yellow pebble shores of Salor and smiled.

"We did it! We did it!" Silvia jumped up and down, opening her eyes wide with excitement.

The beach was covered in cobble yellow crystals, and the waves were large and rough. Several children were playing on the beach, and swimming in the waves. There was lots of laughter all around. Many small houses lined the edge of the beach.

Lily could sense that Silvia wanted to explore and find her family. And obviously, why wouldn't she? But they didn't know where to start, or what to ask.

"What do we do now?" Silvia asked eagerly, looking around to the miniature houses on the beach.

"How do you think we can identify your family?" Lily threw the question back onto Silvia, as she looked at the other pixies playing on the beach. There were so many people around.

"I don't actually know."

"You do know, Silvia. There must be something you remember?"

Lily supported her friend with strength in her words, remembering what Jacques had told her. She had the answer to every question she could ever ask.

"Nothing Miss Lily, I have no memory." Silvia put her tiny hand to her head, and scratched her forehead, messing up her fine pieces of silver hair.

"It's okay, it will come to you when the time is right. Let's just ask someone where to start, perhaps some clues will come forth," Lily suggested, looking around at some of the people playing nearby.

Directly behind and a little to the right of where the girls were sitting stood an old man who was painting a picture. He had a long beard and wore a slanted hat. Lily stood up and immediately walked over.

"Excuse me, Sir."

"Yes?" The old man stopped painting and smiled with small teeth that peeked out from his beard.

"We are looking for someone," Lily explained, and motioned for Silvia to come closer. "How could we find some family members of my friend here?"

"Ah my ladies, family members are best tracked down by the queen you see. She lives far into the Salor woods, up to the top-most point of the mountain. You can see it from over there." The old man wiped the tip of his brush into his white button up shirt as he directed the girls.

The mountain appeared as a tiny speckled dust, very far from where they were now.

"Oh thank you kind sir," Lily curtseyed as she replied. "Please do advise, how do we get there?"

"No problem! Call me Pat," he said, tipping the top of his hat lightly off in mutual respect. "Are you traveling by foot?" He squinted, crunching his teeth down as if suggesting that it was not a great idea.

"Yes, unfortunately. How long do you think it would take?"

"Ah, you would be lucky to make it by moonshine in all honesty. My sister has a zebra you could ride, but you would need to come another day, she is off in town at the moment."

"Thank you, you have been most kindly generous dear Pat." Silvia perked up, excitedly eager with her new options.

"No problem at all dear ladies. Tell me, what is your name, in case I meet some relatives of yours?"

"Silvia, my name is Silvia." She spoke excitedly, with a glimpse in her eye she could feel that she was on the right path.

"Alright Silvia! I will ask around, and come back again soon. Early morning next time!"

The girls thanked the kind old man with the straggly beard and turned back to where they were standing to figure out the next steps.

"What would you like to do?" Lily asked Silvia, encouraging her to make the decision, knowing that such a choice would be empowering for the little pixie.

"Miss Lily, if it takes a long time to get to her, if it's alright with you, I think perhaps it would be best to come another day. We should probably be getting back to Queen Jade before nightfall. If we were gone she would be in an awful temper, and I fear what she would do to the others asking for our whereabouts."

Silvia looked around scared as though Queen Jade had eyes watching over them. And she hurried back to where they originally sat.

"Okay Silvia, if you would like."

"But Miss Lily . . ." she asked, taking another yellow crystal from the beach and placing it in her pocket.

"Yes, Silvia?"

"I am so grateful you took the time to show me this is possible."

"Anything is possible Silvia," Lily said and smiled, taking Silvia's hand to sit on the pebble beach in preparation to tedimeta once more. "I want you to teach this gift to the others," she continued, as she pulled out the green crystal rock and sandwiched it in between the girl's hands. "Now, clear your mind, and focus on the gentle movement of your breath."

The girls arrived back in the land of Tehar with the sun still blaring high in the sky, and they sat on the swaying elephant once more, as though nothing had happened.

"How did it know to take us back here to this elephant?"

"I'm guessing because we believed we would. Once the thought is in place, it is created around you."

Lily listened to herself and heard the words of Jacques speak through again. She didn't really know where the voice had come from, but she spoke her truth just the same.

"Shall we go to Mia? You have such magical energy around you, Miss Lily. I want you to help her the way you have just helped me."

"Okay Silvia, okay," Lily replied, patting the pixie's legs and nodding. She was growing quite fond of Silvia. Lily was grateful that Jade was too busy to have spent the day with her, for it gave her a chance to get to know the pixie better. They stopped in the back of the garden, where the giant hollow tree grew. The butterfly fluttered intensely, her wings a silvery white with black shaded dots, and large orange streaks. The edges of her wings had little lines in a spaced-out pattern, alternating between thick and thin.

"Mia, we are here to help you," Lily whispered, careful that no one could overhear her voice.

The butterfly fairy fluttered her wings quickly and crouched her tiny feet on the branch of the tree trunk. Her face was so sweet, with a pointy little nose and dainty little lips. She smiled. No words.

Lily whispered to the wooden box, asking for the guidance of the spell at hand.

She pulled out the paper—

She is not trapped. The fear is in her mind.

Lily looked to Silvia confused, and then looked back to the butterfly fairy as she recited the words.

"You need to believe in yourself. You are your own prisoner."

But the butterfly fairy stared blankly and Lily wondered if her words were clear enough. She thought about the message, and relayed it to Silvia, explaining that perhaps this outlook on their life was similar to Jade's reign, and that it was through fear alone that she held her power.

Lily spoke the words again to Mia, hoping that her savior would come through for the whole land of Tehar.

"It is not real. You are not trapped here. You are doing this to yourself. It is up to you to fly away."

Lily wanted to reach in and pull the butterfly out. But she stopped herself.

"Why is it that you can't help her?" Silvia asked puzzled, poking her small head in closer to the tree to have a better look.

"Because it is her choice and her choice alone."

She whispered once more to the butterfly fairy before walking away. Perhaps there could be something special about repeating the words she thought.

"I am walking away now, but please. Listen to me. You are not trapped. You can fly. Fly out of here and fly to Otor, find Karisma— she will help you!"

Lily knew there was nothing more she could do. But in the hopes of inspiring the little butterfly fairy, she pulled out the feather that was inside her purse and placed it on the branch of the tree. And she pretended.

"With this feather, I set you free."

Lily turned around with Silvia to head back to the castle. She said goodbye to Mia, wishing her well but Lily did not look behind again.

When Lily and Silvia got back to the castle, they found Jade being pampered by six uniformed pixies all around her. She lay on a giant pillow under a large weeping willow tree to the side of the garden. One pixie was fanning Jade with a huge leaf. Another was standing, holding a tray full of cold colored juices, and a fruit platter. Another was icing a grainy clay facemask on Jade, covering her eyelids with sliced cucumbers. She had one doing her nails, one massaging her arm, and two at her feet. *The day's errands are particularly exhausting!* Lily thought sarcastically. And the feeling of not wanting to be a part of Jade's life was becoming increasingly evident from Lily's daily encounters. Jade's purpose in life seemed to be purely selfish. She used her power to belittle those around her, to make herself appear better than she was, and to gain knowledge and wealth of possessions to satisfy her own greed. Nothing was ever enough. Lily felt quite ready to go home; she was unsure of the choice but knew that she wasn't very happy living with Jade. She didn't feel she was able to enjoy her time to explore and do as she wished.

"I think I'm ready to go home, Queen Jade." Lily spoke quietly, careful not to disturb the beauty regime.

Jade sat up abruptly, and threw the cucumbers to the ground, upon which a pixie scurried quickly to pick them up. "But I was going to take you to see Violetta tomorrow, how about that?" Jade piped up. "We must be invited first you see and she does not know who you are."

Lily had heard so much about Violetta, and the idea of visiting her had grown in her mind to be something of an aspiration. But she reasoned with herself that her purpose in Sa Neo was to be initiated and she was. She was able to see the way of life in the royal affairs and it did not attract her in any which way.

"Thank you so much for the offer but I feel that it is time to go home, back to my father. I am so grateful . . ."

"Nonsense, you are not going anywhere," Jade interrupted, lying back down and continuing to be massaged, although her eyes still darted through the thick facemask. "This is where you belong; you have been initiated to be one of us. I have given you the finest food, the most luxurious bed, servants, the kingdom at your disposal, to do what you like. Now I'm going to take you to visit the other lands, you should be thanking me, not leaving now."

The idea of exploring the other lands was definitely tempting to Lily. *But at what expense? To be a puppet for Jade's entertainment?* Lily didn't really enjoy the conversation with Jade. She felt her to be quite dull, a little boring. There is only so much conversation about one person that she could take, especially when the dialogue was not balanced equally. Lily was never allowed to dine with anyone other than Jade, aside from the pixies who were made to stand by and watch uncomfortably in case anything was needed.

"I really think it is about time I get back to my father. Please know that I am so grateful to have been given the opportunity. I really hope you can understand." Lily started to take a few steps toward the door.

"Oh nonsense, nonsense, nonsense! You are coming with me you silly girl, you must, you must, you must. I will not take no for an answer."

Like a leech, she peeled herself up from the chair and slimed her way closer to Lily, her face now stiffening from the clay, allowing little room for facial movement. The sight of the queen was changing into such a creature that it frightened Lily, and she started to feel herself breathe quickly, as though a fit was about to come on. She slowed her heartbeat down, controlling her mind and she told herself to take some deep breaths.

"I ... I ... I don't want to. I need to leave, Your Majesty," she replied, calming herself completely.

"Where are you going to go? You don't know where you even came from?"

Jade snorted, unable to open her mouth from the dried clay mask on her face. And she turned her head to see what kind of reaction she got from those standing by listening. But the pixies looked away and smiled dumbly, not wanting to disrespect the queen but also held preference for Lily's happiness instead.

Lily felt squashed from being forced into a life that she did not want to live in. Having servants wasn't very fun when she couldn't do anything herself. *The juice tastes sweeter when you squeeze it yourself,* she thought. And within herself she felt strength brewing to overtake Queen Jade, and she heard the confidence from her inner voice telling her to leave. But at the same time, it told her to stay calm and that now was not the right time. She felt extremely conflicted.

"Look at me child. Remember who brought you here." Jade snidely slithered her words out, pointing to a crown that now appeared on her head, reminding Lily of her status and yet threatening Lily's security.

Lily nodded her head, terrified of being turned into the butterfly like Mia. And she curled her fingernails into the fabric of her skirt, reminding herself to take slow, deep breaths. *Inhale, exhale.*

"Here child, come and lie down next to me and let the dwarfs give you a massage."

Jade pointed to an empty space on her right and a massage table appeared before their eyes. A dark green toweling robe was folded neatly with a large flower on top. And two servant maids stood on either side, waiting for Lily.

"Your Majesty, I am quite exhausted, do you mind if I go for a swim and have a rest?"

Lily asked, not wanting to insult the queen, but she also didn't want to spend any more time with her.

"If you're exhausted Lily, a massage is the perfect remedy you silly girl."

Lily didn't like being called silly, especially in front of a crowd of peers, but to avoid further conflict, she did as she was told and changed into the toweling robe and laid on the table.

Crushed gardenia oil was smothered on her skin like butter, and the little pixies went to work, massaging her body in long soft strokes. *It certainly was a treat,* Lily thought. *Perhaps Jade did know best after all.*

After the massage Jade instructed Lily to take a bath and meet her in the dining hall for supper.

During Lily's bath, which overflowed with rose petals, she finally had a moment where she could be alone. Completely alone, with no other interruptions, no one waiting on her (that she could see), and no Jade. She pondered her situation. Was she really trapped to live in this kingdom forever? Did she have the power to leave of her own accord? Surely she could. She thought about Mia Veol, was it a coincidence that such events played out that day? That she told the butterfly the same story that she should be telling herself right now—*you are not trapped; it is all in your head.*

Lily dressed herself in a dark green gown, hand-picked by Jade, and walked to the dining hall to meet her for supper. The queen was already sitting down to a decadently set table, and was holding up a silver mirror, combing her thin pointy eyebrows down with her claw-like finger. Lily's arrival did not startle her, and she continued to look at herself, ignoring the arrival of her dinner companion.

Jade had a line of servants standing to her right, perched on guard, with their backs tall and hands behind, waiting to be spoken to. The room was full of people, but still, Lily could see past it. They did not want to be there. They were forced to be there. And for that reason, Lily could see Jade standing by herself, completely alone.

There was a dark sadness present inside of her, which was invisible to the naked eye.

"Ah, there you are! Welcome," Jade announced as Lily sat down. The movement in the room had disturbed Jade finally.

"What do you think of my new hairstyle? The fairies by the lake gave me golden dust from their wings to give it a bit of za-za-zoom! Looks marvelous am I right?" Jade proudly displayed her new hairstyle, which to Lily looked exactly the same—a tight French knot bun, but dusted with gold specks. Lily could feel the displeasure from the fairies at being forced to give the dust from their wings; but Lily decided she needed to change her attitude, and instead of being agitated, she decided to project love.

"Yes it looks lovely," she said. Something still tugged her inside to oppose, but she pushed back the voice.

"I told them we both want it done for tomorrow when I introduce you to Violetta. If we do this she will know you are royalty."

I'm not royalty. I'm just a normal girl, Lily thought and had to bite her tongue. She didn't care for the riches; surely Violetta would see past the fake exterior too. *How was it that Jade became queen?* Lily thought.

"How do you want your hair done?" Jade asked Lily, pushing for another compliment.

Lily knew she wanted her to say, *like yours.* Saying that small lie would make a huge difference, and mean something to her, but she couldn't bring herself to do it. She wanted to rebel against the expected.

"I don't really mind," Lily replied carelessly. "What's for dinner?" she asked as she sat down, changing the subject and reorganizing the layout of her plate and cutlery with perfect symmetry.

She could feel her words mimicking those of a spoiled child again, and her obsessive control for organization was seeping out in boredom. She knew she had been given everything, except the one thing that she truly needed, to be listened to. And Lily felt herself not wanting to be around Jade or even herself. The purpose of her life felt empty. There was nowhere to go and nothing to do.

"The chef made an enchanted garden for you, look. You have baby trees and sugar snap peas in sesame oil. Eat up."

The plate was arranged like a piece of artwork. The baby broccolini trees stood up straight in a hill of sweet potato mash, and the edges of the leaves were dusted with honey-kissed sesame seeds. The sugar snap peas were open pods, and the small peas nuzzled together soundly asleep. Lily picked at her food and played with it as though she were a toddler. Everything felt irritating to her now that her freedom had been restricted. And although she wanted to leave and felt like she could, there was still something that held her back. *What was it?* The idea of meeting Violetta, perhaps? *Was it really true?*

"What's wrong with you child? You're not eating?" Jade said as she stuffed a fluffy piece of bread in her mouth that was covered in colored sprinkles.

"Why is your meal not the same as mine?" Lily asked, just now realizing the difference.

"I can eat whatever I want, and I want this. You're too young, when you're older you can do as I do," she replied snidely, chewing the speckled bread with her mouth open. Lily watched with disgust as the sprinkles dusted all over the queen's cheeks. Lily didn't even care. She preferred the greens, and all the food she had been eating. It was a different kind of clarity in her mind that she had never felt before from eating such a clean diet. And she voiced her request once more.

"Queen Jade, I apologize. I just really miss my father."

"I know you do, Lily. But, I also know that you want to meet Violetta. Am I right or am I wrong?" She raised her thin eyebrows as she asked the question, knowing perfectly well what the answer would be.

"Yes that is true," Lily replied, popping a piece of baby broccolini into her mouth.

"And I am going to give you the opportunity to meet her

tomorrow. Now, do you want to meet her or don't you?" Jade smiled and continued with a patronizing voice while fluttering her long eyelashes.

"I do, it's just that . . ."

"It's just WHAT?" Jade raised her voice aggressively as she stood up and threw her cutlery on the ground. "Oh I am sick and tired of your spoiled nature." She threw her glass of juice against the wall. "My staff have worked extra hard to create dinner for YOU!" She screamed as she pushed the plate of food under Lily's nose. "And I am taking YOU to see the most powerful empress in all of Sa Neo, yet it is now evident that you do not deserve such a privilege. I don't know why I even bother. Now leave the table at once!"

The queen pointed to the door as her eyes snapped with a flaming red fire and a smoky haze of grey smoke circled around her head. The anger in her voice sent chills down Lily's back, and the hairs on her skin all pricked up at once. She could see the other staff jolt upright as well, and looked to Lily, terrified that she had awoken a beast who had been brewing inside quietly. Lily stood up immediately, holding her self-respect high and walked to the door.

"And just where do you think you are going?" Jade yelled across the twelve-seat table as Lily turned the handle of the door.

"I am leaving like you asked me to," she replied, opening the door wide.

"What are you talking about you strange girl? Come and sit down and finish your dinner," Jade demanded, sitting down herself and snapping her fingers, to which the table set itself back up, and both their plates were now full of food once more.

"But . . . you said . . ."

"I said nothing of the sort." Jade's eyes glistened with a vacant glare, and she picked up the rainbow freckled bread again and took a big bite. "Come here and eat your dinner like a good little girl. It's very rude to leave someone when they are eating. Didn't your mother teach you any manners?"

Jade laughed like a cackling fire. She had never asked Lily about her mother, so it was not her fault for not knowing, but still she hurt

Lily just the same. And instead of explaining what had happened to her mother shortly after she was born, she instead understood the lesson her father was trying to teach her with the gardener. She would never discriminate that which she did not understand again. A part of her wanted so badly to tell Jade to teach her a lesson, but she could hear Karisma in her ear telling her that you can't change someone unless they are willing to change. And Jade was far too set in her ways to learn something new. So Lily turned around and walked back to the table as though nothing had happened. She picked up a pea on her fork and put it into her mouth.

"See that wasn't so hard was it? Now, after supper go straight to bed and we will leave early in the morning."

Lily shuffled the food down quickly, wanting to spend as little time as possible with the queen. When her plate was clean, she claimed she was exhausted and very excited for Violetta in the morning, and she asked to kindly be dismissed for bedtime. Jade agreed, and Lily went on her way.

But she didn't go to bed, as she was far too eager to go see her friend, Crysanthe; she needed some clarity, some comfort and help. There were conflicting thoughts within her head and she was unsure which way to turn. So, past the crystal ball fountain she crept, until she reached the seaside. And she walked far to the right, far from the castle, where the trees hung low. She ensured she was camouflaged, but something did not feel right and she did not feel safe to call upon the mermaid. So she pulled out the yellow citrine crystal, held it tightly in her hand and closed her eyes to tedimeta once more.

She cleared her mind and concentrated hard. A center point came direct to her sight, a bursting circle with firework glitter in multiple colors that spiraled beaming rays toward her. They dove straight past her, from the darkness into the darkness. All around her light danced in patterns, transforming from a circle into a diamond and then a flower into a five-pointed star. The motion spread warmth over her entire body.

And when the sparkles settled, and the kaleidoscope of colors had calmed down, Lily opened her eyes to the land of Salor once more. It was late afternoon, and the sun was setting in a warm yellow sky. Giant puffy balls of white clouds painted the heavenly canvas like dollops of whipped cream. And they moved swiftly around, like ripples of the ocean when a stone is thrown in. The more she looked at it, the bigger it got. And the ocean ahead reflected the sunshine, with strong waves crashing to the yellow-pebbled shore with domination, determination, and force.

Lily sat on the edge of the cliff and immediately felt calm and content with her choice of tedimetaing to another land before calling upon Crysanthe. She had never felt more confident about making such a choice. And she had now realized that the idea of going home to Father was not quite right. She knew that she needed to meet Violetta before such a decision was to be executed. She cleared her mind, threw the seashell and rubbed her necklace. Focusing on her motive, she whispered, *Crysanthe, come to the shore of Salor.*

She breathed deep inhalations and exhalations to calm her mind and envisioned the telepathic cord between the two ignite lively with fire.

Crysanthe, come to the shore of Salor, she whispered the words once more.

The mermaid flicked her hair as she emerged from the water. And Lily stared in awe as her hair sprinkled musical droplets in the ocean around her. Under the moonlight, a glowing frame encased Crysanthe's entire body and it radiated strongly about a hand-width from her skin. The cloud was predominately white, and held specs of purple, sapphire, silver and gold. Lily felt an overwhelming sense of divinity amongst Crysanthe's presence of raw natural beauty. As Lily looked to her own arms she saw that she too was glowing in a similar way, not as bright nor as wide though.

"Why are you at this beach?" Crysanthe asked, staring to the citrine yellow-pebbled shores with wonder.

"In case someone was watching us."

Crysanthe shuddered and ducked her body down low beneath

the water, so only her chunky crystal crown and her violet eyes were above. The glow from her skin flickered softly under the water. She whispered quietly to Lily as she scanned the shores of Salor quickly. "Why would someone be watching us?"

"I felt like I was being watched in Tehar. Jade doesn't like me to be away for too long, she doesn't like being alone."

Crysanthe, realizing she was safe in Salor, pushed her body back up through the water and hovered closer to Lily. "She doesn't like to be alone?" The idea baffled Crysanthe terribly, implying that such a notion was unheard of in her culture.

"She told me I must have every meal with her. And she always has an army of servants around her at all times." Lily sulked as she told her friend about the turmoil of events.

"Do you think she fears the noise of her own mind?" Crysanthe asked curiously.

Lily relived the daunting memory of such a terror in her head. She knew all too well the feeling that Crysanthe was describing. She had often heard voices in her mind that confused her too, prompting a desire to surround herself with people in order to ignore the truth inside.

"Well there is always someone with her."

Lily had never really thought about how Jade was never alone and her conversation with Karisma about being alone now started to ring in her ear. She had once thought that being alone meant that you were unloved. How wrong Lily's idea of love was!

"Do you spend a lot of time alone Crysanthe? Even though you have Zavier?" Lily asked curiously, wondering if the idea was common in Neosa as well.

"I don't *have* Zavier, Lily. He doesn't belong to me. He can do as he pleases," Crysanthe explained in a matter of fact manner. "It is so important for us to be apart. We appreciate each other more, and it helps us to grow. And this kind of mind frame of adapting to change keeps life exciting."

The details of Crysanthe's advice soothed any confusion that Lily had about relationships with others and also with herself. Respecting one another's space sounded right. She didn't need to question it. It didn't sound selfish, or ill-natured. It was the simple truth.

"Crysanthe, I was debating the idea of going home earlier, but then Jade told me she would take me to meet Violetta, who is deemed the most powerful empress in all the lands. Am I wrong to want to stay longer, even though I don't like Jade? Just so I can meet this idol?" Lily confessed. It was the truth she had been battling in her own head. Her words kept arguing against one another, and she felt better to talk about it with her friend.

"Why don't you like Jade, do you think?" Crysanthe asked, handing the seashell back to Lily.

"We spend most of the time drinking tea and eating cake. But it grows a bit boring. She tells me that she is entertaining me and that I should be grateful, but between you and me, I feel like it's the other way around. Could she be lying to me?"

"Perhaps you just don't understand Jade? Try and look for the good in her, and see how it is that she can help you."

Crysanthe swam closer to shore and lay down next to where Lily was standing. She allowed her tail to be massaged by the crystal pebbles, and it flickered up and down in enjoyment.

"Well, I think honestly, the only thing that I am learning is what I don't like. Because I don't like living with Jade or being near her. I wish I could be a mermaid permanently. Isn't there an enchantment that could make me change forever?" Lily sat down near Crysanthe, just far enough for the water to touch her feet. She stared at them, wishing they would turn into a mermaid's tail.

"Oh but Lily, you are so special! You are able to experience both of our worlds, don't you see how lucky you are?"

Crysanthe pinched Lily's feet playfully, and giggled to herself.

"But I don't like the queens here. Well, I like Karisma, she's nice. But Jade is just so awful. She puts people down all the time and she thinks that she is superior. I would rather have one true friend like you, than a million fake followers."

"How is it that she is queen? And yet is so different from Karisma?"

Lily sighed and thought hard, placing the seashell inside her crochet pouch.

"I don't actually know," Lily continued, answering her own question. "For you see, the big difference between Karisma and Jade, is that Jade wants the finished product to gloat to others, whereas Karisma wants to know how it's done, and gets pleasure in understanding the process from start to finish. I guess at the end of the day, they both get the job done maybe?"

Crysanthe nodded in agreement, wriggling her tail down deeper into the water. The waves splashed over gleefully, and Crysanthe shook her shoulders as though feeling a tickling rush all the way up her body.

"What is it about Jade that makes you feel so uneasy?"

Lily couldn't figure out the answer, and she picked up a few crystals from the shore, throwing them into the water, watching the splash roar upwards from the ocean.

"I don't know why, but every now and again she says something or does something that doesn't feel right. And I feel fear, and I get scared." Lily could feel the distress creep into her thoughts, as though the memory reliving it was real, and was happening exactly to her. She shook her head. "I don't know if I am imaging things, but I don't think I should be feeling this way if we are meant to be living in a life of pure love? Why do you think I am drawn to her yet despise her ways? Is there something for me to learn from her? Is there a reason I am here? Is there a reason she is near me?"

Lily stood up discomforted, only now realizing how much her whole body was rejecting the idea of being with Jade. She held hatred for her, and just knowing that she felt that way about someone, worried Lily more than the idea of hatred itself.

"Zavier says that every encounter is here to teach us something. Even though you do not like certain qualities of Jade, you are still learning, right? You are taking in how you don't want to be, and that is just as important as learning what you do."

Crysanthe's words soothed Lily's thoughts, and reminded her of her own advice she handed Silvia, and again, the advice that Jacques had given her when she first arrived. It was necessary to experience the polarity of something, so that she could give the opposite the true credit that it deserved.

"You're right Crysanthe. I am so happy to have met you," Lily said as she sat back down and joined her friend.

"And, I you."

There was an unspoken message of mutual respect, and a light bounced between the two beings vibrating at an extremely high frequency. The gleaming light that glowed around both their bodies, shone brighter and farther than it ever had before.

"Lily, in these brief encounters that we have shared, I have seen you grow so intensely. I think meeting Violetta will be the grand end to your journey here. As much as I want you to stay, I know you will come back and visit."

It was just the encouragement that Lily needed to persevere through to the next day. Yes, she worried about Jade's actions, but there was nothing to harm her unless she let it, she told herself, reciting her friend's words. She knew she needed to see this through to the end, that there was something very alluring that was drawing her to Violetta.

"Crysanthe I will never forget you. I will always come back, I promise. And I will meet Violetta tomorrow. I owe this to the both of us!" Lily said as she waved goodbye to Crysanthe and watched her swim away.

Deep under the current she imagined her swimming. And the memories of the aqua marine life that she had experienced only for a short moment outplayed vividly once again in her mind. She remembered the feeling of floating weightlessly beneath the ocean, sliced between the layers of waves, of water and fish. She felt like she belonged. Amongst the mixed matter of unfamiliar landscapes, and the infinite space of the unknown, here she felt at peace. For she knew that anything could happen, she could become anyone at all. In the darkness there would always be a light to be discovered, and it would shine back up to her, spark through the air and illuminate the way when she least expected it.

CHAPTER NINE
THE CRYSTAL CROWN

Lily woke to the sound of shuffling feet outside her door. It sounded like a crowd of scratching chickens, so noisy along the hallway. Lily didn't allow herself too much time to be worried about the interruption; she was far too excited to meet Violetta. And she leapt from the bed with excitement. Lily opened her bedroom door to a nervously standing Silvia outside it. The pixie fairy was eagerly awaiting Lily's attendance, although she was looking away and fiddling with her finger anxiously, wondering how Lily would be with her.

"Good Morning Silvia!" Lily smiled excitedly as she rushed quickly to give the fairy a huge hug.

"Good Morning Miss Lily!" Silvia replied, embracing her back with equal enthusiasm. "How did you sleep?"

"Absolutely wonderfully! I am so excited to visit Violetta today, and I was thinking just now, that you should go to the land of Salor, because we would be gone for most of the day," Lily instructed as the two walked to the washbasin that was full of sweet-smelling lavender leaves.

"Well . . ." Silvia began, shifting her eyes to the ground.

"And I thought of something else!" Lily interrupted as she began to undress. "The song you always sing, that is going to be the ticket to finding your family! It must be!"

Lily had heard Silvia's song as she awoke that morning. It was as though her dream was telling her to remember it. And as she saw Silvia, she knew that it was so.

"Oh Miss Lily you are so smart, yes, I think you are right. Perhaps if I sing, they will know it is me!" Silvia delicately touched her throat, feeling great relief that she had carried forth an attribute from her past history.

"I don't think you should go by yourself, though. Is there anyone you trust to take you there?" Lily asked with authority, as she squeezed a washcloth of warm water over her skin.

"Umm, I haven't really thought about it before."

"Do you have any friends here?" Lily asked kindly, knowing the feeling all too well.

"I don't think anyone likes me," Silvia replied uneasily, handing Lily a small bottle of sweet-smelling oils.

"I'm sure they do, you just need to find something in common. Has anyone else ever said they are from Salor?" Lily tipped the bottle onto her hand and allowed little droplets of oil to seep into her skin.

"Well . . . Divinia who plays the ukulele guitar, she also thinks that she is from Salor, because her ukulele has the same citrine crystal on the tip of the instrument," Silvia explained, fastening the lid back on top of the oil and placing it on a shelf nearby.

"Does she not know her family either?"

"No, there aren't many of us without a family here, but those of us who don't, we keep to ourselves. Lily . . ."

"Yes Silvia?" Lily stopped what she was doing and put down the washcloth. She could tell that Silvia had something worrying her, and Lily wanted to soothe her, the same way that Lily was being soothed by lying in such a relaxing bath.

"What happens if I find my parents and they don't want me? Why did they leave me in the first place?"

Silvia sat on the tiled seat and rubbed her small hands over her eyes. She pushed the tears away, and composed herself, combing her silver hair back into a tight ponytail.

"Sometimes in order to love someone, you have to let them go.

They might need to go into the world on their own so that when the two of you meet again, you can become different to how you were before. Maybe your parents wanted you to experience more than one land and they were unable to give you that opportunity. And just think, had you never come here, we would not have met, and you would not have known the gift of tedimetaing. Now you will be able to explore both lands, and show others too."

Lily stood up from the bath and dried herself with the towel. A green dress with thin green beads was hanging on the door, but Lily looked to Silvia, discouraged.

"Silvia, I don't want to wear this dress to meet Violetta," Lily said as she rolled her eyes and knocked the fabric with her hand. She could feel the spoiled demeanor coming on again, but it was in protest, she rationalized in her mind.

"Miss Lily, I don't know how to tell you this, but I don't think you are seeing Violetta today," the pixie looked away shyly, and fiddled with her apron once more.

"Why?" Lily asked, frowning her eyebrows with anger. She tried hard not to be too mean to Silvia, knowing it wasn't her fault.

"Because I overheard Jade laugh about it in the mirror this morning as Thimble was doing her hair. She said she only told you that so that you would stay."

Lily felt like boiling water was overheating inside her throat, and steam was smoking out of her ears. She tugged on them roughly, scratching the sides of her ears as though they itched. She had been tricked!

"Well then I am definitely not wearing this dress!" Lily exclaimed as she stormed out of the bathroom. She went into her bedroom and picked up her garnet dress, threw her satchel over her shoulder and walked stubbornly to the dining hall to see if what Silvia had said was true. Silvia rushed after her.

"Oh please, Miss Lily, please don't say I said anything?" Silvia pleaded, looking frightened, terrified of having spread word of something that she was not meant to.

"It's okay Silvia, don't worry. I will not say anything. I will just say I am ready to meet Violetta."

Jade was lying in a large open lounge room, being fanned by a large banana tree leaf. She was facing the door, not the veranda, to look at the view. She wanted to see the people walk past and look at her. Another uniformed staff member was holding a tray of fruit, and the other held three coconuts, each with a different colored straw, although the pixie was sweating from the difficulty of holding such a weight.

Jade knocked the leaf out of her sight and stood up immediately upon Lily entering the space. She coughed loudly, hunched over and pointed her claw-like finger at Lily's outfit.

"Why are you wearing that dress?"

Lily looked down to her dress and held the fabric out to examine. She looked quite fitting she thought.

"Do I not have the freedom to wear as I please?" Lily stared Jade in the eyes, still holding the fabric of the dress out to display the deep ruby colors vividly.

"Not on my land, no. You must represent me, not Karisma." Jade picked a handful of green glittered dust from a small jar on a silver table and threw it onto Lily's dress. The dress immediately changed color to green, although it had dark splotches of red carved through.

"Much better."

Jade turned and laid back down on the lounge bed, and clicked her fingers to encourage the leaf to be waved faster, intensifying the strength of the wind. Lily, although disappointed, wanted to see Violetta, so she ignored the exterior of her outfit and continued on as though everything was fine.

"Now that I am dressed, shall we go?"

Jade didn't move. She didn't even look up to acknowledge Lily had spoken.

"Are we going to see Violetta? She asked for me today, right?" Lily asked, feeling the same form of panic kicking in as how she used to feel waiting to be picked for gym class, eager to be chosen to join the group with the best players. Unfortunately, she was always chosen last and she prepared her mind for a similar defeat.

"I don't know what you are talking about," Jade replied as she sat upright, "I have organized for Rusty in the village to paint your portrait today. We will hang it on the wall over there." She pointed to the wall nearest to her where a line of portraits already hung. They were filled with different images of Jade, looking odd, bored, and ugly. Lily shuddered at the thought of being placed next to such awkward images.

"But, I don't want my portrait painted, I want to meet Violetta."

Jade huffed a great moan and she picked a coconut off the tray, bowling it along the ground to where Lily stood, making her jump out of the way.

"You are so spoiled girl. What more do you want from me?" She picked up another coconut, and threw her arm back as she bowled again.

"Jade, you keep giving me things I do not ask for, and now I am spoiled?" Lily jumped in the air, dodging the second coconut.

"Well if you aren't asking to see Violetta, why should it matter if we go?" Jade replied haughtily, throwing the last coconut with more force this time. Lily jumped up high, missing the coconut by merely inches.

"Do you even know Violetta?" Lily challenged, seeing the anguish of the pixies' faces around her, anticipating the terror that she had just brought onto them.

The light in the room evaporated, and a thick haze of smoke began to seep from the corners of the ceiling, falling down onto Lily and the pixies. But it completely missed Jade, falling around her like a triangle-pointed pyramid. She hunched over, coughed lightly and breathed noisily.

"What did you just say to me? Say it again." She spoke slowly, allowing the pressure of each word to thud loudly on the ground around her. It rattled the ground, as though a giant was jumping up and down creating holes in the floorboards.

"I . . . I . . . I," Lily's voice began to shake and her ears started to itch. But instead of feeling scared, she felt anger pulsating through her veins. And it boiled up through her head, into her skull. She cleared her throat, stood with her back strong and stared at the witch. "I asked if you actually knew her."

Jade laughed with a gush of stale breath and a patronizing wheeze. "Look at this crown upon my head dear child. This is what I am; I am queen. And you, you are nothing."

Jade flicked her fingers in the air, sparking tiny specs of fireworks to protrude from her nails. She rolled her eyes and turned around, hobbling to sit back onto her throne. Lily didn't back down, and instead, she felt her ears burn, her body quiver with such hatred for the beast. She wanted to get even. She wanted to pay her back for all the times that she didn't voice her own opinions, for all the times that she pretended that she was fine. They had bottled up inside of her, they were simmering at the top, ready to boil over, and they were waiting, waiting and ready, ready to flood the house.

"I have seen a far more beautiful crown than that before," Lily laughed, and she turned her back on the sorceress to leave.

"What . . . did . . . you . . . say?"

Lily felt herself be twisted back around to face Jade. The floorboards below had their own circle, and it twirled upon Jade's command. The beast's eyes had rolled to the top of her head, the ink edge of the red pupil bled fiercely into the sclera, until it completely overtook the entire eyeball. Jade did not look like herself. She reminded Lily of Isabella, the fair maid who turned into a toad near Karisma's house, many moons ago.

Lily shuddered. She stood silently, with no response. The queen towered high above Lily, levitating closely, and her fingernails grew longer. She poked Lily, probing her to reply. "Tell me child, upon whom did you see this crown?"

Jade clawed her finger into a long line, as though extracting words from Lily's throat and she lifted her head in response.

"The Mermaid Queen." The words uttered through Lily's lips before she could even stop them. But the fire was already lit inside her belly, and it was smoking up through to her head.

"Nonsense, she is not real. Those stories are just myths," Jade said and waved Lily off, clicking her green claws in response. "Ugh, you are more stupid than I realized. Silly girl."

Jade turned back around to her lounge bed and attempted to sit down, but her hunched back was too uneven to allow her to sit comfortably, and she struggled for several seconds until she got in a seated position.

"Oh really? Well then how come she is my friend? And that I wear this?" Lily pulled down the collar of her dress and pushed the ouroboros to display in prime position for all to see, especially Jade. The crowd gasped and the chatter begun. Jade hushed everyone silent as she stood back up and stomped over to Lily.

"Hand that to me, NOW," Jade screamed loudly. Her eyes protruded closely to Lily, so close that Lily could only see herself inside the mess of blackness.

"No, it is mine!" Lily shrieked as she covered the necklace with one hand, and clenched her fist with the other.

"GIVE ME THAT NECKLACE!" Jade's voice shouted throughout the entire castle, as she screamed like a neglected baby. The walls of the room cracked from the vibration, as the ceiling above begun to shake.

"NO! It is mine!" Lily replied with equal anger, but her voice quivered as she screamed. And like the shark in the water smelling blood, smelling fear, Jade pointed to the necklace held tightly in Lily's hand, forcing it to burn against her skin. The pain made Lily weak, but she wasn't giving up that easily. And she remembered Karisma's lesson in the meadow. The sphere of protection—to ground oneself, so that none may harm.

Lily knew that she needed to clear her mind and envision the protective case. She imagined her body sinking deeply into the ground. She felt her own vibration withdraw from the outside, and the energy pulsate from within. At the tip of her head a violet light crown dribbled down over her stance, through her heart center and down into the ground. The lights from her fingertips crossed through the exterior. And as the light reached the floor, it magically shot out into a sphere, enveloping Lily into a cushioning tight bubble. She felt protected from such outside energies but it almost wasn't enough. She wanted to reflect back what it was that she was feeling. She wanted to use the power that Jade had pushed onto her; she wanted her to feel it too. And without understanding why or whether or not it was real, she imagined the sphere turn into a mirrored ball, reflecting back the outside light. The energy she was omitting radiated and bounced inwards while any outside energy bounced right off. She did not absorb anything.

"Fool!" Jade casually growled back and she twirled her finger around and around. Lily floated up from the ground, and as the finger was twirled, so was she. Although she did not feel as though the queen's power had affected her, she could see herself growing weary. Her eyes felt heavy as the spinning around had disoriented her.

"Rhe non thew," Jade said and flicked her fingers again, as a thick roped net appeared and now held Lily in place. She was trapped!

"Come through child, I will not harm you. I will not take your precious little necklace either," Jade hissed as she drew closely to Lily's face. "On the condition that you do me a little favor here."

Lily could see the pixies standing behind Jade in sheer shock as Jade perched her claws through the rope, pushing her weight down upon it. Lily ignored the queen and looked away hurriedly. She had stopped thinking about the sphere of protection and wondered where it was that she had gone wrong.

"I want you to call upon your mermaid friends. Do this, and I will release you. I will not give you long to think it over child." She turned and stormed off, her heavy green silk dress smashing forcefully on the ground as she thundered down the hallway. "You will be trapped until you obey me." She screeched through the hall as the words floated along behind her, written in smoke drifting through the air.

Lily was trapped, and at a loss about what to do. Her instinct was screaming to tedimeta out of the situation but she had doubt. Could she still tedimeta while under the magic net? Or would she give up the secrecy of her mermaid friends? Perhaps she could pretend they do not exist, say she was lying.

Lily lay in the roped net with an army of pixies staring around. Not one of the faces looked familiar. She couldn't see Silvia amongst that army, or was it that she didn't want to? She didn't want to believe that her friend was holding her against her will. But was she really being held against her will? Confusion kept tugging at her ears, she scratched them again, trying to satisfy the itch.

"Are you ready to do as I say?" Jade demanded as she quickly reappeared in front of her. But it wasn't that Jade appeared in front of Lily inside the room, but Lily had appeared in front of Jade, hanging from a tree on the beach of Tehar. The tourmaline stones looked dull beneath her feet, and behind, Lily could see a line of short pixies standing in front of the entrance of the castle, around the glass bowl fountain. Jade was standing in front of the parade, massaging the body of a slug between her fingers. She held it above her head. An eagle swooped down low and plucked it from her fingertips. Gobbling it up quickly, the bird landed on Jade's arm.

"Well?" She asked tediously.

"I was lying, Your Majesty, there are no mermaids." Lily looked at the bird as she replied, knowing her honesty may have been visible in her innocence.

"Oh really then," Jade jolted her arm as she pushed the eagle away, walking closer to Lily. "Well there is a penalty for lying here in our land. It is considered the most shameful thing that you can do. Did you not know?"

Jade twirled her finger once more, lifting Lily up in the net, high into the sky. She pushed the net over the water, into the sea, and in a swift movement the net unraveled, letting Lily's body drop deep into the ocean.

"Let's see if your mermaid friends will save you now." Jade laughed as she watched the child fall into the water like a pile of stones.

Lily would have screamed loudly if she could. And even though the motion of the net releasing her body and dropping down into the cold ocean played out in slow motion, there were no words left inside of her to scream. The shock of witnessing everything play out around her at a different frequency than before blocked any chance of noise. And the gradual process of everything moving so slowly made Lily question whether it was the correct pace that life had played out always, and somehow we just managed to see things in fast motion. Lily weighed down heavily, falling deep below the current, and the water above her piled up layer after layer. She used the last of her breath to whisper *Crysanthe* through the currents of the ocean in the hopes that she would be saved.

Crysanthe appeared within seconds, or was it minutes? Time and space were merely an illusion. And Lily was close to unconsciousness with the lack of oxygen in her lungs. Crysanthe stayed calm, slowly blowing life back into Lily's chest, and she carried her body back up above to the land of Tehar so that she could rest on the ground.

Jade was waiting unbeknownst to the beautiful princess mermaid. Crysanthe carried Lily to shore, rolling her onto the pebbles to a staring crowd. She knew what was going on, but her goal was to save her friend. And as she turned to dive back into the ocean, a sharp roped net hovered above and captured the delicate creature.

"Good!" Jade smiled, pointing to the net. "Bring her to me!"

Crysanthe squirmed in such a state that her fins bled against the carving of tight restraints on her skin. Lily's eyes spurted tears, as she felt Crysanthe's pain. Lily had betrayed her friend. *Why did I have to speak of their existence?* she thought. With so much anger toward herself, Lily felt a spiraling turmoil of confusion and hatred from her own actions, her regrets saturated her mind and she scolded herself for her own disobedience. Lily tried to make eye contact with the mermaid to show her remorse, but Crysanthe did not look, and instead, she began convulsing, coughing up water, making herself sick.

"Release her!" Lily cried. "You are hurting her!" she pleaded, standing at the edge of the water with tears streaming down her face.

"Release her did you say?" Jade laughed deeply, pretending as though she cared. "You shall be punished for your outburst against my orders!" The queen continued, as a heavy metal cage fell down from above onto Lily, trapping her from moving any further. "Take everything from her." Jade instructed, as she turned to walk back toward the castle. A pixie came and collected Lily's crochet satchel her mother had made and the necklace she had worn as Lily sat on the ground sobbing uncontrollably. Her greatly loved possessions taken from her, and her one true friend was hurt because of her actions. Lily's whole life felt meaningless. She looked to the pixies to find Silvia, but she was not there. Or was she? Lily preferred to blind herself in the hopes that Silvia would have been on her side.

She looked to the giant fountain on the field. She felt so helpless from afar. She looked to the ocean, and the image of Zavier flashed into her mind, as though he were floating above the water in front of her. The idea of contacting him seemed reasonable. Surely he would be worried as to where Crysanthe was. Lily thought about what Crysanthe had said. How we can communicate through our thoughts. She envisioned a line of electrical wires from her mind down into the sea, to find Zavier.

But before she could even request he come to Tehar, there he was. His long hair pulled back like a lion's mane and large muscles protruding with droplets of fresh salt water. Lily felt his anger with her before she had even spoken. And he stared at Lily cast beneath the cage like a wild animal, cut off from the rest of the world.

"Where is she?" he growled, eyes glaring.

"She has been captured by Queen Jade," Lily said timidly as she pointed to the fountain behind her.

Lily was waiting for Zavier to explode with rage, but instead she saw weakness in his eyes, the shared pain of feeling the hurt of his true love. He avoided Lily's eyes and looked away into the landscape, allowing only the skies to see his tears.

"Then I will offer myself in replacement for her," Zavier stated with poise as he turned back to face Lily, trying to get the attention of the pixies standing guard by the fountain.

"No! There must be another way," Lily pleaded, pushing her little arms between the wired cage. "I will use my power."

"To do what exactly?" he asked pompously. "And why haven't you done it already if you are so powerful?" He raised his silver eyebrows as he dove into the ocean, moving closer to the castle and ignoring Lily. He swam as close to shore as possible and jumped through the air like a dolphin, creating a commotion. Two giant sharks joined him in the dance of intimidation. Quite soon after, one of the pixies came to shore to examine and promptly produced a flute, playing several chords. He was communicating through sound. Jade appeared wearing the green cloak cape identical to the one she had worn the night of initiation. She was not fazed in the slightest, confidence outpouring with her every movement.

"Ah another one I see. I already have a fish for my fishbowl, I guess I could take another." She laughed, pointing to the crystal ball fountain behind her shoulders where Crysanthe was held against her will. She clicked her green fingernails as the net appeared once more. Zavier pulled out a sharp seashell and threw it directly to the net, slicing the mesh into two. He swam back slightly from the shore, keeping his distance, showing he was ready for war.

"Release her," he commanded bravely, although Lily could clearly see past his heroic demeanor. He was in agony seeing his beloved floating amongst the stench of warm algae water. She felt as though he too were experiencing the pain of Crysanthe. "Release her and take me instead," he concluded, lifting his hands in the air showing his surrender, while the two sharks behind crept up to the surface, standing guard.

"I give myself to you," Zavier said again as he took the chain and a large crystal rock off from around his neck and handed it to the pixies.

Jade grinned with a devilish smile, "Take him to the bowl and Crysanthe will be released."

"No, release Crysanthe first," Zavier growled back, the sharks behind him now growing in size.

"I am true to my word, what kind of queen do you take me for?" she snorted back with her eyes gleaming, red veins pulsating around her iris.

Lily felt the back of her neck tense up as a cold shiver sped down her spine. The stillness in the air spoke to Lily, telling her it was a trap, and she closed her eyes trying to communicate with Zavier. *Do not give in*, she thought as she imagined an electric cable shooting from the crown of her head to his. But he wouldn't listen. His head held high and proud, ready to sacrifice his life in exchange for his love. The net hung over his head, and weaved through the water, rippling down in miniature squares, and lifting back up, carrying the heavy weight of the King. He looked like a fish stuck in a fisherman's net, but this time, there was no struggle. He had accepted his fate.

Jade laughed as she took the jewelry from his hand.

"Ugh," Jade shrieked. "It's disgusting and slimy."

She threw the necklace carelessly in the face of the closest pixie. Zavier's eyes grew faint and the scales of his tail turned from a silvery purple to a dull grey from the lack of water.

Jade cackled with a deep evil laugh, which turned into a cough as her back hunched over even more. She pointed her green claw-like nails to release him into the pond to join the weltering Crysanthe who was barely moving.

Lily felt the despair once more as she watched her last resort move into the giant fountain bowl. She knew there was no agreement in place as such.

"Well it looks like I have two fish for my fountain now. Perhaps we should make a statue from them?" Jade spoke out loud to no one in particular and yet the pixies continued to follow her as she walked back up to the castle.

Lily sat on the ground kicking the green pebbles with her feet as she contemplated her next move. There was nothing calling out to her. She felt so hopeless, trapped inside the cage, as she stared from afar at the giant crystal fountain in front of the castle. Zavier held Crysanthe tightly, although she seemed less alive than he was. Their tails were twirled into each other, with no room for space in between.

An image of Silvia flashed into Lily's mind and she wondered whether she could contact her through the same technique of the mermaids. She imagined an electrical wire from her head into the pixie fairy. But the stress of the situation and the people around her confused her greatly and she saw the wire continue to be chopped off. It wasn't working! Distressed, she looked to the bowl and thought about Crysanthe.

"I am so sorry," she whispered into the wind. "Please forgive me."

Lily looked to the ocean, where the mermaids lived. She thought to contact Indigo. Maybe they could bring more force, or maybe he would just get trapped too. She begged once more for forgiveness. "I am so sorry. Please forgive me."

"It's okay, Lily." She felt a deep noise vibrate through. "It is not your fault. We have chosen this fate." Lily heard the male voice strum in her ears. She wondered whether it was the tide crushing the pebbles at shore, or whether she actually heard Zavier.

"What can I do?" Lily thought again, remembering the beautiful world of Neosa underneath the water.

"We do need your help," Zavier spoke again, more distant, more faintly. "This is a slow death. Please find some poison and make this pain disappear."

Lily shook her head with despair.

"No, I don't want to. There is still hope!" Lily pleaded.

"Lily, think of the ouroboros. It is our time. Help move us along quickly," she heard again, but this time distorted, making Lily question whether she had imagined the whole conversation to help herself feel better. She imagined Silvia once more, and looked back to the ocean, praying for help from above.

"Miss Lily," came a whisper through the trees. "I came as quickly as I could." The little pixie fairy shuffled her feet as close as possible without intruding in visible sight, and she threw the crochet bag from a distance to reach Lily.

"Silvia, I was wondering where you were!" Lily exclaimed, relieved as she saw her friend.

"I did not forget your kindness Miss Lily. I just needed to make sure all was not lost," she said and smiled. "It will be okay. Use the power from the crystals!"

And with that, she was gone. Lily opened up her pouch. All was intact, even her necklace had no scratch on it. She fastened the ouroboros around her neck, and pulled out the first crystal she could feel. It was a purple amethyst.

Lily didn't allow herself to think much longer and she closed her eyes. Gripping the stone tightly, she imagined the color purple and thought of the land Neveah. She had very little time left to tedimeta to Violetta, but she would try. She focused hard, closing her eyes and clearing her mind. The wind around her body twirled in a tornado, faster and faster. She felt herself completely immerse into nothing.

CHAPTER TEN

VIOLETTA & THE LAND OF NEVEAH

When Lily opened her eyes to the land of Neveah, she felt an intense wave of energy calm her quickly. Swirls of sparkling stars moved all around her, as though she was floating in a stream of white light and purple streaked space. It was unlike anything she had ever seen or felt before and she automatically had ultimate faith in the universe. She trusted that all was happening as it was meant to, for the right reasons. It was the exact same feeling that she felt that day when she awoke from the dream. The fear inside of what was to come had disappeared. She almost forgot what it was that she was meant to be doing there. *What was my purpose to travel to this land?* she thought.

The ocean ahead rippled like a million snakes slithering, and they swirled out from the horizon, directly toward her. The currents traveled so quickly, running back and forth, but when she looked away, they didn't seem to be moving at all. On either edge of the water to the left and the right were giant snow mountains, well; it looked like snow. Lily turned her back to the ocean and stared at the wondrous landscape all around— white floors, walls, cliffs and mountainside. The trees were blanketed in white snow, white leaves, white flowers, white everything. Innocent and pure. The absence of color was strangely calming.

In one blink, a beautiful lady appeared. She was dressed in a tight covering of black wool, which reached over her toes, right to her fingers and up to her neck. The skin of the fabric was decorated with pale clear crystals, very thin and very subtle. She glided along the path moving closer to Lily. Her legs bicycled mechanically in a soft pitter-patter, looking almost detached from her body as her upper waist floated along in a smooth sailing line. Her hair was stark white with metallic purple streaks and her skin was a dark charcoal. She wore no crown upon her head, no jewelry on her body at all, except for tiny little crystals above her eyebrows and cheekbones, framing her violet eyes delicately. The color of her eyes reminded Lily of Crysanthe's, cold yet warm at the same time. They were inviting but studious, and she slowly looked Lily up and down. She did not smile. There was no emotion. She looked inquisitively at the child. It was at this moment that Lily realized that she had not been invited to enter this land. Is this a problem? *No*, she heard a voice say inside. And then the words, *I am Violetta,* spoke through to Lily's mind.

"Dear Empress Violetta, please forgive my intrusion," Lily curtseyed, hoping the gesture would forgive her impolite nature. But such actions did not faze the queen, and Violetta stared with the same exact expression, a calculating expression, one from which Lily felt her mind flutter with insecurity as she continued to explain.

"I seek your help, your advice and your expertise," Lily pleaded, looking down to the snow on the ground as she asked.

"It is not my place to get involved," Violetta responded with a therapeutic tone, and she smiled gently, beautiful white teeth contrasting her smooth calming skin. Her smile was not patronizing, but was offered in a loving way, in a way that Lily knew that she would not be swayed to change her mind but still she had to try.

"The ruler of Tehar, Jade, has . . ."

"I know."

"But . . ."

"I know." She opened her hand, showing her surrender as she continued. "It is not my place. Let the water level itself out naturally.

Let the rivers run until they are dry, let the raindrops fall from the clouds until they can fall no more. Let it be." Violetta shrugged her shoulders ever so gently, and as she breathed, her eyelids fluttered lightly in the wind, slowly coming to a close as she inhaled deeply. Completely lost in the moment, Lily felt as though she were merely a witness to the scene. And she felt unworthy. The unworthiness forced fear to interfere with her thoughts and she rejected such advice displeasingly.

"No!" She spoke assertively, disrupting the harmony between the two. "We must do something," she pleaded again. "How is it that Jade can do such evil in this land?"

Violetta did not react to the outcry, and she stared back at Lily peacefully, as though the words had not registered with her.

"It all happened because of me though?" Lily tried again. "It did not happen by chance, it happened because of me. I came into this world. I walked through these shores." Lily stressed the words and pointed to the ground where her footprints lay. "There must be something that I can do?" She continued, holding her palms out open to show her remorse. She wanted to be heard, and she wanted to be saved.

Violetta held patience, and took Lily's hands within her own. "Take some crystals from the beach and hold them tightly," Violetta instructed, as two crystals appeared within Lily's hands, cradled between hers and Violetta's. "Whisper the worries that you wish to be taken away from you. All of your fearful thoughts, speak them aloud until you can talk no more." Violetta lifted Lily's hands to her mouth. "And then, release them to the water." She threw the stones to the shore, shooting them like firing arrows into the horizon, exploding with fireworks as they landed. "Let the oceans carry your burdens for you, so that you may fly lighter than before. Let your wings soar fluidly in the sky, and watch them bang brightly. Watch them crash into the stars, so that the bustling lights of stardust that explodes may fall through the onyx night sky. And onto the tips of your eyelashes they will rest, so that you may see the world differently, so that you may see the world as it truly is, spectacular and perfect in all its glory."

The empress waved her hand above, allowing speckles of amethyst sand to fall down from the sky, as white birds flew overhead. The power Violetta possessed was like no other she had ever felt, nor did Lily know were even imaginable. Her beauty was exquisite, and the color of her skin was captivating, glowing against the white backdrop of the snowy mountains. She assumed the position of an almighty creator, knowing all to be known yet willing to release the information carefully, when the time was ripe. As Lily looked into the violet eyes of the empress, there was a lightning explosion as she connected as one, and the rest of the world around her just melted. The compass of beauty and of love together bound, felt so familiar, so profound, that it felt like a reflection of herself. She felt such warmth and calmness and familiarity, all in one look. All in one movement, one moment, one touch, without touching. *How is it so?*

The space around twisted suddenly, and Lily felt exhausted, light-headed, and ready to faint. She couldn't recall the last time that anything made sense to her, and she just wanted out. Wanted to run away and never look back. Wanted to forget about Jade and Crysanthe and Zavier and Violetta. *Why did she have to care so much about someone who may or may not be caring about her?* She knew thinking that way wasn't true to her intentions and she looked down disheartened. The serpent's eyes on her mermaid necklace shone brightly, reflecting a new color, a light violet. It appeared to be different than she remembered. Nothing felt familiar. The symbol of life that she held close looked completely different now; it was different again and different still. The serpent was eating itself, hurting itself, consuming itself and loving itself. All in one.

She looked to Violetta and saw the circles of her violet pupil eyes turn into flowers, and then into diamonds and then to stars. She was traveling very quickly and for a single moment she felt peace. She had fainted.

When Lily came to she was lying on a large circle bed that felt like soft billowing clouds of cotton wool, but looked transparent liked a clear-threaded nest. A thin praying mantis-looking lady was standing above, holding a cool washcloth on Lily's forehead. She handed Lily a glass of water and smiled lovingly, speaking no words.

After awhile of drifting in and out of consciousness, the praying mantis lady helped Lily stand, holding her hands in between each of hers. She lifted Lily's arms open and moved forward to hug Lily tightly, the same way that Jacques had taught Lily earlier. A tight closure of one heart crossing against the other heart. And she breathed deeply, encouraging Lily to do the same. Lily heard no words, but a voice spoke inside of Lily's heart, and it said . . . *I love you, I love you, I love you.* After three deep breaths and three loving chants, the lady disappeared. Lily stood, in absolute white light, completely alone. The emptiness of nothingness suffocated her mind with no room for thoughts and she felt completely weightless, a re-energized kind of floating. And then, Violetta appeared, standing tall with graceful white hair, and piercing white eyes.

"I'm sorry for . . ." But Lily's mind drifted off to the right, and she couldn't find the words she was searching for. Silence demanded the space, and Lily surrendered willingly, as the two just stared at each other.

"Never apologize for something beyond your control," Violetta ushered the words through therapeutically.

Their conversation from before had come back to Lily. Her memory did not fail. The desires to control and help began to creep inside her thoughts once more, and she felt herself speak with distress, re-energized from her fall.

"Violetta . . . I don't understand. If I have the power to change what I like, why can't I control this?"

Violetta pursed her lips faintly, and in slow motion she opened her right palm and pointed to it with her left finger. A sphere of clear glass appeared.

"Try and stop this ball from breaking," she said as she threw the sphere of glass up high. The ball fell down quickly, smashing onto a freshly formulated floor into thousands of tiny pieces, showering the room with a waterfall of glass droplets. It moved in slow motion, and Violetta continued to repeat the process.

"Try and stop this ball from breaking," she said again. Each time, the ball was fresh in her hand, and the splinters of glass were not on the floor. Each time, it happened slower than before. The floor would form into a flat surface of white concrete cement. And the ball itself looked as though it grew heavy with weight, pushing itself to fall over the edge due to Violetta unable to hold to it. The splinters of glass danced around, glistening brighter than a dark sky full of stars.

"Try and stop this ball from breaking."

The lessons Lily had learned with Karisma and Jacques sifted through in a directory sequence of flash cards. She knew she had to use her mind to think about it not breaking, and that she already had the power to do such a thing. She stared at the glass ball carefully. Violetta threw it up high up into the air as expected. Lily forced every thought into her mind to stop the ball breaking. She screamed for it to stop, commanding the object that it had to stay afloat. But alas, it continued to fall down and break, adding glitter to the empty space all around.

Lily looked at the sphere again, seeing the weight of the crystal, the perfectly outlined edge, and reflective nature of transparent glass. It glided through the air, gracefully making its way down to the ground and finally colliding with the concrete floor. The pieces of glass shattered quickly, and floated back up around the girls. The ball appeared in Violetta's hand, Lily stared at it until her eyes blurred. The edges of the ball blended into the backdrop of white, and she concentrated hard, clearing her mind so that she could not see the ball anymore.

Lily waited to hear the noise of the ball smashing below, but it did not. And the ball was no longer visibly moving; it hovered up above, a blurred empty space. Somehow there but not there at all. Lily moved her eyes to Violetta, ignoring the ball, yet she remembered that it was waiting to fall. She knew it would fall eventually, but for now, she had managed to stop it.

"It's not breaking," Lily whispered, hoping Violetta would acknowledge her achievement.

"Very good." Violetta returned Lily's smile with little enthusiasm. She brushed her purple streaked white hair with her fingertips, revealing an open hole where her ear would be. The sight tormented Lily, and she looked away, back to the sphere of crystal that was floating in the air.

Alas, when she turned back to look at the floating ball, it started to fall, once again, toward the ground. And the motion repeated itself as before, smashing into tiny thousands of pieces.

"I don't understand."

Violetta smiled. "You do."

Lily looked down at the smashed pieces of small broken glass disheartened, consumed in her own misery. She doubted herself. *Am I not powerful enough? Smart enough? Strong enough?*

"No Lily, that's not it."

"What is it then?"

"You are telling yourself that the glass will break, and so that glass is destined to break, regardless of anything that you do to it. You can pause it in time for awhile, but ultimately, what is meant to happen will happen, and there is nothing you can do about it."

Lily looked to the empty space of nothingness, staring at the miniature pieces of smashed crystal bouncing up and down, floating through the air.

"And before? When I did make it stop?"

The pieces of glass disappeared, and only Lily and Violetta were standing there in the empty space.

"Before, it did not exist." The crystal ball flashed as though it were real and then disappeared again. "You focused your attention elsewhere. It was no longer a part of your world."

Lily couldn't quite comprehend Violetta's advice, although somehow it seemed to make sense, she didn't want to believe it. Sadness chained her eyes to the ground, and she couldn't bear to look back up. She envisioned the failure of not being able to help her friend, and the responsibility for such a turn of events forced a pain in her chest, making it uncomfortable to breathe.

"What do I do now?" Lily asked, her eyes sewn to the ground, seeing the smashed particles reflect like sparkling seas of confetti, and she pushed her hand to her chest to ease her breath.

"Nothing," Violetta replied soothingly.

But the words could not be heard by Lily; and instead she felt herself immersed in warm water, a complete and comfortable sense of knowing. She shook it off quickly, remembering her friends in distress inside the water fountain.

"Violetta it is because of me that this happened," she pleaded once more, finally looking back up to meet her eyes.

"Think of the crystal ball," Violetta said as she pointed to the glowing stars that surrounded the two and continued. "The destiny of the sphere is to break; this is meant to happen."

The stars grew in depth as Lily stared at them. They danced with beauty, flickering lights amongst the empty space.

"There is nothing I can do?" Lily reached her hand up to touch one, it seemed so close. But her hand moved through it, as though it never existed.

"There is no outside force that you can unravel that will help you. You must deal with it from within." Violetta held her hand up upon her chest to show her truth, and a small beating fire ignited inside, growing with each breath.

Lily was still too overwhelmed with her emotions to comprehend and she pleaded, begging to bargain with the empress to change the world.

"Can you not change the outcome with thoughts alone?" Lily appealed with distress, recalling the lessons from Jacques and Karisma.

"Yes, but that concept it much more complex than you are allowing yourself to understand. And until you realize what that means, it will continue to happen until the message is transparent."

Lily stood and stared at the pieces of glass scattered on the floor. The longer she looked at it, the more they changed. The concrete floor began to disappear, and the glass had floated up around the two, spinning ever so slowly.

"And so the glass will always break?"

"In your world, yes."

"And in yours?"

"You and I do not see things the same," Violetta stated as she opened the palm of her hand, and the two watched in silence as the pieces of broken glass moved in a reverse motion to form the crystal ball once more. Lily felt herself grow frustrated under such riddles.

"So did the glass break or did it not?" she asked impatiently, placing one of her hands on her hips and the other out in front, as though she was ready to receive the information in a tangible state.

"Both," Violetta replied casually, folding her fingers around the glass ball and shrinking it in size until it was no longer visible.

"How can both have happened?" Lily asked, almost ready to dismiss the empress as being almighty powerful.

"In your world, the glass broke." She said, as the room filled up with glistening particles of glass once again. The floor turned into a hard shell of concrete and the edges of the room became defined inside a square. "But in my world," the room emptied back into empty white space as she continued, "it did not."

Lily looked around confused and felt her ears start to itch again. She tugged on them lightly, as she stared to the blank canvas. She knew that she was seeing the situation through the eyes of the empress.

"How can it be both here and there in the same moment?"

"You and I do not see things the same way," Violetta said as she held Lily's hands once more and stared into her eyes.

Lily blinked. The landscape of empty space changed once again, and the two were standing on the shores of Neveah. Rocks and spheres of amethyst crystals lined the shores of the white mountainside. The sky was a pale white, and only in the shadows was the edge of the mountain able to be seen.

"We do not see things the same?" Lily asked, staring at the marvelous landscape and wondering whether in fact Violetta was seeing the ocean, the pebbles, and the trees in the same light.

"No, we do not," she replied, not taking her eyes off Lily.

"And anyone else?" Lily looked around. There was no one else around them, nothing but pure landscape.

"In someone else's world, the glass sphere does not exist." And with those last words from Violetta, she disappeared into nothing. Lily was standing alone. Completely alone, on the shores of Neveah, with only the purple pebbles, and endless white mountains around her. She was so alone that Lily began to question herself as to whether Violetta even visited her in the first place, where did she come from? Or was she having a conversation with herself?

She stood on her own for several minutes trying to process what had happened. But she wanted her friend to help, she wanted to tell Crysanthe, and ask her what she thought. And then she remembered what had happened. For a brief moment, she had forgotten. *Would it be possible to forget about her forever? No.*

She looked to the ocean. There was something magical about this land; she knew that for certain. It was unlike any other beach that she had stepped on in Sa Neo. And the advice of Violetta, as profound as it was, was not completely clear to her. She wasn't ready to give up and she knew she needed to seek outside help once more. So, she closed her eyes and held her garnet crystal tightly between her hands. She felt herself float up into a patchwork pool of rainbow colors where she swam leisurely through. They continuously connected, molding one into the other. Slowly one color overtook them all and she felt herself float upwards. Pushing through her body, the mind drifting within an unlimited compass.

CHAPTER ELEVEN

THE CRYSTAL BALL FOUNTAIN

Lily opened her eyes wearily to the land of garnet, but the forestation that once lay so heavenly lush had now dried up. There was no visible abundance of green leaves or merry flowers, the land felt empty and frail with life. She hoped for Jacques and the pyramid to be there as she ran along the path. It only just dawned on her that if the pyramid and Jacques weren't there as she walked up, how would she ever get home? She didn't worry about that idea too much, though, as she had bigger problems on her mind. Were Crysanthe and Zavier still alive? Were they mad at her? The same questions rolled over and over in her mind as she bustled along the pathway ahead.

High up on the hill above she could see the tipping point of Jacques' pyramid. The sight of hope nuzzled quickly in her tummy like nourishing warm breastmilk, and she moved even faster toward the house. She walked hurriedly straight through the sphere door, disturbing Jacques in a peaceful meditative state.

"Oh Jacques!" Lily sobbed as she rushed into him, tears flowing uncontrollably. "I have thought of you all through my travels and now I have come to you, desperately seeking your help."

Jacques opened his eyes slowly, feeling the heavy distressed energy from Lily, stronger than the words that she spoke.

"Li-ly, calm yourself my dear. Here, here, don't cry," Jacques cooed, ushering Lily to sit down on a giant feathered pillow. "Tell me sweet Li-ly, whatever could be wrong?"

The distraught Lily sat down in the pyramid home that she first walked into, however so long ago. She felt immediately safe, undisturbed from the outside affairs. But the idea of abandoning her friends now was inconceivable; there was no turning back, she needed to keep moving forward.

"The mermaids . . . I . . . I . . . Oh Jacques . . ." Lily wailed. The truth of what she had done now shone through clearly in her mind.

"It's okay, my dear. Take a deep breath," Jacques said. He held Lily's hand up to his chest and inhaled deeply, allowing the soft drum of his heartbeat to calm her nerves. "Now my dear, let's start from the beginning."

He handed Lily a tissue made of soft spider web silk, and she patted it under her eyes delicately, letting the teardrops suckle to the web like morning dew.

"It exists. Everything that you think is possible exists!" she announced with exhaustion, allowing herself to rest immediately as though now she had passed on the baton.

Jacques' eyes widened with excitement and his fat lips pursed over his teeth as he opened his mouth wide.

"And the mermaids?" He asked, jumping up and down, clapping his hands gleefully while a series of miraculous myths he was told as a boy fluttered through his head.

Lily nodded with exhaustion, the flooding tears ceasing momentarily.

"I knew it! Oh this is so fantastic to finally know Lily! Thousands of years of speculation and I am the one to find out that they exist! Meeting you has meant more to me than my entire 587 years of living!"

Jacques wrapped his arms around Lily in a tight embrace, but hearing his praises just made her hate herself even more. She couldn't understand how life could be so cruel. How was it that she could have done such a horrid thing to her true friends? Everyone was living so peacefully and happily, so kind and lovingly, and yet she had to ruin it.

"But Jacques, I did wrong. I told Jade they exist, and she was furious." Lily explained between blubbering sobs, the turmoil of events that led her up to this point. She was expecting Jacques to turn away in horror but he made no such movement, and instead, he stood right next to her, holding her hand and listening to her speak with no interruptions.

"Why do I relive the story in my head when it does nothing but hurt me?" she asked as she continued to cry. Lily was unable to stop replaying the moment that she fought back to Jade, the moment that started it all.

"It is only a thought in your mind, do not give it power. Let it go. Let it go," he said. He patted her hand abruptly, as though he was knocking the thought right out of her body. Lily didn't budge and she thought back to Crysanthe and Zavier, trapped, helplessly because of her. And the request sang through to Lily, telling her to ask Jacques for a quick ending to their time in Sa Neo.

"Crysanthe and Zavier desire a potion that will make them die." Lily spoke the words automatically with no emotion, as though the words did not belong to her. And she watched unfazed as Jacques' face turned into shock at such a vulgar request.

"A potion to make them die?" He responded ensuring that he heard the words correctly. "I would not know how to create such a thing."

Although Lily didn't want to kill the mermaids, she had no other plan of how to proceed. She questioned her power against the sorcerer and now only wanted to please the mermaids. The mermaids' fearless nature of change had started to settle within Lily, and she was beginning to believe that death was a natural evolution of the soul. No longer did she feel the need to mourn her loss to disrupt her life, she had accepted her fate and was eager to allow life to flow. But alas, upon finding that the potion was unavailable she immediately wanted it more, her spoiled child streak shining through.

"But you have to!" she pleaded desperately. "I have no other choice! What else can I do?"

"You have the power within you," Jacques said and stroked Lily's forehead. Still holding her hand, he looked deep into her eyes, as though he too were looking for the answers inside her mind.

She twitched uncomfortably and mocked his response. "You sound like Violetta."

"She said that?" Jacques replied smiling with dumbfounded pleasure that he had echoed words of the master.

"She said that no outside force would do any good." Lily thought back to the discussion with Violetta, still trying to grasp if such a conversation actually existed. But the memory of what had been discussed was blurry in her mind. She could only remember the way that she felt around the empress—such a feeling of security and contentment.

"You are stronger than you think Lily. You are wiser, and smarter than you care to let on," Jacques nudged, helping her stand upright. "I believe in you."

Lily held Jacques' hands as she stood and used his vibrant energy to help her think. She closed her eyes to attempt a foreseeable outcome in her vision. But her mind was too cluttered with emotion, and her voice inside was flooded with tears.

"Be clear with your intentions," Jacques whispered.

She peeked at his eyes. They gleamed through as shining crescent moons, radiating hidden wisdom and excitement.

"You once said I was a gift to this world Jacques. Some gift! I am destroying everything that I touch."

Jacques squeezed Lily's hand tightly, and pulled her arm to focus.

"It's your world Lily, don't you see that yet? And *you* are the gift. Only when you see both love and conflict under the same umbrella will you be at peace. They equally demand your respect."

Lily rolled her eyes with dismay and tugged on her ouroboros necklace, tapping the pearl eyes with her fingertips. She found herself stroking the piece of jewelry around her neck quite regularly since she had been troubled. It seemed to exude some form of comfort from the repetition. He handed her some crystal stones, one for protection, one for intuition and the last one for courage. And then he told her that it was time for her to go.

"To go back home?" Lily asked, terrified that his response was to be yes.

And it was only now that she realized how fond she had grown of not just Crysanthe, but of the land too. She still felt there was more to learn, seek, and experience. She wanted Crysanthe and Zavier to get out so she could go back under water with them again, and dance to Neo.

"You can go home if you want to. You can do anything you like Lily. This world, this life here, it only exists if you choose for it to."

The definition of the room around Lily wobbled. The lines blurred as though her vision was fading and she squinted her eyes to keep the memory vibrant.

"But my friendship with Crysanthe, it's real isn't it?" she asked, looking concerned to a smiling Jacques, who was standing next to the sphere door.

"Come with me," Jacques said as he held Lily's hands tightly in his own and walked her to the edge of his house where it overlooked the seaside. It was the same point of view that they had spent on her first day when she had arrived, and he was pushing her to leave, to go explore. This time, there was no such push. She felt comfortable standing in the exact moment that she was standing. She held both his hands in her hands and looked into his eyes, feeling the depths of his essence oozing pure loving energy.

"If she dies, I don't know what will happen to me." She felt a burn in her chest, pressure from the outside collapsing on her lungs at the sheer thought of her best friend being taken away from her so quickly.

Jacques remained calm, staring at Lily with a straight face.

"You will continue living and that is all. Another change in your life will take a turn. But that's not for you to say whether it is bad or good. It is just change. It is inevitable." His eyes darted back and forth from left to right as he spoke calmly. "You can choose your attitude as to how it will affect you emotionally."

The knowledge, advice, and wisdom that he delivered in sharp sentences did not scare her. It was truth, bold and heartfelt. And she admired her fellow peer for speaking so honestly to her.

"If I left this world, what would happen to everyone though?" She asked cautiously, knowing the answer had the ability to destroy.

"If you did not see us?" Jacques asked, ensuring she wanted the answer he was ready to provide.

Lily nodded in response.

"And you walked away right now?" His eyes began to light up mischievously, as though he could see something from afar that provided him great pleasure.

"Yes." Lily's eyes pleaded with kindness. She knew the answer clearly, yet the glass was misty, she needed to wipe the dust off in order to see it properly.

Jacques looked back to Lily and ignored the outside path, his pupils zoomed completely into the back of her mind. He opened his mouth, hovering carefully before he spoke, ensuring she was listening to his every breath.

"Everything would be as it always was." Jacques turned to face the horizon, and Lily mirrored his actions. Together, they stood silently, both looking out from the top point of the hill, onto the valley below. The soft noises of wilderness surrounded the two. And as she looked to the green bushes of the treetops, of perfect leaves and flowers, they moved ever so gently. She could feel the energy of liveliness all around her moving constantly. *Everything would be as it always was,* she heard again in her ears. She breathed deeply, inhaling the air around, with its vibrant aroma of life massaging the senses of her nose. She closed her eyes, breathing in the moment of clarity. She looked to Jacques, but he was not there. The pyramid, once again, had disappeared, and in its place lay a beautiful garden full of flowers. Lily picked a flower and held it in her hand.

The outer petals of the flower curved inwards, and were spread out graciously. Touching each other close to the center and thinning out to the edge to a diamond-like point. The fingertips of the petals merged like stained water paints, a soft pink mixed with a deep magenta hue. And the second layer of petals pointed out like whimsical eyelashes, colored in a pretty indigo blue. standing soft and thin as if protecting the center point as their purpose. And the heart of the flower was the most unusual of them all, with bright yellow sticks holding a fluffy pollen globe on their head. The scent was intoxicatingly sweet, overpowering, and addictive. Lily smelled and stared at the flower, longing to dive right through the middle and disappear forever. She gently caressed the textured petals with the tips of her fingers. She was unable to look away, deep in thought; she continued to stare, allowing the beauty to take control of her mind.

"Do you realize the beauty of this flower that which you hold in your hand is created only in your mind?" Jacques appeared once more, standing by her side. "It is a reflection of your world. You are in love with your own reflection of the universe," he continued.

"How can I create this flower when I have never seen it before?" Lily asked.

"Because you are the creator, anything is possible."

"I created this flower?" Lily pulled off the petals and crumbled them in her hand, smelling the sweet perfume as it absorbed into the pores of her skin.

"You are continuously creating every second. There is endless potential inside of you."

"I'm not sure I quite understand." She held the flower to Jacques, allowing him to inhale the overpowering perfume as well. Instead, he looked to her palm. The love line bled fiercely. As though it had been carved by a razor blade only moments ago. "You understand more than you realize." He smiled, and pushed her along the path gently, waving goodbye.

She accepted his dismissal, and waved farewell. She held the flower in her hand and walked toward the ocean once more, she was no longer crying. Instead, the red slithers of light from the sky reflected directly into her eyes, and a streak of madness with anticipation of excitement trickled through her blood; and as a wolf hunts through the night in order to find prey, she too had the same thirst of hunger, this time, to see what else this world was going to show her. This time, she would welcome in the fear and turn it swiftly into love, for she knew that love killed all. It consumed hatred and fear, the way the light demolishes the dark, never to be seen again.

She was ready to face Jade, she had the strength to witness how this adventure was going to play out. She was willing to embrace the change. Lily sat cross-legged on the garnet pebble beach, and closed her eyes. Her mind cleared effortlessly, so quickly and steady that it made her wonder as to whether she really was consumed with such emotional turmoil from the events. *Am I numb to the pain?* she thought. *Or has my mind accepted the fact that I cannot change this?* She pondered the various possible outcomes and ultimately came to the same conclusion every time—to surrender. *It is beyond your control,* she heard a voice inside her head that sounded like Violetta. *Was she communicating from afar? Or has she been with me the whole time?* The question after question seemed to distort Lily more and more. She had to quickly take focus. Clearing her mind, she held the crystals from Tehar and tedimetaed herself back to Jade, holding the sphere of protection around her body.

Before she opened her eyes she was greeted with ghastly chills from the North, colder than before. In the short period that she had been gone, a strong shift in the weather had erupted. The trees looked barer, no flowers were in bloom, and any that were once alive and thriving were sad and droopy. She felt like the soil in the ground was dryer and the buzzing noise of animals, birds and insects that were once alive, were now silent. *How long have I been away?*

The beautiful palm trees that once lined Jade's castle in perfect symmetry were no longer there, and an empty shell of rubble, dried out twigs and rough pebbles were in its place. The giant crystal ball fountain was still intact, with Crysanthe and Zavier holding each other tightly, no movement at all. The water in the sphere looked contaminated, as pieces of algae and slime covered along the sides. Lily held her protective bubble around her body and cast the spell of invisibility to hide her movements.

She walked up to the sphere, and touched on the glass. The case of water felt warm in contrast to the cold land upon Lily's feet. She pressed her cheek up against the fountain and imagined the wire between her forehead and Crysanthe's. She would use her mind to communicate with the mermaids.

"Crysanthe, it is me, I am here."

The mermaids did not move in the slightest. There was no response, no movement. Nothing. Crysanthe's head had rested on Zavier's chest and their arms were embraced in a comforting grip.

"CRYSANTHE! ZAVIER! It is Lily, I am here with you!" she tried to yell louder.

No movement, nothing.

Lily felt herself begin to panic, and she tapped on the glass hurriedly, humming at the same time, trying to move vibrational frequencies from her body through the water inside the sphere. But there was no movement from the inside that she could see. And she rested her forehead on the glass, allowing tears to sweep down her cheeks. *Are you still alive?* she asked.

Don't you remember? We never die, we are just reborn into another life. She heard a voice inside her head, but it didn't sound like Crysanthe nor Zavier, and Lily wondered as to whether it was her own voice, telling herself a story she would like to hear. *Or was it the truth?*

Lily pressed her skin against the fountain that was being guarded by uniformed gnomes. Lily knew they could hear her but she didn't care. There was a sense of calmness still settling inside of her from the meetings with Jacques and Violetta. As she looked to the top most point of the crystal bowl, she had a strange feeling of familiarity. She had stared at that exact point of the bowl before, not only stared, she had a feeling of an entrapment, of a struggle. The vision at Karisma's! And immediately, the lightning sparked as a voice from above, she knew what to do.

Lily's hand floated up beside her, allowing her initiation ring to shine dominantly. The tiny compass in front of her eyes represented the magic that had manifested itself into her world without her knowledge. The way it fit so snugly around her skin that when she squinted her eyes, the edges blurred, exuding the illusion that perhaps it had been there for longer than she realized, perhaps right from the day she was born she held the power. And instead of knocking the silly ideas from her head, this time Lily listened, and agreed, and respected the notion. She rubbed the crystal on the surface and thought about what it was she needed to do. And a hopeful image of the crystal fountain shattered in her mind, and a waterfall came gushing through the field, carrying the mermaids back to their ocean.

Lily stood strong upon the ground. She envisioned her feet on the grass grow roots and tear deep beneath the soil below. Threading through the rocks and dirt, her roots grew, until she connected with the other lines from the plants around her, and the spider web below of a thick tangled net supported her vision. She whispered to the ground, through her feet, into the vines and asked for strength. And still the vines grew down, they created a caged lattice that held the fire inside the core of the world. And the warmth and light from the fire seeped up through the wires, like a fast moving electrical current, sizzling as it moved. The energy sparked through her body, pressing out through her ears, her eyes, and her nose with each breath. She was alive, charged with electrical vibrations, from the core of the world, with the joint energy from every frequency that was around.

And when she opened her eyes, the land of Tehar was completely different, the world of Sa Neo, unlike anything she had witnessed before. The crystal ball stood intact, but the inside of it swirled with dark matter. The mermaids were unable to be seen against the lighter grey backdrop. The white and black edges blurred together, molding into one. She couldn't see. All that she could see was a circle. A fuzzy lined circle. Nothing outside, nothing inside. She knew what it contained; it was the case that held the mermaids, the one she needed to break. It needed to be smashed, shattered, so that they could go on living.

She opened both palms of her hands wide to face the ball, slowly, allowing the fingers to bend, so that she could feel the energy of the ball take weight into her palms. And then, she spoke. "Sa Neo, tel eb mar o ekyu."

The words seeped from her lips effortlessly. She did not know what they meant but she knew they must have been right, for the vibration of sound moved beyond her control.

She repeated the words three times while she thought of the light that she held inside of her. The one that started from her heart, moved up through her head, and shot back down to the ground, into the web of chained roots below. And she watched as light pierced through the tips of her fingers. But instead of the light piercing through the center of the bowl, shattering the splinters of glass like the lesson from Violetta, it insulated the circumference, cushioning the sphere with a layer of glowing purity. But she did not hold enough force, and she could not smash the glass.

She sprawled open her fingers and imagined holding the ball in her hand. She could feel the entire sphere weigh heavy on her fingers, and the world that trapped the mermaids inside was waiting to be acknowledged. So much power was taken, so much responsibility was given. And for a flash moment, she thought about giving up. Her arms began to weaken, the weight was too much, and it crushed her bones to the ground. She could feel them want to surrender. Her mind preferred the attachment of failing. But she could hear Karisma in her ear, telling her to clear her mind and to focus. To not think. To just do. And slowly, very slowly, she raised her arm back up. And the reflection of the bowl lifting her hand was mirrored on the ground, a raw sound of ripping concrete as the crystal ball fountain levitated toward the sky. The base of the fountain crumbled loudly, resonating through the air as it broke free from the soil, which rested on the land of Tehar.

She lifted it high over her head, higher than the trees, up, up, and above. Her hands moved swiftly toward the ocean, motioning for the bowl to move over, and it did. And then with great relief, she let it go. The murky layers of swirling water inside the sphere began to subside, and the outline figures of Crysanthe and Zavier were once again to be seen. The giant crystal ball hovered over the water with Crysanthe and Zavier inside and Lily could foretell the future events. The ball would shatter into thousands of tiny pieces once it hit the rocky surface of the ocean floor, and the mermaids would swim back into the world of which they came from. But it did not touch the simmering bubbles of gallant waters beneath, and it stayed floating in the air, above Lily's head. She held her grip tightly to the ball once more, and with all her energy pushed it down to the ground. But it did not move, and instead, it reluctantly started to hover back toward Lily, toward the land. And in the shiny glass sphere of reflective windows, she could feel the horror once more.

Lily saw the claw-like fingers first before she saw Queen Jade. And they pointed to the bowl, a dark green smoke pushing through from her wrinkly hands. She was trying to take back the control and she was succeeding. The crystal sphere floated back toward the fountain, over the pebbles, and onto the dirt. The great sorcerer was too powerful against the young girl. And as hard as Lily tried, she had to let it go. But as she did, the sheer force of the two having pushed their energy together into one, forced the crystal ball to collapse.

In extreme slow motion the ball shattered into miniature pieces of finite glass, spreading far and wide over the entire field of dirt-ridden land, the pebbled beach, the forest and the ocean. Inside the sphere, the bodies crashed down too, and both Crysanthe and Zavier closed their eyes to commence their never-ending sleep. Queen Jade shrieked a high- pitched scream, swaying her head in disbelief of having been overridden by the foreign girl.

A scowling flood of tears poured from Lily's eyes as uncontrollable waves of sadness washed over her stance. She stood frozen, unable to move, barely able to breathe. The cold wind whipped her wet face, and it howled as it flew past her ears, a spinning turmoil of touch and sound. It was overbearing. But strangely, she began to like feeling the pain. It helped to deter her mind, and in the moment of feeling ever so lost, and so insignificant, she somehow felt more alive than she had ever felt before. Her eyes rolled heavy with madness, the spinning of glass around the sky disoriented her mind. And before she could focus her attention back to defeat the evil empress, a golden net floated above sweet Lily. The thick gold-plaited chain lifted high in the air and stretched out far and wide, directly above where she stood. And as the net fastened down to the ground, the sheer weight of gold crushed Lily's head. The powerful force knocked her down hastily, she could not hold herself up anymore and she collapsed.

Lily understood what was about to happen next, she had seen it before, in the vision. She knew how it could play out and for that reason; she felt no fear. She accepted the situation exactly as it was. For everything that it was and was yet to be. She did not refuse, did not object, and she released any ounce of energy that was in denial. And she closed her eyes and continued to breathe.

But instead of seeing the restraints around her body that existed in her reality, she imagined the energy of the lights bouncing below. Like the first day she walked under the house and the crystals all lit up, guiding the way. They were doing it again. And she saw herself as a buzzing glow of energetic light too. The light inside of her stretched out into an infinite space, and then it squashed back together, into a tiny miniature ball, smaller than anything she had ever seen before. She focused on another beam of light, as far away from herself as possible, and she thought of how a magnet can pull something from afar, she pushed herself there, with the hope to connect. And slowly, very slowly, she felt herself float closer to the light. And when she opened her eyes, she was no longer crushed on the ground beneath the net on the shores of Tehar, but she was standing next to Violetta, looking out onto the land of Neveah.

"Did I tedimeta?" Lily asked Violetta, as she looked down to her body, which had transported itself as well.

"You did not need to tedimeta," Violetta replied, staring straight ahead into the horizon at the white chalk-like cliffs.

"I did not?"

"You did not."

Lily looked to her body again. It was intact perfectly, only now she was wearing her nightgown she wore when she entered Sa Neo.

"How am I here?"

Lily looked to the white snow covered land that encompassed her surroundings. There was nothing to be seen for miles except the white mass of snow and faint contrast of smooth grey sky.

"You shifted dimensions. You changed your consciousness. It happens all the time."

The white-chalk horizon slowly faded, as though the wind was carrying it away from the girls. It continued to move further away, dispersing the edges into the cloudy sky. And it wasn't until the sky had turned into a thick, clouded mass that Lily realized that perhaps the sky wasn't moving at all, perhaps it was she that had moved.

"It happens all the time?" she looked up to the beautiful empress, asking the question, knowing perhaps Violetta would be able to explain more than just her question. But alas, once more, the familiar sense of calming noise blanketed Lily's mind like a warm watered bath. She felt relief, and a strong sense of already knowing the answer to every question rang clear inside her body.

"Yes. Give me your hand. I will show you the way."

Lily opened her right palm to allow Violetta to take hold of it. But instead, her left palm opened and a hand went into that one as well. And she was standing with identical marginal cutouts of herself, all holding hands in one great big row. From one side to the other, the line of Lilys continued, stretching out past the edges, continuing on for an infinity as far as she could see left, and as far as she could see right. And Violetta was standing in front of Lily, with her hands down by her side. Lily was holding hands with only herself.

The beautiful queen stood strong in front of Lily. Her purple eyes perfectly framed with her long thick black eyelashes. And Lily looked deep within her eyes, in calming silence, she allowed her mouth to open and the words to roll out although she did not know where they had rolled from.

"Am I still on the ground in Tehar?" Lily asked, knowing this kind of question was usually one to send the doctors to fill prescriptions. But she wasn't scared with Violetta, she knew any question that she carried would be brought to the surface with patience, and answered without laughter. And before she could start to feel the fear of thinking so foolishly, the powerful empress confirmed her thoughts to be true.

"Yes," she said, although no movement was visible. The noise was loud, and the sound of Violetta's soothing song of affirmation seemed to echo in the many cutout Lilys that lined up beside her. "Yes," she repeated. Knowing that Lily's mind was ticking to keep asking more questions.

Lily imagined herself still stuck on the land of Tehar, inside the golden net that weighed her down to the ground, crushing her bones, her mind, and her toes. And then she floated back above her own body that held so tightly the hands of the others.

"How can I be there and here as well?" She wondered, still not satisfied to accept all that there was, all that there is, and all that there ever will be.

Violetta moved her eyes around the white space, looking to each of the other Lilys who held her hand so tightly, and stared with awe at the sight of the beautiful queen.

"You are everywhere," she replied, the sentence echoing through the girls all around, reminding Lily of the truth that she already knew.

"And Crysanthe, is she dead?"

Violetta shook her head slowly, no emotion in her face and her soft purple eyes, calm.

"She is still swimming under the ocean."

The image of Crysanthe waving from afar flashed into Lily's mind. Her skin glistening from the water, a thick crown of crystals covering her head. She felt so real, and so radiantly alive that believing Violetta seemed easy.

"And you knew about the mermaids?"

"I know everything."

The chalk-like cliffs from afar moved closer, closing in on the two, and gradually eliminating the cut outs of Lily, one by one. But the distance between the horizon and the girls stayed intact. They continued to travel in a long drawn-out line, moving at a great distance and yet not moving at all.

"Come. It is time for you to go back to your father." Violetta held her hand out to Lily while both of them stood by themselves in an empty space of white nothingness.

"But, if I am everywhere, aren't I already there?"

The queen smirked with a satisfied look. "Yes. But you want to be present with him at this time. I know you miss him."

The memory of living with Father felt almost odd to her now. She was a completely different person than how she was before she had arrived in Sa Neo. But the love that she felt for her father burst through her thoughts. As though each cut out person that she had once held hands with was still visible, she could feel they all shared the same vibrational field. The overwhelming desire to visit her father engulfed her essence, and upon being told that was where she was meant to be, she agreed that it was so.

"Can I come back here?" she asked, looking around the room for recognition, searching for the land that she once knew. But it seemed distant now, as though she had already left Sa Neo.

"A part of you will never leave," Violetta replied, as she pointed to the ouroboros necklace on Lily's neck.

"The white will bring you back to Neveah. And the black pearl, to Neosa."

Lily bowed her head in gratitude. "Violetta?" she asked, wanting to voice the question inside that burned from the moment she ever laid eyes on the ouroboros. "Is the serpent really eating his own tail?"

The corners of Violetta's mouth stirred upwards lightly, as though she was going to smile proudly, and she titled her head with admiration for Lily's question, ready to answer.

"Lily, you are right, the truth behind this symbol is far greater than many think. The serpent really isn't eating its own tail." The image of the ouroboros appeared floating in the sky as Violetta spoke, the slithery skin etched in gold. "For you see, he does not know outside of his own being. So the tail that you and I see him eating is different in his reality. And it is his reality that only exists to him. There is no world outside of his tail, so his tail is not his tail. And yet his tail will continue to exist somewhere else." The serpent swirled, munching on its own tail, as though it had no idea the two were watching him. "Now, take a deep breath. And close your eyes."

CHAPTER TWELVE

MIA VEOL

"Lily, wake up." It was Father. He was combing the hair back from her face, lightly stroking her cheek. She opened her eyes slowly, adjusting to her surroundings.

"Oh Papa," she shrieked, hugging her father ever so tightly, as though for the first time in a very long time.

"My goodness that is a tight hug," he replied, smothering her equally in an embrace. He was just as she remembered, with the small wrinkles by his green eyes that curved as he smiled, and the short stubby beard around his face.

"Papa this house is absolutely incredible!" she said and smiled, sitting up quickly, excited to think about going back down and exploring once more. "I must show you under the house."

"We did it last night, remember?" he replied, handing her a glass of water to drink.

"We did?"

"Yes, you showed me last night. You screamed when you fell down and I found you."

"I did?" Lily looked to her father puzzled, and she rubbed the back of her head and felt a small bump.

"Yes darling. Now, come and get dressed. The owner of the

house is here; she wanted to have a look at it one last time. Did you have any questions for her?"

Father stood up and opened the window next to the bed, allowing a soft draft to breeze through. He picked a small flower from the bushes outside the windowsill and placed it on the nightstand next to Lily. She smiled with admiration of such a beautifully perfect gift.

"Look Papa, a lady beetle," Lily said as a tiny red beetle with black colored spots crawled out from underneath the petals.

"Yes darling. Remember your grandmother used to say that lady beetles are good luck." He smiled, letting the beetle crawl onto his hand so that Lily could get a better look.

"But Papa, are they really lucky?" she asked, putting her hand alongside her father's so that the beetle crawled onto it. "Or perhaps just thinking that way changes your day because your attitude is now different and you start looking for the good in things?"

She jumped up and carried the beetle over to the open window, letting it crawl back onto the hedges, releasing it into its natural habitat. And she searched sight of the gardener, smiled and waved happily, yelling out good morning.

Her father smirked with his hands in his pockets. "Who is this girl and what have you done with my Lily?" he asked, his eyebrows slightly raised.

Lily spun around excitedly. "Papa, last night something wonderful happened to me."

She skipped back to her bed, and smelled the sweet gardenia flower. The small white petals exuded such a strong scent of exotic perfume. She placed it back on the draw and began to make her bed.

"After you fell?" Father asked, taking hold of the duvet and pulling it into the corner.

"Yes, after I fell."

She nodded, fluffing the pillows one by one.

"What was it darling?" he asked surprised, sitting on the edge of her perfectly made bed.

She walked back over to the window and looked to the garden, holding the ouroboros necklace around her neck. She felt the edges of the tail and the crackles of the skin, and looked down to the eyes; the colors were exactly as they were meant to be.

"I was shown the universe," Lily said, as she kissed the snake's head and turned to face her father. "I was shown how we are meant to listen to ourselves, to our bodies, and our mind." She stopped, and rubbed the serpent's eyes over her lips, feeling the energy from the crystals ignite on her skin.

"Go on," Father said eagerly.

"I want to touch heaven every day," she said proudly, moving closer to her father. "I am in control of my own thoughts. It's up to me to think clearly. And I will seek happiness every day. I will, Papa. I want to breathe in only love forever."

Father looked to his little girl, not as his child, but as his equal. And with tears in his eyes he smiled.

"It sounds like you have had an epiphany," he replied, seeing the presence of untouched innocence that she held once as a newborn baby.

"I did. Papa, I don't want to go back to the doctors. Let me try and figure this out on my own?"

Father did not say anything. He wanted to believe her, he felt like he was going to believe her, but he was cautious.

"How can we do it, do you think?" he asked, slanting his chin down to the floor and lifting his ear toward her.

"By not thinking," she replied blankly.

Father didn't move and he kept his eyes fixated on his daughter's face.

"Explain it some more to me," he encouraged, combing her curl behind her ear.

"Well, my thoughts are not pure," she confessed, turning to look at herself in the mirrored doors on her wardrobe. "I listen as I tell myself that I am unworthy. It is not true. I know it is not true." She turned back to face her father. "And now, I can remove this hatred. When I close my eyes, I clear my mind, and I imagine vibrant white light pouring down into my body from the heavens above, and I can feel love inside of me. And it gushes out, so strongly, so magnificently powerful that it overflows rapidly. The light moves within me so fiercely that nothing else has room to exist. Except me and myself. It is my choice, Papa. Let me try Papa, oh please let me try." She leapt directly into his arms, and cuddled him tightly. "I hear Mama telling me it is right," she continued. "I feel it in my bones that it is right. Listen to your heart. What does it say?"

He patted her head as she nuzzled in, smelling her hair. "Okay Lily, I trust you. Let's try it out," he replied as he kissed her forehead. "Get dressed and come and meet me and Rosalyn in the lounge area, okay?"

Lily nodded as he walked out the door. She promptly dressed herself in a white loose summer dress with embroidered lavender flowers and joined the two in the living area. The old lady was sitting on the maroon velvet chairs. Father was already seated, and he stood up upon Lily's attendance.

"Lily, I'd like you to meet Rosalyn, she grew up in this house. In the exact room that you are in now."

Lily looked to the old lady who appeared to be in her late eighties. She was frail and wrinkly, and her skin was soft and cold. Her eyes were slightly closed, and were colored a very faint blue, the kind of color that a wispy white cloud amongst the clear blue sky would make.

"It's a pleasure to meet you, Rosalyn." Lily smiled and curtseyed while bowing her head, in the same manner that she did when she had first met the queen. She remembered that an immediate respectful nature when meeting someone for the first time was the best approach.

"What a delightful young lady you are," Rosalyn spoke softly, reaching her hand out to Lily so that she could join her on the sofa. "Tell me, do you like that room? It was mine when I was your age. I used to love looking out the window to the garden, staring at the beautiful flowers and the butterflies!" she exclaimed, her voice shaking as she did so.

"Me too. I saw the most beautiful butterfly there just the other day actually." Lily smiled. She wanted to say it was many days ago, but she knew that her father would think her strange. So she kept her real thoughts to herself, knowing the truth.

"You know Lily, I still remember the most beautiful butterfly I had ever seen that used to visit me in that room. It was a yellow butterfly with long green legs, pale pink wings with speckles of green. It used to tap against my window, almost as though it wanted to come in and swap places with me or something, yet it was right where it was meant to be,"

Rosalyn explained, her eyes wandering over to the window as she related her memory. The story reminded Lily of Mia Veol, and she hoped the butterfly would finally have realized, she was holding onto a false reality in her head.

Lily smiled, feeling a strange connection with the older lady. "Rosalyn, I have a question perhaps you could help me with?"

Father stared with confusion as this polite-mannered girl who spoke so confidently to the old lady. Lily's whole persona had changed. Her eyes gleamed with excitement, and her body language was open, eager to interact with another.

"Of course my dear, anything," Rosalyn replied, taking a sip of tea from the blue and white painted teacup in her hand.

"Where did you get this from?" Lily took the ouroboros off from around her neck and handed it to the old lady. "I found it in your room. Up on top of the bed frame."

Rosalyn placed the teacup on the coffee table and lifted her glasses up that were hanging around her neck. The wrinkles around her eyes opened wide as she looked with astonishment.

"Oh my, I haven't seen that in over sixty years! I always wondered what happened to it. I remember hiding it away but I forgot where I put it." She fiddled the snake in both her hands, and rubbed the eyes gently. "Oh it's so beautiful to see it again, it brings me right back to that age. I would like you to keep it, darling, you have it." She folded the necklace back into Lily's hands and winked at her, smiling as she did so.

"Thank you so much! I've grown quite fond of it," Lily replied, ecstatic at being able to keep it. "Can I ask where you got it from?"

Lily fastened the necklace back around her neck, and rubbed the snake on her cheek, feeling the crystals once more. And she smiled, thinking about how powerful the stones could be. She really had no idea.

"Well dear I made it in school one day. We had a silversmith class, and the teacher helped me quite a bit. You see, these edges around here I couldn't get quite right."

Rosalyn pointed to the edges of the snake, the imperfections that Lily had liked most. And the two smiled together, as though in on a secret.

"So you made it yourself? No one gave it to you?" Lily asked surprised, although when she thought about it, it made more sense to her than she realized.

"No one gave it to me. I gave it to myself," Rosalyn replied, shaking her head proudly. "I saw it in a dream one night, and when I awoke, I decided to create it."

Rosalyn's eyes wandered back to her teacup, and she picked it up. Staring at the leaves as though remembering the dream vividly. She was lost in thought for awhile.

"It's beautiful Rosalyn. It's definitely made my little girl happy," Father said, and grinned as he looked to Lily, seeing a change in her stance yet unsure as to where it had come from.

"Yes, it's so beautiful, I really love it. Thank you again," Lily replied to the lady as she moved to the edge of the seat, trying to see through the veranda doors. She turned to Father and asked, "Papa, I think it's raining outside, do you mind if I go and watch?"

She could hear the pitter-patter sound of water dripping on the roof. It was creating beautiful music for all to hear and she was itching to go and watch the sky replenish the garden.

"Not at all. We will have some tea here, come back when you are ready." He nodded, picking up an almond cookie from the middle of the table.

"Please excuse me," Lily replied as she stood, bowing lightly to say goodbye. "It was lovely to meet you," she said as she walked through the kaleidoscope stain glass windows onto the veranda.

Lily stood on the far edge, overlooking the garden, and she watched the rainfall of water float down gracefully from the clouds in the sky. Drifting down ever so slowly, a gallivant parade of bubbles floating. They kissed the ground in a therapeutic chiming noise, like precious musical notes clinging together harmoniously in high-pitched yet soft metal-like clinks. And as Lily looked at the waterfall it reminded her of the feeling she had when she was a small child, staring with anticipation of what such a shape and illuminated rainbow light could mean. And her imagination ran through hurriedly like wind whispering through leaves in the trees, ongoing with the direction but no idea where it would settle, if it would settle. And the feeling she received from staring at such peaceful surroundings filled her with warmth and love and joy, in an indescribable way, like maybe there is something bigger than herself in this world, bigger than her mind and her life. This world had existed before she arrived and would continue to do so well after she was gone. Does her being here make a difference? Did she stumble upon it accidentally? And for the first time since she had arrived she realized that she was meant to be here, right here, looking at these drops of rainfall with wondrous lust, realizing that there is something bigger than just her, and that she is connected with it. For without her staring at these shapes of light, who would they be dancing for, if not for her? And without her gaze upon such dreamlike figures, would they exist if there was no one alive to watch them? For without her stare, they would not be there. Which means that she would not be here, and this world around her as she knew it would cease to exist.

ABOUT THE AUTHOR

Phoebe Garnsworthy is an Australian female author who loves to discover magic in everyday lives. She has travelled the world extensively, exploring eastern and western philosophies alike, while studying the influences that these beliefs have on humanity. The intention of her writing is to encourage conscious living and unconditional love.

www.LostNowhere.com

Made in the USA
San Bernardino, CA
16 May 2017